# HOUSE OF HARMONY

# HOUSE
## OF
# HARMONY

*Concordia-Argonaut's First 130 Years*

### BY

# BERNICE SCHARLACH

*Western Jewish History Center*
*Judah L. Magnes Memorial Museum*
*Berkeley, California*

Design by Roger Templeton and Diane Scheiman
Edited by Elaine Korry
Printed in the United States of America
by The James H. Barry Company, San Francisco

*To the memory of Reynold H. Colvin*
*who exemplified for me all the best*
*that is Concordia-Argonaut.*

# CONTENTS

Contents

# INTRODUCTION

ABOUT TEN YEARS AGO, as Editor of the *Concordian*, the Club's news-letter, I did a series of profiles of pioneer Club members and their families. I recall the stories of Harold Zellerbach, Walter Haas, Sr., S. Walter and Edwin Newman and their families, of Harry Hilp, Daniel and Robert Koshland and Joseph Bransten and the Bransten family. Then, sadly, because I so enjoyed doing the profiles, professional pressures compelled me to discontinue the newslet-ter. The conversations with members of the families, the library research, the review and study of the extensive memorabilia — all have imprinted in my memory a most absorbing series of experiences.

Proud of their heritage, distinguished as bankers, merchants, builders, from humble beginnings, these and other Concordia-Argonaut founders and pioneer members were adventurers, strong and independent; men of vision and courage who in their lifetimes saw dreams become realities. And with these realities, these founders and pioneers and their families also became models of responsible citizen-ship creating new dreams for their frontier City, State and their Nation.

These personal histories, interestingly enough, slowly raised the consciousness of Concordia's Officers, Directors and members of the Club's historically unique and significant past. More and more, the question was asked, "Doesn't this Club have a published history — with all the colorful personalities and events of the past 130 years?" and the startling answer, "No, in 130 years, never a history, the people and events never recorded. Never."

Then came the discussions, the debate and deliberations — "Should there be a history? If so, is this the time? Who would do it? What's the budget? Etc., etc." All this went on for several years. Finally, at a Board of Director's meeting on July 25, 1979, approval was granted for a history and President Rick Colsky ap-pointed a Club History Committee.

The Committee was directed to proceed with the selection of an author and the eventual publication of a history of Concordia Argonaut. Almost four years in the process, here it is at last, the first history of the Club and perhaps the last in the lives of most of us.

The 130 year span covers in microcosm a remarkable period in the history of this City, Nation and the World. Several of our living members remember the carriages, the delivery wagons and cable cars, all horse drawn, of an earlier San Francisco, captured in these pages. They remember the devastating 1906 earthquake, two World Wars, through to today, the bewildering age of the 1980's, of electronic media, of television as the current miracle or perhaps opiate, and of the pervasive computer that permits our society to function even in the confused world's economy. And with all this speed and the comforts in our lives, there is a veiled nervousness, tension and fear of a second holocaust, this one called "nuclear." All this within the 130 years of Concordia-Argonaut.

As of today (and it will always be so), there are constant reminders of our Club's continuity and history. At a "Concordia East" lunch on a Wednesday in January of this year, I asked Bill Green and Allen Meier, "How long have you guys been having these Wednesday lunches at the Club?" Bill and Allen and about seven friends have met for Wednesday lunches at the Club since their Stanford and University of California days, their World War II service and even before. "Let's see; it's a long time," says Allen, "somewhere, I'd say, just beyond forever."

And Larry Nestel, answering the question of how long he and friends or Club members drifting casually onto the volleyball court had been at that weekly game, checks his memory: "We're into the third generation of players. How long has this game gone on? Hell, I think we invented the game," he answers.

The poker game of Dick Goldman and friends . . . that one has been around for a while too! The players and their families have known each other since their Galileo High School days and they too are World War II vets. Even some grandparents of these players knew each other in early San Francisco. I looked in on their game one night in February, 1983 to listen to the reminiscenses of the old days, stories told by Dick Goldman, Stuart Erlanger, Bill Green, John Greenberg, Allen Meier, Al Hayman, Harold Baer and Bill Peiser. Their hero and the hero of many other boys in the 1920's and 30's was Hoyt Wood, the Athletic Director. A friend and teacher for the boys, a superb role model, he was dedicated to his boys. As the "boys" reminisced about Hoyt, their respect and love for him was reflected in stories of trips, of basketball league games and of learning to swim — "he tied me to a rope and told me to get going." There was quiet introspection and the memories were cherished ones. Back to the poker game. "Deal 'em around again, Dick — many, many more years."

We see the imprint of our founders' and our members' contributions to the history of San Francisco everywhere in the Club: the photographs of early San

Francisco, the collection of classical literature, the furnishings, appointments, the ambience, the style, the feeling is something special. Some call it "Old San Francisco."

In the Club's long history many gave much of themselves, but none more than Marcel Hirsch. Marcel had many interests — business, civic, philanthropic and social — but next to his family, for Marcel, Corcordia-Argonaut was central to his life. He was a member for 61 years and President for a decade (1938–1948). These depression and war years were the most trying in the Club's history. With one or two others, it was Marcel who not only saw that Concordia-Argonaut's problems were resolved, but Marcel refused to tolerate any lessening in the quality or style of the Club. "Our standards are the highest of any I know, and they will remain so," Marcel insisted. This leadership and the commitment of Marcel Hirsch has been reflected in many Directors and Officers for whom Marcel was both friend and mentor. After a long life and a full one, Marcel passed away March 1, 1980 leaving a substantial bequest to the Club. This book is, in part, possible because of Marcel's bequest. In these pages of a Club history, truly for you, Marcel, "a second home," we remember you with respect and love.

A Club project of this scope required, of course, the helpful hands, minds and experience of many Club members and friends of the Club. And an acknowledgement of the support and assistance of these good people must be made a part of this history.

To Presidents Rick Colsky and Marvin Nathan, thanks for your commitment to the history and for your help in removing or getting us through a long series of obstacles.

The History Committee, and bless them all, were: Edward Bransten, Jr., Brian Getz, Robert L. Goldman, John F. Rothmann, Daniel E. Stone and Myron Wacholder. The Committee was a faithful, devoted, working Committee that met eighteen times during the four years of the book's preparation. It was this Committee that conducted the search for and the interviews of eight candidates for the appointment as a historian. The choice, Bernice Scharlach, was unanimous and, in the Committee member's reading of the history several times, it's apparent to us the choice was fortuitous, just right. Bernice's patience and happy disposition were tested in her several meetings with us, (how did you ever put up with us?). Bernice once said, "you guys are not easy, but remember, this book had to come through an earthquake (1906) two World Wars and a fire (1982) so I've been through a lot."

Special thanks to John Rothmann, Brian Getz, Daniel E. Stone and Myron Wacholder for their many hours of help in their areas of special competency: in research, proof reading, design, costing and liaison with the Judah Magnes

Museum, the publisher. Thanks to you, Club Manager Douwe Drayer for your administrative and logistical support; to you Cliff Barbanell, House Committee Chairman and liaison to the History Committee, for providing the important communication link to the Board of Directors.

Roger Templeton and Diane Scheiman, thanks to you for conceptual, design and production counsel and maintaining our target dates for completion of the book. And to you, Seymour Fromer of the Judah Magnes Museum, for your cooperation and that of the Museum Directors in arranging for the publication of this history.

One goal of the history is to lend depth and significance to our understanding of the traditions of the Club with the expectation that all of us will preserve and continue these traditions. They stress respect and consideration for Club members and the Staff; they call upon us to maintain and enhance the special qualities and stature of Concordia-Argonaut; they ask us to experience the Club as "my second home."

For our lives beyond the Club, our traditions encourage a sharing of ourselves with our communities, city, state and nation through responsible and involved citizenship. This too, please remember. This history is our history, it is an extension of our past into the future, ours — yours and mine.

Well, now it's over — enough Diamond, enough. Read on Concordians, and enjoy.

Stanley Diamond
Chairman,
Concordia Argonaut
History Committee

# FOREWORD

"Americans of all ages, all conditions, and all dispositions constantly form associations . . . of a thousand . . . kinds, religious, moral, serious, futile, general or restricted, enormous or diminutive," noted Alexis de Tocqueville one hundred and fifty years ago after his visit to the United States. Ever since, what James Bryce called, "the habit of forming associations" has come to be regarded as the hallmark of American nationality. By whatever measure, we have been uncontestably a nation of joiners.

At the Golden Gate where, in J. S. Holiday's celebrated phrase, "the world rushed in," in the turbulent golden mid-nineteenth century years, and as often rushed out, the urge to associate with one's own kind as well as with others was contagious. More than anywhere, in San Francisco, the most cosmopolitan city in the Western world in the 1850's, that impulse was generously and instantly gratifiable. At land's end, a continent and as frequently an ocean away from their places of birth and countries of origin, amidst a multitude of uncommonly purposeful strangers, even the most adventurous and individualistic newcomers at times experienced a sense of profound isolation and unbearable loneliness. Only through active association could the preponderantly single male pioneers and sojourners be assured of mutual support, comradely amusement, humanizing companionship, and on certain time-honored occasions, religious solace and renewal.

In the premier instant American metropolis of the West, an uninhibited array of benevolent societies, fire companies, congregations, secret societies, and lodges — Masons, Odd Fellows, Hibernians, Knights of Pythias, Ancient Order of Druids and B'nai B'rith, not to speak of Committees of Vigilance — sprang promptly to life. For the more fastidious, gentlemen's clubs, as well, in imitation of the English model, early won their share of devotees.

Among the many pioneers from Germany, especially, were those who yearned for the cogenial more select company of their peers. A few years after the founding of the First Hebrew and the Eureka benevolent societies and of Congregations Emanu-El and Sherith Israel, the City's premier Jewish institutions, Jewish and other German immigrants established the City's first German and second gentlemen's club. Organized just one year after the founding of the Pacific, the City's first Anglo-American club by Southerners, and a year before the launching of the second, the Union, by Yankees, the San Francisco Verein, the first direct ancestor of Concordia-Argonaut, apparently attracted young men who aspired to large affairs as well as a sprinkling of professional and university men. A decade later, swelled by former members of the short-lived Alemanian, the City's first Jewish club, the Concordia was organized and became the namesake and second ancestor of the present club.

By the late 19th century, San Francisco, like the other great American metropolitan centers, harbored a British Protestant, a German, and a Jewish elite, as well as smaller coteries, with their complement of social clubs and institutions. Yet the City projected an openness that was singularly its own. San Francisco's first *Elite Directory*, for example, inclubed both a Calling and Address List and a Jewish List of 455 names with two leaders of the Jewish community, Levi Strauss and Abraham Weil, listed on the Christian but absent from the Jewish list. Most notably reflective of the City's cosmopolitan business, civic and social milieu was the esteemed Philip Lilienthal, founder of the Anglo-Californian Bank and son of Cincinnati's renowned Rabbi Max Lilienthal, who was especially famed for the breadth of his associations. A "prominent member" of the Bohemian, the Pacific Union, and the Union League, he was also a leading member of the Family, the Argonaut and the Commonwealth clubs, and "his membership in each meant something," noted a local historian.

In the early decades of the 20th century, however, a growing contraction of social attitudes and horizons led to the hardening of what earlier had been permeable social and group boundaries. The prestigious social clubs, progressively adjuncts of a nationwide managerial corporate way of life, were bent on social and religious homogeneity and intolerant of any kind of group individuality. Inevitably, the unabashed exclusion of Jews from membership in the more fashionable clubs throughout the country had a proscriptive impact in San Francisco as well. For those leading Jews impeccably equipped to meet society's most exacting prescriptions and committed as well to Jewish identity and historical consciousness, an era of free-flowing good will had come to an end, to reemerge again only after the implications of the greatest Jewish catastrophe in all history revealed the depths to which mankind had fallen.

After World War Two, a resurgent vitalized new America opened the way to the growing acceptance of Americans of all kinds into circles where they had formerly been excluded or at best kept at arm's length, most notably in the corporate business and professional worlds. More widely and more earnestly then ever, mature Americans were coming to discover in the nation's social and cultural diversity the virtues of pluralism, opening the way to the attainment of a new equilibrium among the unusual multi-ethnic mix of peoples that has become emblematic of San Francisco.

These significant changes contributed to an enhanced Jewish self-regard — for the Jewish community, for Concordia-Argonaut, and for its ever more varied membership. Unlike some Jewish clubs in other cities, the Concordia has played no role in the development of philanthropy and has never had a Jewish agenda. Those matters traditionally were left to other agencies. However, the delayed trauma of the Holocaust and the problematic state of Israel, in an age when democratic nations are so few, have come to serve as perpetual reminders of the fragility of civilization, of the critical need for eternal vigilance, and of the continual necessity for the renewal of personal ties in a world that fragments human relationships and threatens to make all associations anonymous and sterile. Since the Middle East crisis of 1973, club members have had a chance, thanks to the initiative of young John Rothmann, to listen to speakers who have forcefully and responsibly addressed and analyzed the dilemmas of that troubled and critically important region whose fate and destiny is never too far from Jewish consciousness.

In an era when the disappearance of old and distinguished clubs has frequently been remarked, Concordia-Argonaut, for a host of reasons, has more members on its rolls than ever before. If neither quite as stately nor quite as dramatically situated as is the club building atop Nob Hill, the Pacific Union Club, which counts an unprecedented, if modest, number of Jews among its members, the Concordia takes extreme pride in its persistent occupancy of the identical site and building since 1891, a record of continuity that marks it as unique among the City's clubs. Both the historic earthquake and fire of 1906 and the conflagration of 1982 have left Concordia-Argonaut undaunted.

A civic landmark in its own right, 1142 Van Ness has become a prized edifice in a city that takes immense pride in its rich architectural heritage. For its members, as for so many other San Franciscans, the club has also become a symbol of a splendid tradition of professional and business integrity and elan of which there are so many distinguished examples and of civic steadfastness inseparable from the City's sense of its best self.

•     •     •

There has never been a full-dress history of any of San Francisco's many social clubs or, for that matter, of a Jewish club anywhere in the country. Carefully done recent centennial histories by Maxwell Whiteman of the Union League Club of Philadelphia and by Wilcomb E. Washburn of the Cosmos Club of Washington, authoritatively illuminating the role of two of metropolitan America's best-known and most reputable clubs, have not been matched elsewhere. In San Francisco, the extensive chronicles of the Bohemian Club and the Family Club and an elegant centenial album for the Olympic Club are useful but fall short as genuine histories. For Jewish clubs, a few mere pamphlet chronicles, a booklet issued by New York's Harmonie Club on its 125th anniversary, and a handsome picture book published on its centennial by the Standard Club of Chicago are even less adequate.

Bernice Scharlach's history of Concordia-Argonaut is therefore especially welcome. It has the double distinction of being both the first comprehensive history of a Jewish club and of a San Francisco club. In Mrs. Scharlach, Concordia-Argonaut has been fortunate to find a charming and gifted author with both a flair for spirited popular writing and a genuine passion and commitment to historical research. In the face of formidable obstacles, she has pursued every surviving record and living witness to document and illuminate the club's 130 year history. As in the case of so much in the annals of San Francisco, the 1906 earthquake and fire tested Mrs. Scharlach's capabilities to their limits. Unlike the Gesellschaft Harmonie (the original name of the Harmonie Club of New York) whose complete records in German for the first four decades of its history have survived intact and are housed at the New York Historical Society, the Concordia-Argonaut is virtually recordless for its first half century. Even for more recent decades, an undeveloped sense of history and an indifference to record-keeping have made Mrs. Scharlach's task inordinately difficult. Her history is all the more remarkable therefore because she has had to exercise uncommon ingenuity and patience in ferreting out fact from fancy. Yet, by imaginatively drawing on a host of fugitive sources and people, Mrs. Scharlach, in her sprightly composed and richly detailed narrative, has allowed us to enter for the first time into the inner councils of one of San Francisco's most venerable institutions by making its workings comprehensible and significant to her contemporaries. Surely Schiller's Bell will ring out again on this splendid historic and civic occasion.

Moses Rischin
Western Jewish History Center
Judah L. Magnes Memorial Museum

# ACKNOWLEDGMENTS

**W**HEN I FIRST UNDERTOOK THIS ASSIGNMENT, it was readily ac-
knowledged that it would be a formidable task since the Club could
provide little in the way of historical records. Although it was said
that in the early days, board minutes were kept in German and English, unfortunately they did not survive. So while I am indebted to many people for their help
in piecing this history together, my greatest thanks must go to the scores of people
who were gracious enough to share with me their memories of the Club. (A
complete list of those interviewed, Club members, staff and others, appears
elsewhere in this book.)

I am extremely grateful to members of the History Committee, whose members include: Stanley Diamond, Chairman; Edward Bransten, Jr.; Brian H. Getz;
Robert L. Goldman; John F. Rothmann; Dan E. Stone (referred to in the book as,
Dan Stone, Jr.); Myron Wacholder, and to Clifford Barbanell, who acted as
liaison between the Committee and the Board of Directors. Each was a delight to
work with, and the fact that Committee meetings were held over sumptuous
luncheons at the Club only added to the pleasure of those conferences. I would
especially like to single out for special thanks three members of the Committee:
Chairman Stanley Diamond for always being available to offer his help in arranging interviews, in mediating differences of opinion and for making my task the
enjoyable one it has been; John F. Rothmann, a descendant of numerous founding
members, for his insights into Club traditions, and for his willingness to share the
expertise he acquired during the publications of two of his mother's books; and
Dan E. Stone, for not only supplying me with unpublished material from his
personal files, but for his diligence in seeing to it that this book conform to his own
high standards in his role as liaison between the Club and the Western Jewish
History Center's Board of Directors.

The Club's staff of employees was extremely helpful in providing assistance,
often without being asked. While I am grateful to all of them, I would especially like to thank Club Manager Douwe Drayer and Club Secretary Carolyn

Tokusato, who were never too busy — even during the hectic days and weeks following the fire — to answer my incessant phone calls or to drop everything to look for information I needed.

I owe much to Seymour Fromer, Director of the Judah L. Magnes Memorial Museum, for founding that splendid institution now entering its third decade, with its renown Western Jewish History Center; to Ruth Rafael, the Center's archivist, for her cheerful help in locating rare documents and records, and to Norman Coliver, Chairman of the Center's Advisory Committee, for his cooperation. Special thanks must go to Dr. Moses Rischin, Professor of History at San Francisco State University, the Center's distinguished Director, for his encouragement, for his wise suggestions and for urging me on to further and further research. To the extent that this book has any merit as social history, the credit is his.

Thanks is due also to Gladys Hansen, San Francisco City Archivist, and the staff of the California Historical Society for the use of materials available in their respective collections.

One member of the Club has had a tremendous influence on this work. Now, lamentably, deceased, Reynold H. Colvin, was a dear friend to whom I dedicate this book. Although he didn't live to see it completed, Renny's wise counsel from the beginning set a course to which I tried to adhere. How I miss his ability to puncture pomposity and to cut through to the essentials, always doing so gently and with humor. Renny took great pride in his Club, but he knew its limitations. That never stopped him from trying to make it better, to infuse it with some sense of higher purpose, to insist that those people with whom he found cameraderie and fellowship measure up to his own high standards of community involvement. Renny's decency, his unflinching honesty and his sense of the nobler purposes of life remained with me as I wrote this book. Although I will never know, I can only hope this effort would merit his approval.

I wish that I might have been able to list Marcel Hirsch in these acknowledgments, but to my deep regret, he became mortally ill when I began this book and died shortly thereafter. But to Bert Rabinowitz, Marcel's close lifetime friend, I am very grateful for helping me to see Marcel as he did.

Four other people helped to make this book a reality. My thanks must go to Dr. Norton B. Stern, editor of the Western States Jewish Historical Quarterly, for his friendship, for the excellent material in his publications, and his eagerness to share with me information which pertained to the Club or its early membership. My friend Ernest H. Weiner, Bay Area Director of the American Jewish Committee, offered valuable editorial suggestions and insights into the San Francisco Jewish community. To my brother-in-law, Adrian Scharlach, goes my gratitude and admiration. With his customary grace, tact and fairness, although a member of the Selection Committee to choose an author for the Club's history, he never succumbed to pressure or influence.

My last word of thanks goes to my husband, Arthur, whose support and encouragement have always been my mainstay in all my endeavors. His willingness to relieve me of all the tedious details—the hours of xeroxing he did, or caused to have done, for me; the attention to tape recorders that were miraculously restored to functioning; the research trips that he turned into pleasure jaunts—all these expressed better than words his faith in me and in this project.

Bernice Scharlach
Walnut Creek, California
May, 1983

# PROLOGUE
*"All burnt over*
*Is the Place."*

T WAS SHORTLY BEFORE eight o'clock on Sunday morning, January 31, 1982. Marvin Nathan was shaving and thinking about stopping at the Club for a swim before going to his office in the Jack Tar building. For Marvin, the head of an accounting firm, this was his peak business season; all of his clients were clamoring at once for their income tax information to be compiled. A relaxing swim and then a quick walk across the street for a few hours of work without the usual distractions, would give him a good headstart on the busy week ahead.

As the razor glided over his face, Marvin thought contentedly, "What a time to be president of Concordia-Argonaut, the best club in the best city in the world!" Just last Sunday the Forty-Niners had captured San Francisco's first Super Bowl championship; the excitement of victory was still in the air.

The Concordia-Argonaut was world class, too, Marvin mused. He thought of the men on the membership waiting list; as long as five years before some could be admitted to the Club. Marvin was proud of the Club's recent successes; excellent athletic facilities had been added, and the Club was in the best financial condition in its history. He looked forward with relish to the excellent dinner he would enjoy there tonight with his family, cooked by a chef who could boast — with reason — that he served the finest food in the City.

He was thinking about all the presidents who had preceded him in the 130 years of the Club's history. He thought about the membership, some of whom were fifth-generation San Franciscans: men with names like Haas, Magnin, Newman, and Liebes; Bransten, Koshland, Sinton, and Lilienthal; Stone, Zelinsky and Zellerbach.

Marvin was congratulating himself for the honor of heading such a prestigious, well-run club, an organization with a sense of permanence.

Then the telephone rang.

It was his business partner, sounding very agitated. "You'd better get down here fast. Your Club's on fire!"

Douwe Drayer, the handsome, young manager of the Club, had just been informed of the fire. At 7:30 that morning, switchboard operator Bobby Max-well, sounding panicked, had called Drayer at his home in Orinda, to tell him the awful news. He had opened the Club that morning and smelled smoke, which he traced to the dining room on the third floor. Faulty wiring behind a hot plate had ignited nearby napkins and linens. At first, Bobby tried to extinguish the blaze himself, but when he soon realized it was futile, he called the fire department.

Across town, Richard Goldman, president of the Jewish Community Federa-tion, was getting ready to go to the Fairmont Hotel for "Super Sunday." Along with his committee chairpeople, Goldman had long been preparing for this day, when scores of volunteers would be telephoning local Jewish citizens to solicit contributions for social welfare programs, both in the Bay Area and in Israel. Goldman had just pulled his car out of the garage when his phone rang.

"I'll have to make a detour to the Club," he thought, torn between his responsibilities to the Federation and to his Club. He was motivated not only by personal concern ("All the years of pleasure I had experienced there were en-gulfed in that conflagration," he later said), but also by professional considerations. Goldman was Chairman of the Board of Richard N. Goldman & Company, the Club's insurance broker.

Meanwhile, Stuart Seiler, the brokerage company's president, was also on his way to participate in "Super Sunday" when he heard the news. He drove as close to the Club as he could before going to the Fairmont. Watching the smoke and flames pouring from the roof, he suddenly remembered that the insurance in-spectors from Mission Insurance Company, carriers of the Club's policy, would not be available. Indeed, the entire Mission Insurance operation was temporarily shut down following the awful events of the previous Friday. The crazed hus-band of one of the firm's employees had killed two men and wounded eight others before the police killed him, ending a twenty-minute blood bath on January 28.

"We'll have to hire an independent adjustor," thought Seiler, "and get our Account Executive right on this so we can get the ball rolling immediately to determine the amount of the losses the Club has suffered."

Jack Lipman heard of the fire from a fellow former Club President, Ben Baum. "I was in bed when Ben phoned. My first thought after hearing the news was that if that baby caught, she'd go — and go quickly," said Lipman, a retired building contractor. He then thought of the Club's wine cellar. A food and wine connoisseur, Lipman had helped over the years to see that the wine cellar was stocked with choice and rare vintages. "The 1955, 1957, and 1960 Chateau

LaFittes and other vintage French Bordeaux wines were later discovered floating in the Club's flooded basement."

Club Vice President Ted Euphrat was buckling-up aboard the early morning Western Airlines flight to Acapulco. Just before take off he was startled to see a friend of his arguing with the stewardess to let him aboard the plane. The friend, who had just arrived at the airport to catch a later plane, heard about the fire enroute. He finally persuaded the stewardess to let him relay the news to Euphrat before the plane took off.

"I grew up in the Club," Euphrat later said, "and it was a frustrating experience having to sit for hours on the plane not knowing what was happening at home. But by the time I checked in at my hotel, I had a message with all the details waiting for me." (Two weeks later, shortly after his return to San Francisco, Euphrat became fully involved in the rebuilding plans.)

Franny Green, chairman of the Red Cross Disaster Corps, responded to a call from headquarters that morning about a "huge fire on Van Ness." A Jewish community leader, her indignation at being refused admission to the Club dining room for lunch when one of the boards on which she was serving held its meetings there, was one of the factors that eventually led to the opening of the Club's dining rooms to women.

Franny did not know the exact location on Van Ness of the disaster until her coffee canteen truck was speeding toward Post Street. When she realized the burning building was the Club, she quickly set up operations and then telephoned her husband, member Bill Green with the news. His sleepy response was, "That's a hell of a thing to do just because they wouldn't let you have lunch there!"

Joe Ferrero, tall, loose-limbed "Super Joe," the Club's athletic director, bounded out of bed in San Jose at 7:45 that morning, in response to a call from his father informing him "your Club is burning down." Jumping into his clothes, Joe phoned Niels Ploug, the Club's chef, in Burlingame and told him he would be out of his house in five minutes, and would pick the chef up on his way into town.

During the drive up Highway 280 to the City, the car radio reported that the blaze had become a five – alarm fire. Joe was worried about a case of matches in the Club's storage area. "I've got to get to a fireman right away," he told Niels.

Joe parked his car a block from the Club, and tried to push his way inside the roped-off area. As he explained who he was and what he wanted, he was passed from one fireman to another until he relayed his message to then Fire Chief Andy Casper. The Chief told him not to worry, since in a fire of that magnitude, a case of matches couldn't make it much worse.

Ferrero was ushered back behind the protective ropes, where he joined a group of sixty to seventy Club and staff members. Drayer was there, as well as

Arnold the Bartender, who had retired one month earlier, after serving the Club for fifty years; Carolyn Tokusato, the Club secretary, accompanied by her husband Paul the Houseman; Craig, their young son, and Ted, the security guard.

"We stood there talking about all the good times we'd had in that building," said Walter Newman, a former Club president who had been a member for some fifty-two years. Newman's family, including two other past Club presidents, went back to the very founding of the Club. "There was a great deal of sadness, yet nobody was discouraged. We knew we'd build it better and have a chance to correct some of the things we couldn't do in the first place.

"We watched from the sidelines, terrified that somebody would be hurt. They were carrying firemen out and giving them oxygen on the street, and still others were going back up those ladders. We saw the flames shooting out the windows and the roof into the alley on Cedar. Two of the firemen were trapped on the roof. It was terribly frightening."

For two and a half hours, the firemen fought the blaze. At its height, Fire Chief Casper had forty-four pieces of equipment and 160 firefighters on the scene. Fire Captain Tom Bogue was on the roof when it collapsed. "All of a sudden I told everyone to get to the firewall, and, bingo, the roof fell in."

Ten firemen were trapped inside the building. A special unit used chain saws to cut a passageway for two firemen, and prying bars were used to extricate the remaining men from the burning wreckage. Five of the firefighters, suffering cuts, bruises and smoke inhalation, were taken by ambulance to St. Francis Hospital, where it was determined that none of their injuries were serious. (Afterwards, the firemen told Club members they were close to abandoning the building, but they decided to fight it into the corner — the southwest corner.)

Shortly before the $2 million blaze was under control, firemen sought out Joe Ferrero. "They wanted to know if we manufacture our own chlorine. A man from OSHA was there. He was concerned about a pipe with green gas that erupted, and he though it might be chlorine. Fortunately, it wasn't. We don't make our own chlorine. The green stuff was Freon from the air-conditioning unit.

"Finally, I was permitted downstairs into the Athletic Department. I opened the main drain valve and emptied out two feet of water. The drains were overflowing. I had to empty that much out to prevent the pool from overflowing. There's 93,000 gallons of water in that pool. Then the arson squad wanted to talk to me. They wanted to know where the power was."

By 10 a.m., the firemen permitted President Nathan, former President Rick Colsky and Manager Drayer to look inside the building. They draped towels over their heads to protect themselves from dripping water and falling glass.

"We went into the athletic department, where the damage was minimal — mostly water damage," said Colsky. "Then we went up the back stairs (constructed of iron) through the balcony to the back of the stage, where the fire had ignited. It was a mass of blackened ruins . . . .

"I had very mixed feelings. I thought about the bravery of the firemen, how they would bring the wounded out on stretchers while others would keep going back in; I thought about how awful it was to see the Club burning down before my eyes. And at the same time, I found myself looking down the road to the future. You always want to put things back together again.

"I am in a unique position," continued Colsky, who, at age 39, was the youngest of the Club's presidents. "First, I grew up with most of the employees and I feel very close to them. Then, I am probably one of the few who uses both sides of the Club equally — the athletic side and the social side. I had very strong feelings about keeping all the employees together.

"We have an astounding record of employment here. Cliff, the Bartender, has been here thirty years; head Houseman Paul, twenty-three years. Houseman Rudi has worked here twenty-three years; Nino, seventeen and Eddie, thirteen. Carolyn, the Club secretary has been with us twenty-two years; Niels, twenty-one; Romero, the sauceman, thirty; and Ysmael, the dishwasher, has been doing our dishes for thirty years. People like that you can't — you don't — let go."

"All my beautiful carving knives — that hurt the most," said Niels, the chef. Realizing there was nothing he could save in his kitchen, he turned to his next concern, the Club's art work on the main floor. He headed for the drawing room and library and with the help of security guard Ted Loeffler, began removing the pictures from the walls. Joe Ferrero, having accomplished his work in the basement dashed to the office.

"The next day was the first of the month, and I knew all the bills were in there waiting to be mailed out. Chief Casper told the firemen to let us in. I got to the office and the firemen asked for the key. Looking at the water we were wading in, and all the other mess around, I said, 'Hell, break the door down!' We got the bookkeeping records out and Niels removed all the art work, and we took them next door to Adeline's Bakery. Tom Lembo, the owner, is a Club member."

Now that the fire was over, Drayer had his own concerns. He was thinking ahead to the emergency board meeting Nathan had called for the following day. Leaving Nathan and the others to answer the questions of the newspaper, radio and TV people who were swarming over the area (the newspapers the next morning would also be quoting Newman, Club Secretary Allen Meier and former Vice President Adrian Scharlach), Drayer went across the street to Nathan's office to notify board members who weren't on the scene about the meeting on Monday.

"I thought of the effect the fire would have on the lives of the old-timers, on men like Edgar Gould and Irwin Stern who were down here every day. And I thought of William Bransten; the high point of his day was when he came to the Club at noon for lunch and a visit with his friends. I thought of all the private parties that would have to be cancelled — we were booked until 1983 — and wondered how I would find alternate locations for them. I thought of how I would handle the problem of correlating decisions since I couldn't give yes or no answers.

"But my greatest concern was to keep the family together — both the membership family and the staff family. We learn and we grow. Now my job would not only be to take care of routine Club matters but also to cope with this emergency."

Drayer's first act was to find temporary headquarters. Tom Lembo volunteered the use of a room in his baking plant behind the bakery. Although the space was small and one's senses were assailed by the tantalizing odors and sights of freshly-baked cakes and pastries, Drayer grabbed the opportunity to use the room. From his vantage point he could look out the window and oversee the operations at the Club, while remaining accessible to the adjustors and others who would need to meet with him. (For almost four weeks, until a suite of rooms could be secured at the Grosvenor Inn, formerly the Richelieu Hotel, Drayer, Carolyn and one other rotating staff member worked out of the bakery, trying to put the Club's business affairs back in order.)

By Sunday afternoon, Dan Stone, Jr., a bachelor who had grown up in the Club where his father had been a past president, was still on the phone "undoing all the plans I had made for the week ahead at the Club." Dan had decided against going to Van Ness Avenue that morning, not wanting to add to the confusion there. Besides, he had all those calls to make.

"First I had to select another location for the family birthday dinner I had planned at the Club that night. People had to be notified. Then I looked at my calendar: I had a haircut appointment at the Club on Monday; a lunch date on Tuesday; a dinner date with my Stanford scholarship program winners on Wednesday, and on Thursday I had an appointment with the Club's masseur."

(The birthday dinner was transferred to a little French restaurant out in the Richmond District, Le Tricolor, where five tables in the tiny restaurant were filled with groups who would normally be dining at the Club. "We all sat around saying, 'Isn't it awful?' and commiserating with each other," Stone reported.)

Carolyn Lisberger is the widow of past president Sylvan Lisberger, in whose honor the Sylvan Room, adjacent to the Club's main dining room, had been named. The redoubtable nonagenarian was taking her usual Sunday afternoon drive when she passed by the burnt-out building. Looking at the collapsed roof, she sighed deeply. "Poor Sylvan," she said, "his lovely room! They'll just have to name another one after him when they rebuild again."

It was late Sunday afternoon when Stanley Diamond, editor of the Club's newsletter, *The Concordian*, learned about the fire. It was, for Stanley, the climax of an emotionally draining weekend. As Special Assistant to Senator S. I. Hayakawa, Stanley was at the California Republican Convention in Monterey with a secret draft of the senator's withdrawal announcement from the upcoming Senatorial primary election in California. At the Convention, and then at a network TV and national press conference called by Diamond, the dramatic announcement was made to shocked audiences by Sen. Hayakawa. Sunday, on the long and lonely road from Monterey to Mill Valley, the Senator's home, the two reminisced — between periods of silence — over their twenty-five years of close association.

"Mrs. Hayakawa greeted me at the door with the news of the fire. It was almost too much to absorb," said Diamond. "I should have been stunned, shocked, but I was just numb. The full impact of it didn't hit me until I got home and saw the devastation on the six o'clock news. I realized I was going to have to restructure my way of life. I swim and work out six days a week. I have been very active in Club affairs. I love the staff . . . my closest friends are Club members. I entertain guests — visitors of the Senator and friends from Latin America — each week at the Club. It's the best dining room in town and it's so easy to be spoiled. . ."

(Within a day of the fire, Stan knew the alternative clubs to which he could take his guests. Club members were soon invited to use the facilities of the Press Club, the Metropolitan Club, Lake Merced Golf and Country Club, the Family Club, the University Club, the Commercial Club and the Athens-Nile Club in Oakland.)

●　　　●　　　●

When Club members awoke the next morning, they realized they were not alone in their sense of loss. The whole City seemed to share in it. The building that had stood for so long, so unobtrusively and with such dignity, had been a respected landmark.

Banner headlines in the *San Francisco Chronicle* of February 1 proclaimed, "Five Alarm Fire at Historic San Francisco Club." A picture of the burning building was spread across the front page, with two additional pictures on inside pages. Most of the paper's third page was devoted to a side-bar story on "The Burned Club's Historic Ties to San Francisco."

*The San Francisco Examiner*, in its evening edition, headlined the news that, "Directors Plan to Resurrect Historic Club Ravaged By Fire."

The *San Jose Mercury* headlined their coverage somewhat inaccurately, "100 Years of History Razed by SF Club Fire."

There was an outpouring of sympathy demonstrated in letters and telegrams to members from guests of the Club throughout the years. The underlying message was summed up in the letter received by Ben Baum from Robert Branch, treasurer of Ventura County, who wrote, "San Francisco lost part of its heritage through this disaster . . . ."

When he could at last step back and assess it, Marvin Nathan realized the loss would only be temporary. Just as a previous generation had rebuilt the Club after the 1906 earthquake, so it could be restored once again.

"There is a sense of permanence about this Club . . . whose roots go back almost as far as those of the City its members have loved and served so well . . . ."

**PART ONE**

# PIONEERING THE GOOD LIFE:
# 1853–1906

# CHAPTER ONE

# THE SAN FRANCISCO VEREIN

 R. JACOB REGENSBURGER was a man of refinement and quiet tastes living in a town of young men gone wild. The doctor had received his medical training in Germany, but left his homeland in 1853 to settle in California. The San Francisco he discovered was a frontier community in the throes of gold fever, a mecca for prostitution, gambling and drinking. Of course, not everybody cared for such decadent recreation, certainly not Jacob Regensburger and the German-speaking men of his acquaintance. They were of solid, middle-class virtue who appreciated the subtle pleasures of good food and cards. While other men frequented the bawdy houses or gambled on the cock-fights, bullfights or bear-baitings, the German settlers stayed in their bleak boardinghouses, and over sauerbraten and steins of beer, planned the San Francisco Verein (German for "club"), the forerunner of the Argonaut Club.

During the City's youthful days, one could find over twenty Vereins listed in the City directory. Among the more notable were the San Francisco Turn Verein, the Grutili Verein, the Deutscher Verein, the Wagner Verein, and the Eureka Turn Verein. There was even a women's association called Der Israelitische Frauenverein, which, by 1858, had the good sense to simplify and anglicize its name to the Ladies Society of Israelites.

The principal Verein, the one that endured the longest — for half a century, until it became the Argonaut Club — was the San Francisco Verein, which from its inception in 1853, described itself as a men's club "composed largely of prominent German citizens."

The circumstances which spawned the overnight development of hotel life in San Francisco in the 1850s also fostered the growth of clubs. In an article entitled "Our City's Clubs," which appeared in the *San Francisco Morning Call*, on January 16, 1887, reporters noted that "for the sake of conviviality and economy secured by association, men began to form clubs here and to lead club lives even before the club system was dominating Eastern cities."

Of course, the sudden and rapid accumulation of wealth by San Francisco's early settlers contributed to make the trend fashionable. But the fundamental motive for the formation of clubs, the article noted, was remarkably similar to the reason for Concordia-Argonaut's existence today: to provide an environment where members could enjoy good food and a game of cards.

"Whereas the normal purpose of the English clubs was to drink and be merry," the article stated, "and the normal purpose of the French clubmen was to gamble, and the purpose of the New York clubs was to furnish a place where they may gossip, the essential aim of the San Francisco club appears to be to provide the members with lunch and a place where, at night, homeless outcasts may play a rubber."

From its inception, the San Francisco Verein was comprised of both Gentiles and Jews. That Jews should have socialized on equal terms with Gentiles was not without precedent. Dr. Regensburger and several other German Jews had earlier joined with the Gentiles in collaborative efforts, such as the founding of the German Hospital (later Franklin Hospital, now the Ralph K. Davies Medical Center), and the German Benevolent Society. Jews could hardly be considered "intruders" when everyone was a newcomer.

Gaining acceptance in this pioneer community required a willingness to work, but it didn't hurt to have money, too. In 1855 Daniel Levy, a French Jewish intellectual, wrote to the editor of the *Archives Israelites* in France, describing the first business ventures of Jewish San Franciscans:

"There is one branch of business to which Jews seem to have been given the password. They have cornered it, made a specialty and almost a monopoly of it, and they exploit it at every level, wholesale, retail, commission and peddling. It is the business of textiles and ready-made clothes. This preference for dealing in soft goods has reached the point that, in some mining areas, where there are convenient terms for everything, these types of stores are called 'Jewshops,' even when run by Christians.

"After this favorite line come cigars, and tobacco, foods, groceries, liquor, etc. The Polish Jews are almost always tailors . . . at least when they are not shoemakers. They are truly wonderful men, knowing a little about everything and embarrassed by nothing.

"The Jew is a little like the ant: active, organized, far-sighted, thrifty. His goal is to become rich, and he succeeds by patience and effort; more rapidly than the tortoise of the fable, but not as fast as the hare — the speculator and gambler who expects to attain wealth in one leap."

His feet firmly planted on the path to riches, the German immigrant left his "Jewshop" in the care of relatives from the old country, and he moved his base of operations to San Francisco. It was a pattern followed by several Jewish pioneer members of the San Francisco Verein. One such settler was young August Helbing, who established a thriving crockery and dry goods business in the City after making his start in a general store in the Gold Country. However, Helbing's business success was not without setbacks: four times his entire inventory had been destroyed by fire. A true philanthropist (he was the founder of the Eureka Benevolent Society for needy *Baiern*, or Bavarian Jews, Helbing succeeded Dr. Regensburger as president of the Verein in 1872.

Joseph Brandenstein was another pioneer who joined the Verein in 1854, after moving to San Francisco from the mining country. Brandenstein, an educated man from Germany, was an avid scholar of Shakespeare. He formed a partnership with Albert and Moses Rosenbaum in the wholesale trade of leaf tobacco and cigars. His sons would later form the MJB coffee empire. From the day Brandenstein joined the Verein, the family name would remain on the Club's roster through its evolution into the Argonaut Club, and up to the present Concordia-Argonaut.

As Jews arrived, they became respected members of the San Francisco community. An article from the *San Francisco Herald* of 1851 demonstrates the regard which they enjoyed: "The Israelites constitute a numerous and intelligent class of our citizens and conduct themselves with great propriety and decorum. They are industrious and enterprising and make worthy members of our community."

While well-received by the San Francisco community at large, the Jewish population soon experienced divisiveness within its own ranks. By 1853 when the Jews living in San Francisco numbered about 3,000, San Francisco had not *one*, but *two* Jewish houses of worship: Congregation Emanu-El (for the Germans, or *Baiern*); and Sherith Israel (for the Poles). There were two benevolent societies to aid the needy, care for the sick and bury the dead — again, one for the Germans and one for the Poles. While the German Jews may have been considered equal with Gentiles in the burgeoning city, they did not share that perception of equality with their Polish counterparts. In the opinion of prominent pioneer German families a "Polack" ranked only slightly above a "Chinaman."

●     ●     ●

The needs of the Jewish community having been cared for, Dr. Regensburger and several of his friends felt it time to look to their private comforts. They turned to Gentile "landsmen" to share relaxation and company. These men all spoke the same language, read the same books and newspapers, and enjoyed similar food and recreation.

The German Gentiles, for their part, welcomed the Jews. As historian Rudolf Glanz points out: "All too often the official (Gentile) bearers of German culture in America had to admit that without the assistance of the German Jewish immigrants, their work would have been to no avail."

German Jews, together with those settlers who Dr. Norton Stern, editor of *Western States Jewish History Quarterly*, refers to as the "pretenders" (Jews from Prussian Poland who posed as Germans), "created and affirmed German culture and language in America when German Gentiles were beginning to be doubtful of its worth on the new continent."

The quarters on Sacramento and Kearny Streets that Dr. Regensburger and his friends rented for their first clubhouse were very modest, consisting of a dining area and a smaller space for card-playing and reading. The dining room occasionally served as a dance hall. Although the atmosphere of the clubhouse was little better than that of the members' boardinghouse rooms, it offered certain advantages, privacy being one, and *Gemütlicht* another. In addition, it was a place where respectable women could be entertained.

The diary of Helen Levinson, one of the so-called "pretenders" provides an insider's view of the club's early days. In 1855 Helen and her sister arrived in San Francisco, from Posen Prussia, to join their brother Jacob Levinson. Jacob, newly established as a leather merchant in the City, took his sisters to the San Francisco Verein for social activities. In her memoirs Helen Levinson writes, "My younger brother Jacob was one of the founders of the club. When we entered the hall our (dance) programs were taken by the gentlemen, and we did not receive them back until they were completely filled. It was all very pleasant."

At the time it was also very noteworthy, since the Levinsons were Polish Jews. Many years would pass and great quantities of *sauerbraten* and *damfnudel* would be consumed before Poles would be welcomed knowingly and openly into the ranks of what was to become Concordia-Argonaut again.

The men of the San Francisco Verein were not entirely selfish about their club. With patriarchal largesse, they occasionally shared their private arena with wives and other female relatives. *The Hebrew* of February 17, 1865, noted one such event when it announced that, "Tomorrow evening the San Francisco Verein will give their Fifth Annual Masquerade Ball at their hall on Sacramento and Kearny."

In 1869 the Verein moved to more spacious quarters at 430 Pine Street. Among the luncheoners one could find such men as Lewis Gerstle and Simon

Greenewald, former Sacramento merchants who had formed a partnership in the Alaska Commercial Company. (The third partner, Louis Sloss, however, was a member of the Concordia Club at that time.)

By 1874 the Verein clubmen were anxious to improve their surroundings once again. The club members had profitted from the financial opportunities of the Sixties. In California, a state not ravaged by the Civil War, business had flourished as a result of the war-time demand for finished goods and raw materials, as well as by the Comstock silver strike in Nevada and the completion of the first transcontinental railway. These factors had combined to produce a climate in which budding entrepreneurs had blossomed into full-fledged tycoons. The tycoons of the Verein left their Pine Street clubhouse to the newly-organized Bohemian Club (formed in 1872) and moved into more elaborate quarters at the corner of Sutter and Dupont (now Grant) Streets, which were refurbished "at a cost of sixty-five thousand dollars." Leading Verein members then included the financiers Isaias W. Hellman, manager of the Farmers and Merchants Bank in Los Angeles, and later, president of the Nevada Bank of San Francisco, (which he then merged with Wells Fargo); and Philip Lilienthal, founder of the Anglo London and Paris National Bank, predecessor of the Anglo California National Bank.

Philip's father, the famed Rabbi Max Lilienthal of Cincinnati, a leader of the American Reform movement, visited San Francisco in the summer of 1876 and wrote of his son's club:

> "That the Israelites, and especially the German Israelites, will not forget and neglect the pleasures of social life is a matter of course. I have visited two of their clubs, the Verein, which consists of Jewish and Christian members, and the Concordia, which consists only of Jewish members. Both are most elegantly furnished and excellently managed and fully rival even the Harmonie of New York."

15

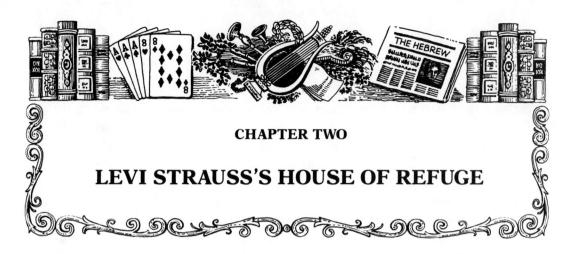

## CHAPTER TWO

# LEVI STRAUSS'S HOUSE OF REFUGE

EVI STRAUSS was a bachelor. In 1864 he had little reason to be dissatisfied with his life, being free to pursue his booming mercantile business — and at liberty to pursue the ladies. He lived with his sister, Fannie Stern, who created a fine home for him, as well as for her husband David — Strauss' business associate — her four sons and three daughters. The one ingredient missing in his life was a place to relax in an all-male environment.

By 1864 San Francisco had come a long way in its struggle to become an urbane city. But, scratch its surface and one still found a bawdy frontier town. The wild state of the City prompted urgent pleas for "a house of refuge for the spiritual improvement and social gatherings of the Jewish young men of this city." One such plea appeared in a letter to editor Philo Jacoby, publisher of *The Hebrew*. A person, using the pseudonym "Truth," railed against the recreational choices of the day:

> "When the store or shop is closed, the mind of the young man is relaxed. He seeks recreation. Where does he find it? . . . The fife and drum on the balcony of yonder melodeon attracts his attention; his steps are led thither and he breathes the compressed foul air of the 'temple of fun' for hours, while the 'galaxy of stars' entertain him with their stale and equivocal wits. . . .
>
> "Disguise it as we may, the extent of the licentiousness indulged in by many young men is truly appalling, and it is notoriously known that they are amongst the most liberal patrons of these incarnations of infamy and vice."

The author finally proposed a "house of refuge, a hired hall in a decent location" that would contain, among its amenities, "a select Jewish library, lectures of Jewish content, debates and games of chess." The letter ended with a direct challenge: "What say ye men of learning? What say ye wholesale merchants, ye men of princely fortunes and income?"

Whether this sermon influenced Levi Strauss and a group of young friends to organize the Concordia Society later that year cannot be known. But when the Concordia Society was incorporated on January 10, 1865, it was largely comprised of wholesale merchants building princely fortunes. Echoing "Truth's" plea, the society's objectives were: "promoting of social intercourse, cultivating literary taste and diffusing useful knowledge among the members thereof". No mention was made of chess.

The incorporators, in addition to Strauss included: J. H. Neustadter, Sig Greenebaum, J. M. Rothchild, Daniel Bloch, Herman Newbauer, Edward Kalisher, Joseph Napthaly, Rafael Peixotto (a Sephardic Jew, the only non-German in the group), Lippman Sachs, Henry Sinsheimer, Sol Wangenheim, Simon Newman, Walter Levy, S. H. Ackerman, Max Brooks, Leopold Weil, Henry Dinkelspiel, Leopold Haas, A. Schwabacher, A. A. Son, Abe Spitz, Fred Toklas, R. Samson and Herman Waldeck.

Simon Newman, barely 18 years old at the time of incorporation and working for his uncle, Sol Wangenheim, was just beginning an illustrious career in the cattle and grain business. He went on to become Concordia president from 1901 to 1907. His grandson, Walter S. Newman led the Club from 1963 to 1965. Currently the fourth generation of Newmans are preparing to carry on the family tradition of Concordia leadership.

Henry Sinsheimer, associated with wool merchant Simon Koshland, was another member whose progeny have remained within the ranks of both Concordia and Argonaut from the very beginning.

Israel Steinhart, great grand-uncle of present Club member John Steinhart, was named the president of the newly incorporated group. Other officers included Levi Strauss, Vice President; Leon Ehrman, Treasurer; and A. W. Michaels, Secretary.

The first home of the Concordia Society was a large room on the second floor of the Odd Fellows Hall at Bush and Kearny. It was not luxurious, but to the young men, most of whom were bachelors like Strauss, living with families or in bleak boardinghouse rooms, it provided a most desirable "house of refuge." The Club also afforded married men a respite from the demands of family life. There was a room for cards and a room for conversation where talk frequently turned to the Civil War that was tearing the new nation apart, and to its repercussions in the West.

●　　　●　　　●

As the "Merchant Princes" organized the Concordia Society, another group of prospering Jews formed a social club they called the Alemania Society. According to *The Hebrew*, their first recorded affair was a soirée held at Platt's Music Hall, January 27, 1865. Two months later, the club elected its first slate of officers: President A. Wangenheim ( brother of Concordia founder, Sol Wangenheim); Vice President L. Schwartzchild; Treasurer J. Neustadter (also a Concordia founding member); and Secretary I. M. Franklin. According to the newpaper account, "the Club is now in a most flourishing condition. The members are evincing a great interest in its welfare, and have proposed to soon give an entertainment." They did so the next month: a picnic in Belmont Park in San Jose. They placed an announcement in Jacoby's paper and invited the entire Jewish community to attend.

In September the Alemanians were given extensive publicity for their forthcoming subscription ball — doubtless because the Arrangements Committee had the good sense to provide the editor with a ticket. Thus we read, "A subscription ball of the Society will be given at Platt Hall tomorrow evening which will surely be graced by the beauty and fashion of the elite circles of Jewish society in this city. The Committee of Arrangements embrace some of the leading men among our co-religionists, and furnish a guarantee that the attendance will be of the most select and polished character. With pleasure we shall avail ourselves of the courtesy extended to us. Dancing, for which a large and splendid band has been employed, will commence at half past nine o'clock."

The following November, the Concordia Society elected a new slate of officers, headed by President M. Esberg, and celebrated its first anniversary with a grand ball at Platt's Music Hall. Presumably the editor wasn't invited since *The Hebrew* commented only that "The affair passed off very pleasantly and there was a good attendance in spite of the inclemency of the weather."

The Alemania Society remained independent another year and then merged with Concordia. Its second Anniversary Subscription Ball was its last affair. *The Hebrew* rhapsodized about the "twenty-two piece band playing for the elite of Jewish society." At great length it described the decorative national and German banners, and the food prepared by the best cooks of the day, Strauss Caterers. Finally, it mentioned that since the regular supper room was too small, the main hall of Platt's was partitioned off for the overflow crowd.

In 1868 the Concordia Society, augmented by those excellent party-givers, the Alemanians, moved to larger quarters in Dashaway Hall, 212 Sutter, between Kearny and Dupont (now Grant) Streets. A number of clubs and social groups held meetings in the building, colorfully named for a volunteer fire company whose members had pledged to "dash away" the cup of alcohol, an attitude that carried little weight along Sutter Street! On one corner of Sutter and Kearny Streets stood the Arion, "a beer saloon pure and simple," the haunt of the City's professional musicians, where the first musician's union was formed. On another corner Concordia member and tobacconist Moses Gunst had his store, which he established in 1872. In time Gunst joined the ranks of the tycoons as millionaire owner of the United Cigar Stores.

Nearly everyone who bought a cigar in the 1860s was a sportsman at heart, and upstairs was one of the oldest true gambling fraternities on the Pacific Coast. A few doors down from the hall was the American District Messenger Boys office, "its bevy of nascent Mercurys, eternally playing craps between assignments." In the days before the telephone put them out of business, the messengers were continually dispatched with messages for wives whose husbands sent word that they were "delayed at the office" and would be late for dinner.

In five years the Concordia outgrew Dashaway Hall. By 1873, the same set of economic conditions which, during the '60's, enabled the members of the Verein to become the City's leading bankers, insurance brokers and stock brokers, also moved the merchants of Concordia up to new heights. Levi Strauss became a nationally recognized pioneer in the field of men's work clothes; David Livingston, and Solomon Gump opened the City's leading department stores where merchandise from all over the world was displayed. These men wanted club accommodations befitting their stature. In 1873 they decorated two floors of the Howard building at the northwest corner of O'Farrell and Stockton Streets at a cost of $30,000. There was a reading room replete with magazines and newspapers; a wellstocked library; a billiard room, a dining hall; and not least of all, card rooms. The Club was only open evenings and Sundays.

According to the listing in the *Social Manual of San Francisco*, "The membership is entirely Jewish, and chiefly composed of wholesale merchants . . . . The entertainments are monthly or bimonthly parties, at which are seen the elite of the Hebrew residents of the city."

The term "wholesale merchants" was not a casual description. By the 1870s occupation and wealth became fundamental requirements for membership among the "elite." The story of a rich man recounted by author Rudolf Glanz is a fitting one: "A wealthy man who had a large circle of acquaintances but, realizing that he could not invite everyone, declared, 'We must draw the line somewhere, you know.' He drew it bravely between wholesaler and retailer. The man who sold soap and candles by the box was deemed within the 'sacred pale' of society's most elect. The man who sold soap and candles by the pound was voted a social Philistine."

The Turn Verein clubhouse shared the block with the Howard Building, giving "that section a distinctly GermanAmerican atmosphere," according to a journalist of the day. The old Orpheum theater, which was built like a beer garden reinforced that feeling. It had "a stage with a good orchestra and a few variety performers, as many chairs and small round tables as the auditorium could hold, and all the beer the audience could drink."

A decade later the appeal of the old world had faded for Concordians. The most fashionable residential area of the City by 1880 was Pacific Heights, where wealthy San Franciscans, Jew and Gentile alike, built stately homes. Van Ness Avenue, named for former mayor James Van Ness, was the focal point of the area. A broad boulevard, five feet wider than Market Street, lined with a double row of trees on each side, Van Ness Avenue was the setting for the magnificent Claus Spreckels mansion, the Hobart mansion, and the elegant residences of Louis Sloss, Lewis Gerstle, Leon Sloss and Ernest Lilienthal. Its flower-gardens and private entrance gates were imposing. It was ornamented with fine equipages and glamorous women, creating a dazzling background for the parades which streamed down the avenue on special occasions. When Concordia members decided to establish a club house of their own in 1887, they looked for land on Van Ness Avenue.

If they needed a blue print for what such a building should contain, it was outlined for them in B. E. Lloyd's description of club life in San Francisco, in his book, *Lights and Shades.*

"The aristocratic club-rooms are temples of luxury. The members are generally men of wealth able and willing to share with each other any expense that is necessary to add to their comfort. Besides the offices, reading and reception rooms, there are bar-rooms — stocked with choicest wines, liquors and the milder beverages — a billiard room, gaming rooms, music room, restaurant, and numerous lodging rooms, all furnished in costly elegance."

When the first Concordia Club building opened in 1891, it not only met these requirements, it refined them and raised them to new, elegant heights which set the standard for club life in San Francisco.

The Union Club, organized the same year as the Concordia Society had just completed its new quarters on Union Square. Rated as the club with the "highest social rank" in the City, it boasted a two-story dining room and interior decorations by a New York designer, who fashioned each principal room after a theme: there was a Francis II renaissance sitting room, a Persian style cafe, and Celtic cardrooms to name a few.

The older, more exclusive Pacific Club on Post and Dupont Streets "affected such a hefty reserve" that little was written about its interior. It was stated that the club is "gorgeously appointed, the table is good, lawyers predominate among the members and all the statesmen are to be found here." The Pacific Club had a reputation for being stuffy. One columnist reported wryly: "We are in a position to deny the story that on one occasion when Mr. — — was telling one of his stories at dinner at the club, all the old gentlemen in the room fell asleep simultaneously, and had to be awakened by the waiter when bedtime came."

A livelier club, one exclusively devoted to athletic sports, was the Olympic Club. Founded in 1860 as the San Francisco Olympic Club, it merged in the mid-Seventies with the California Olympic Club, which was conceived in 1871. It had been extensively reconstructed to the club members' specifications by landlord Mike de Young. Special attention was given to the gymnasium by John Hammersmith, one of the club's most outstanding athletes. Even so, this was just a temporary location until ground could be broken for a building of their own on Post Street.

The Bohemian Club, known as an artistic society, was established in 1872 by newspapermen. Doubtless biased, a columnist for the *Morning Call* noted that "like everything else newspapermen attempt, it was of course, a success. Those who are not members can only gaze like the Peri at the gates of Paradise . . . The brightest men in the city belong to it, and more wit has flashed under its roof than under any roof in town." Describing the interior of the Bohemian Club, writers highlighted such things as the picture bought each year at the Paris salon, the music library reputed to be the best in the city, and the club's symbol, the owl.

"You find the owl in the rugs, in the paintings, in plaster and in marble, in oil and in charcoal; sometimes blinking, oftener gazing out of the depth of its melancholy eyes at the clubmen as if to say that it had its high jinks, too, at the time of Minerva, and to warn the kindly member not to believe the scandals circulated about its character by La Fontaine (a gossip columnist of the day)."

•      •      •

There was a plethora of luxury clubs in San Francisco, and each group vied for community support. In this competitive atmosphere Concordia Club members launched a funding drive which was so successful that within three years they were able to build and furnish a clubhouse at a cost of more than half a million dollars. The success of the drive pointed to a new self-awareness among Bay Area Jews. While Jews played an increasingly prominent part in San Francisco's business and civic life, their social world became more self-contained. Choice was a factor in this development, but discrimination played an important role. Wealthy Jewish merchants, in every way the peer of their Gentile competitors, were made to feel unwelcome in Gentile clubs.

Discrimination at the Olympic Club reaches back to 1864, when in a letter to the editor of *The Hebrew*, a Jewish member of the Olympic Club wrote that,

"An assembly composed principally of inexperienced, self-conceited individuals misnamed American, amongst them a goodly number under twenty-one, passed a resolution that no Hebrew shall become a member of the Olympic Club hereafter." (There were eleven Jewish members at the time.) "A gentleman who did not participate remarked whether it wasn't necessary that candidates should thereafter undergo a medical examination before being admitted." The writer went on to say how the eleven Jewish members retaliated: "Blackballing Jews led to Jewish members looking at the proposer not the proposed, and horrors, *Christians* were blackballed."

There were Jews in some exclusive clubs, but they were exceptional. Frederick Castle, first president of Mt. Zion Hospital, who operated the leading California dried fruits firm with his brother, once served as president of the Union Club. Banker Sigmund Steinhart was a member of the Bohemian, Pacific Union and the Argonaut Clubs as was banker Philip N. Lilienthal. But these men were exceptions not unlike the select handful of Jews at the Pacific Union, Bohemian and Olympic Clubs in the 1980's

Another reason for the success of Concordia's building drive was the pride members felt for their organization, in spite of constant denigration by members of the Verein. Although the members of both clubs were German Jews who, predominantly, attended Temple Emanu-El, and were associated in the business world, there were schisms within the group. Because the Verein Jews arrived on the scene ten years before the Concordians and made their money ten minutes sooner, they viewed themselves as the elite. Nonetheless, the Concordians considered themselves no less exclusive. The acerbic prose of journalist Isadore Choynski is illustrative. Writing about the formation of yet another Jewish organization in 1875, he explains the rationale which led to its inception: "The Standard (is) the name of a new society, distinct in name and membership from the Concordia, which boasts of its pure blue blood and its mahogany tables and linen double headers . . . . The Concordia, being an old aristocratic establishment, is loath to affiliate with modern shoddy, hence this desire on the part of the newcomer to establish an independent clubroom where caste and circumstances are not to be taken into consideration."

Nevertheless, the "old aristocratic" Concordia Club smarted under the superior attitude of the Verein. Alice Gerstle Levison, whose father, Lewis Gerstle, was a member of the Verein, reflects that attitude in her personal memoirs:

"I seldom went to the Concordia because it was just a little bit—I don't want to use the word, but—below the standard of the other club, and my father wasn't a member. His partner, Louis Sloss was. I got to know

23

some men who invited me to come to the Concordia, and I was allowed to go to it, but I think my father always looked at it with a little doubt. He would just as soon not have his daughters go to the Concordia . . . ."

The construction of their own building offered Concordians the opportunity to provide themselves with facilities that would not be below the standards of anyone — including the Verein! How well they succeeded was apparent when the *San Francisco Examiner*, covering the informal housewarming on October 1, 1891, reported:

"Last night was one which will be long remembered by the Hebrew colony of San Francisco, the members of which form so prominent and influential part of the populaton of the city.

"It was the Concordia Club's opening night at their new building, and those who compose this popular and steadily growing organization had determined that the occasion should be one in every way worthy of themselves, of their race, the City and of the beautiful new home of which they have just come in possession.

"They succeeded."

## CHAPTER THREE

# 1142 VAN NESS

HE MEMBERS HAD worked for more than four years to acquire their new home. It was the Club's original intention to lease, rather than build the property. According to a story in the *Jewish Progress* on April 29, 1887, the Concordia Club "leased from Mrs. Albert Mann the property at the corner of Van Ness and Post Streets for ten years — 120 feet on Van Ness and 100 feet on Post. The lease runs from February 1, 1888, for $600 per month, and she will erect a building for them."

However, the idea of paying that sum of rent to a landlord — $72,000 over ten years — evidently didn't sit well with members like Levi Strauss or attorney J.D. Neustadter and banker Eugene Meyer. Following a year spent discussing the findings of a "Feasibility Committee," the clubmen decided instead to buy the parcel of land and build their new quarters themselves. Accordingly, a new corporation called the Concordia Building Association was formed for the purpose of subscribing bonds. Sam Sachs was designated as agent and treasurer of the newly formed corporation. Mortgage bonds upon the prospective property were issued in the value of $100 each, bearing interest at six percent per year. An escape clause in the contract provided that "this agreement shall be void and said subscriptions be deemed withdrawn unless the sum of $60,000 in bonds of $100 each shall be subscribed hereto within sixty days from this date, October 22, 1888."

Sixteen members signed the papers incorporating the Concordia Building Association, pledging bond subscriptions totalling almost half the sum required by the agreement — $29,000. Levi Strauss bought $5,000 worth of bonds, and Treasurer Sachs, $3,000. Other subscribers included J.D. Neustadter, S.W. and E.L. Heller, Eugene Meyer, M. Heller and M. Hyman.

Once the $60,000 was raised, the Club purchased the lot from Mrs. Mann for the sum of $147,000, according to Choyinsky's column of December 14, 1888. Club members expected to pay an additional $300,000 to erect and furnish the building.

Choyinski, who could always be counted on to strike a sour chord, categorized the proposed club as a "half million dollar gambling and banquet hall." Scoffing at the *raison d' être* of the men's club, he continued,

"The Concordia has been in existence for the last twenty years and their rooms — parlors, sideboards and all — are second to none in this city.

"The married men, chiefly, contribute to the maintenance of that temple of threes, fours and flushes, the very men who have most elegant homes, accomplished wives and lovely daughters. What answer can they make when, after midnight, they return to their elegant homes with swimming headaches? But it has been thus from time immemorial, in this country, and what can you do or say about it?

"Levi Strauss is a millionaire bachelor, and he has a constitutional excuse. So have some benedicts who have hell on earth, though they live in marble halls. But what shall we say of those who have good, virtuous wives, wasting their cold knees while they are betting against heavy odds at the Concordia, while their buttons are being sewed on and their socks darned?"

In the absence of any organized outcry by the "good virtuous wives" to slow the momentum, the fund drive accelerated into high gear. Another document in the Club's vault, dated April 21, 1890, lists an additional $14,000 subscribed to by a group of men including Leopold Michels, Simon Anspacher, Charles Blum and B. Triest.

The following month, Concordia President, attorney J.M. Rothchild, compiled a list of young members who had not yet subscribed. Rothchild sent the list to Chairman J.H. Neustadter with the suggestion that it be turned over to "Charles Sutro, M. Heller, Jr., and Henry Sinsheimer, who can solicit among them" from their young contemporaries.

Edgar Sinton, son of Henry Sinsheimer, saved a copy of the letter from Neustadter to his father, which reads in part: "I hand you a list of names who have not yet subscribed for Concordia Bonds and whom it is desirable that you in connection with the balance of the committee, should interview as early as possible, since you are well aware we have not yet placed the full amount of bonds, and it is absolutely necessary that money should be raised."

Commenting on that fund drive, Edgar Sinton, now one of the elder statesmen of Concordia-Argonaut, recently said, "It is surprising to see from the list of the donors that they gave very sizable amounts for young people. People were giving $500 and $1,000, which they barely had. $1,000 then was worth at least $20,000 today."

• • •

The architect retained to design the first Concordia building was J.H. Littlefield. Littlefield was renowned for the luxury buildings he had designed including the Hotel Pleasanton, the Raymond Hotel of Pasadena and the Hotel Larkspur.

Construction work progressed slowly, due to the incompetence of the building foreman. In November 1889, a year after construction began, only the basement had been completed. Finally, after two foremen had been fired, the building committee learned of Daniel Cameron, who, at the age of twenty-seven was already acclaimed in his field. They rushed to employ him and he, in turn, moved quickly to oversee the building's completion, "personally directing the erection of the building and the finishing of every one of the thousand details where absolute accuracy was required."

The building was a splendid red brick structure, embellished with granite facing, rising five stories above Van Ness Avenue. There were three full floors, plus a high-ceilinged basement and an attic. The cement work was done by a Sacramento Street firm which was the sole agent for Dyckerhoff Portland cement, the same material used in the construction of Stanford University. The firm's most important customer was the German government which, characterizing the Dyckerhoff cement as the strongest and purest available, used it in their military fortifications, acqueducts, etc.

Entering by the front door, a visitor to the Concordia caught a first glimpse of the beautiful etched glasswork appearing throughout the clubhouse. The artwork was done by the Haussmann Brothers, who were members of both the Concordia and the Verein. The main entrance was flanked by a pair of windows. One window panel represented a portrait of Johann von Schiller, from whose poem, "The Bell," christened Concordia, the Club derived its name. The other window depicted Wolfgang Mozart, the master of harmony, who inspired the Club's motto, *Harmonie Sol Walten* (Harmony Shall Prevail").

*Harmonie Sol Walten!* was the toast drunk again and again during the night of October 1, 1891, when Club members welcomed their friends and the press to an informal gathering to showcase the new building. Because its purpose was to display the building as it would ordinarily look, little decoration other than vases of roses on the mantlepieces and a few potted plants, adorned the halls. An orchestra stationed near the main staircase on the second floor provided the atmosphere of a promenade concert. To the strains of the "Coronation March" from Giacomo Meyerbeer and a "Good Times Medley," the visitors wandered through the cardrooms, cafe and billiard rooms, moving in a continuous procession from the parlors on the second floor to the great ballroom, eventually finding their way to the dining rooms on the third floor.

The following evening the *San Francisco Examiner* provided this description of the guests' reaction:

"On every hand was to be heard expressions of practically the same sentiment — that the club has now, if not the absolutely ideal clubhouse, certainly something as nearly approaching it as can very well be.

"This great building is more than that. There are many of its appointments, of course, peculiar to a place of rendezvous and entertainment used by men, but in innumerable other features, the beautiful interior so nearly resembles the private mansions of the wealthy and cultivated that one could find nothing at all strange in the presence of hundreds and hundreds of lovely and brilliantly costumed ladies who last evening mingled with the throngs of elegantly dressed and courteous-mannered gentlemen who were either doing the honors of the occasion, or, as guests, accepting them at the hands of their friends . . . .

"In the spacious entrance hall into which the visitors were first ushered, the most striking object is the great mantle of carved mahogany which surmounts and surrounds the vast chimney place. The richness and the beauty of this feature, costing as it did over $7,000, made it famous even before it had been entirely finished.

"The first apartment opening off of the lobby on the left is one handsomely furnished and fitted up for the especial use of the directors of the club. It is called the Directors Room, and opens back through sliding doors into a suite of three other handsome apartments, all furnished with comfortable chairs and greentopped tables, at which many of the ladies looked with demure smiles.

" 'This is where we will sit when we want to play solitaire,' said a director suavely."

A more detailed description of those rooms to the left of the lobby is offered by the *San Francisco Chronicle*'s account:

"The entire north, or Post Street side is devoted to four cardrooms, three of which are furnished and finished exactly alike, with many square tables of oak and chairs of the same wood and richly carved oak mantles. The fourth room, on the corner, is of black walnut finish and has a quaintly figured Turkish carpet and huge chairs upholstered in patterns to correspond. This apartment, when not used for cards, will be used by the directors as a board room and for that purpose has a long writing table.

"Opening from the opposite or south end of the lobby, is a corresponding suite of apartments, yet more handsomely furnished, in oak and mahogany. The first is the gentlemen's sitting room; the second, the reading room; the third, the cafe; and the fourth, the bar and billiard room. The latter is furnished with three billiard tables, the bar occupying a recess at the north end, the walls of which are formed of enormous mirrors in which the wealth of crystal and glassware is reflected and rereflected innumerable times.

"Nearly everyone next took at least a flying trip downstairs and through the spacious basement for a look at the bowling alley, shooting gallery and gymnasium. All were perfect in their way, but there was known to be such superior attractions on the upper floors that the majority of the guests, particularly the ladies, were anxious to hurry thither. So the grand staircase leading up from the front lobby soon became thronged with smiling groups, strolling upward, yet pausing at every landing, almost at every step, for another look at the bright scene below . . . .

"There were two great attractions on the second floor—the ladies' parlor and the ballroom. The former was really two apartments, furnished with soft couches and lounges. The windows and archways were draped with curtains of raw silk, while the chandeliers of crystal and gold shed a flood of soft light over all.

"Across the corridor was the ballroom, a vast apartment seventytwo by seventysix feet in size, with a stage at the eastern end fourteen feet deep and fortytwo feet wide, and walls which rose upward through the story above to an arched and decorated ceiling. Five great chandeliers furnished light for the vast apartment, in the center showing no less than seventy gas jets, the fixtures being all of brilliant crystal and gilt.

"Up another flight of steps and the thronging guests found themselves in the dining room, a vast apartment in the form of an 'L,' capable of seating many hundreds of guests. This room is not yet entirely furnished, but even as it is, it speaks eloquently of scenes of feasting and good cheer, of which it will many times and oft in the days to come be made the theater.

"Adjoining the dining room on the east side is the spacious kitchen, with its ample ranges and every other known modern appliance of culinary convenience."

Another noteworthy feature of the clubhouse was its fine plumbing, particularly in the gentlemen's lavatory on the second floor, reportedly "the finest to be found in the city, and, from an artistic and sanitary point of view, it is hardly to be excelled. The wash basins are arranged along a marble slab . . . the closets are marvels of neatness, and supplied with a patent tank and have a perfect system of ventilation. In the stalls, at the side, the partitions are of glass, and the water supply is not only available through the faucets above each receptacle, but there is also an automatic feeding tank which emits its regular portion of water at intervals."

The floor-coverings also were accorded their portion of praise: "No clubhouse, nor in fact any house in the city, is as richly and elegantly carpeted as in the Concordia Club building." Some of the rugs were "three inches thick, and marvels of art in this line."

Even the elevator received a share of attention, described as "the latest improved style . . . of the direct-acting, vertical hydraulic ram pattern."

The last word on the last word in clubhouses read: "In all its appointments and details, the new home of the Concordia Club is solid, substantial, luxurious and elegant. From roof to basement, outside and inside, it is of the best and most costly material, yet there is not in it one effect which mars the quiet, subdued tone of elegance. There is nothing florid, nothing that jars on the artistic sense."

Little did the newspaper reporters or the three hundred Club members and their guests dream that such splendid elegance was to be enjoyed for less than fifteen years . . . .

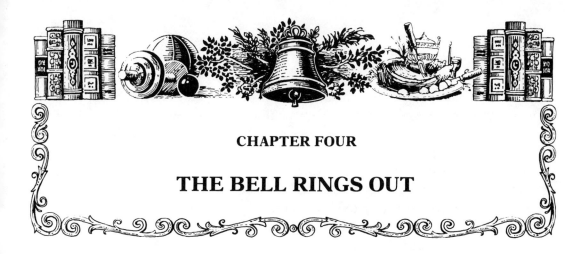

# CHAPTER FOUR

# THE BELL RINGS OUT

HAT MASTERFUL USE the members made of that building! From the floor to the gables, the luxurious rooms rang with laughter and music. It was the scene of sporting events, theatrical perfor-mances, balls and weddings, the Club soon becoming a second home not only to members but to their families as well.

Of prime importance, of course, were the four cardrooms on the main floor. Edgar Sinton, seated in his law offices, recalled the importance of these rooms in his father's life:

"He went there every Wednesday night and Saturday afternoon. All his friends did, because they had a card game arranged. No one would miss it — that was very important. I remember him taking me out to the Cliff House or to the park, but he always had to get home in time to get to the Club, because if he didn't . . . he wouldn't get in the game. (They played poker.) They had lunch there on Saturday before the cards. I remember going there to lunch on occasion with him."

A contemporary of Sinton's, Edwin Newman, son of Simon Newman, who was president at the turn of the century, recalled the nature of the Club's athletic activities when he was a young boy.

"I attended gym there when I was about eight — back in 1896. It was held in the ballroom. The first instructor was a man by the name of Sparks; then Mr. Smythe took over. They drilled us in calisthenics, weight pulleys, parallel bars — everything that goes with a modern gym. There were contests, and we would perform before our fathers and mothers. They didn't have separate memberships for boys. You came because your father was a member."

Harry Hilp also recollected those days. "I remember the three Stanton boys and the three Newman boys. The reason I remember the Stantons is because the instructor, Smythe, was a gymnast, and he had the three Stantons and me doing acrobatic standups and everything that went with it . . . . We received token medals and prizes."

Remembering the hours spent in the Club's bowling alley Newman said, "We youngsters, as well as the older people, would go there to bowl frequently. There was one sad thing about it, as I think back now. We would employ orphans as pin boys from the orphanage at the corner of Post and Franklin. What was sad was that the orphanage dressed the children so you'd spot them on the street as orphans. The boys wore almost shaved heads and short little gingham trousers. We paid the children five or ten cents to pick up the pins."

Women, as well as men, bowled at the Club. There was a Friday Night Bowling Club, which, according to a report in the *San Francisco Chronicle* December 1, 1893, was the only bowling club for ladies in San Francisco. (That the men turned the alleys over to the ladies on Friday night is some indication of the clubmen's enlightened attitude toward women.)

Unlike the token medals won by the young Hilp, fine prizes were awarded in the athletic events to older competitors. In the Club's archives is a large gold medal with the figures of two wrestlers engraved on it. Made by George Shreve and Company of San Francisco, it was awarded in 1898 to the twenty-one year-old L. Greenebaum of the Alaska Commercial Company. The medal, beautiful and elaborate in design, is especially impressive because it was awarded for second place!

The Club was a splendid setting for the frequent weddings held there. In December, 1896, *The Emanu-El* carried a description of one, proclaiming:

"Under the softened glow of countless fairy lamps and twinkling wax-lights, in a bower of fragrant buds and blossoms, Miss Gerturde Napthaly and Lionel B. Feigenbaum spoke to each other last night the solemn, binding words which united them for life.

"The wedding took place in the elegant home of the Concordia Club . . . . The guests entered under a canopy of crimson cloth into the main entrance hall, which, like the landings of the wide staircases, was adorned by numerous potted palms, the windowseats and mantels being banked with rare exotics in rich settings of ferns and mosses. The promenade surrounding the main ballroom was transformed into an avenue of palms and tiny cedars amid which shone electric lights and countless flowers, producing an effect uniquely beautiful . . . .

"The Rev. Dr. Voorsanger received the vows of the happy pair" . . . (in a scene illuminated by) "five chandeliers, in which were as many hundred wax lights, connected with each other by graceful, flashing festoons of star-like electric lights, entwined with smilax . . . .

"At eleven o'clock, the guests, to the number of 350, sat down to a sumptuous repast in the banquet hall, which had been magnificently adorned for the occasion."

While Joseph Napthaly, the noted attorney, spared no expense for his daughter's wedding, Mr. Napthaly's Club did not lag far behind in the lavishness of its own social functions. There was the annual Thanksgiving Ball, and the Washington's Birthday Ball. (It was at one of these that Henry Sinsheimer proposed to Nettie Koshland, who accepted his hand on the Club's dance floor.) The inauguration of a new slate of officers was another cause for a ball.

●　　　●　　　●

Concordians began welcoming visitors from all over the country to their new building. Those initial guests came to San Francisco to attend the City's first World's Fair, officially known as the California Midwinter International Exposition, which opened January 24, 1894. The fair site was a 200 acre expanse of sand dunes in Concert Valley, Golden Gate Park, now known as the Music Concourse.

To these sand dunes came exhibits from all over the world displaying the latest developments in manufacturing, agriculture, the arts, and other fields. Twenty countries participated including Brazil, France, the Ottoman Empire, Serbia, Montenegro, Rumania, Canada, Austria-Hungary, Great Britain, Russia, Portugal, Siam, Spain, Switzerland, Belgium and countries of Asia.

Actually, it was a second-hand fair. These countries had participated in the Columbian Exposition in Chicago the previous summer. M. H. de Young, a vice-president of the Chicago Exposition and Publisher of the *San Francisco Chronicle* believed that San Francisco could capitalize on a duplication of the Chicago exposition: it would emphasize the temperate winter climate here, highlighting the desirability of the region, yet cost the City very little money to sponsor. There were no state or federal funds to support the fair. The necessary money, approximately $361,000 was raised by a Citizens' Committee through popular subscription. Among the members of the Citizens' Committee were Louis Sloss, Philip Lilienthal and Dr. Martin Regensburger.

One of the highlights of the Midwinter Fair was the Japanese Village (its Tea Garden is a major attraction in the park today), which included "the splendid private residence of a native nobleman" and artists studios.

The other highlight was the "Midway Plaisance" which featured such diverse attractions as a replica of a village from the former French colony of Dahomey and a '49er mining camp with saloon, gambling and fandango houses. Other highlights of the Midway were the Electric Theater which featured Mlle.

Fontaine and her troop of French Folly dancers, the Heidelberg Castle, and the "Streets of Cairo" bedecked with bangles, beads complete with camel rides, and the astonishing Persian Palace with "muscle dancers" led by La Belle Fatima, performing "astonishing anatomical gyrations."

●　　●　　●

New heights of entertainment were reached in San Francisco with the Mid-Winter Fair, and to satisfy raised expectations Concordia social committees strived to generate exciting, original ideas for events. One such event was the Inaugural Ball of November, 1898. That night there were flowers arranged in a Japanese motif. A professional mind reader, and two well-known actors, who performed a "rehearsal scene" from their stage show were on hand. But the highlight of the evening was the "Concordiascope," described by *The Emanu-El* as: "an improved animatiscope, picturing upon the screen interesting scenes from club life, including a stormy session of the Board of Directors; an animated card game participated in by devotees of the game; proud young fathers exhibiting their pretty children, and the departure of the vanquished from the clubhouse." According to the newspaper report, "participants were unaware of the camera's presence when these scenes were enacted." Al Ehrman acted as floor manager, and the following men comprised the Entertainment Committee: H. G. Dinkelspiel, Leon H. Cook, Louis W. Neustadter, Max Koshland, Mel Toplitz, Henry C. Ahpel, Max Blum, Milton Bremer and Henry Sachs.

The most lavish balls were those on New Year's Eve. Wives and adult daughters began preparing for the occasion months in advance, selecting the fabrics and patterns for their gowns at the salon of Madame Baer, San Francisco's leading couturier. The expensive gowns kept dozens of seamstresses bent over their machines for weeks in the huge basement workroom of Madame's residence at the corner of Geary and Franklin Streets. Madame herself was kept busy seeing that none of the ladies had duplicate gowns! Hansom cabs and limousines were rented weeks in advance from Kelly's Stables on Sutter Street. A few of the members came to the balls in their own horse-drawn carriages. Herman Heyderman, a tobacco merchant, had his own turnout, and "Bonanza" Levy, would trot his rig down the block from his home at Franklin and Post.

The New Year's Eve Ball which celebrated the coming of 1897 was vividly described in *The Wave*, a weekly society publication. There were "innumerable girls in gorgeous gowns," and a "bevy of debutantes, including Miss Daisy

Schweitzer and Miss Edna Blum." The "beautifully decorated and spacious hall" was the site of dazzling entertainment provided by a fun-loving group of performers called the Calliopeans, who had recently merged with Concordia. One month earlier, at the annual Thanksgiving Ball, the Calliopeans had staged a variety show including impressions, song-and-dance numbers and a show-stopping "illustrated josh on thirty-five of the club members."

The theatrically-minded Calliopeans were probably drawn to Concordia by the elaborate burlesque staged by the Club earlier that year entitled, "The Misfit Monarch." The musical, which was produced at a cost of almost $3,000, was "an original burlesque satirizing *The Prisoner of Zenda*." The music was written by William Lorraine, a popular composer of the day. While the play was cast with men of Concordia, professionals did the rest. The book from which the play derived was written by John P. Wilson, long associated with the Tivoli theater.

Shortly before midnight New Year's Eve, the guests took part in the Grand March to the banquet room. A few minutes later, as the chimes began to ring out the old year and announce the new, the lights were turned down. "Father Time" appeared amidst a brilliant glow to bid farewell to '96. He was "habited à la Santa Claus." As he faded, a startling white light flared, illuminating "a charming young woman who represented '97." Fully clothed of course!

The account of that event ends on an interesting note: "The attendance was excellent, quite a number of people coming over from the Verein after the vaudeville there, remaining to the end." Though the Verein still condescended to the merchants of Concordia, Concordians, reveling in their beautiful, new building, and enjoying glowing publicity in the city's press, could not be ignored. Indeed, there were a few Verein members who also held membership in Concordia, such as Max Brandenstein, Charles Adler, M. Esberg and J.H. Neustadter, who was a Concordia Vice President. The young people of Alice Gerstle's set were not going to miss any of the fun, her deprecating remarks nonwithstanding.

## CHAPTER FIVE

# THE VEREIN JUMPS ON THE WAGON

HE SPLENDID EVENTS sponsored by the Concordia Club were matched by equally grand affairs staged by the Verein. On New Year's Eve of 1896 the Verein held a ball heralded by *The Wave* as "one of the most agreeable affairs" it ever gave.

"The dance was preceded by a vaudeville performance which lasted almost until midnight. The most striking features were Miss Alice Friedlander's imitation of (dancer) Loie Fuller and Mrs. Marcus Gerstle, who appeared as a music hall songstress. Both were very clever . . . Mrs. Gerstle has lots of talent and chic and her number brought down the house. The New Year was ushered in during the supper and, afterwards, the dancing was kept up until milk wagon time. There were any number of pretty girls present, but a scarcity of dancing men. The damsels who especially struck me were Miss Norma Bachman, in white tulle with myriads of ruffles, Miss Olga Triest in white tulle over pale blue and Miss Shainwald in white and grey. Of the matrons, Mrs. I.N. Walter looked stunning in pink and green brocade. . ."

It is no mere coincidence that only Jewish names appeared in the *Wave* article. By 1896 there were no longer any Gentiles in the Verein; the club was comprised entirely of German Jews. The changes unfolded gradually, although Jews had assumed leadership roles in the club from its inception. Dr. Jacob Regensburger, became the organization's second president in 1865. He was succeeded by August Helbing seven years later, and by Dr. D. Cohen in 1877. William Haas, a prominent wholesale grocer, was elected treasurer of the club in 1878. Six years later the Verein had both a Jewish president (Isadore Gutte) and a Jewish treasurer (Louis Sloss, Jr.). The membership roster of 1888 reveals that the club — without altering its charter — had become entirely Jewish.

What factors account for the withdrawal of Gentiles from the Verein? Their departure was perhaps inevitable, since for the scions of the wealthy members, the preservation of German culture had become unimportant. Moreover, there were other clubs eagerly soliciting their membership: the Bohemian, for the fun-loving; the Olympic, for the athletic; or the Pacific and Union Clubs, for those who were sufficiently blue-blooded and subdued.

However, for the Jews of German heritage, as well as for their American-born sons, the Verein represented a cultural bond they preferred to perpetuate. Throughout the late 1880s and the 1890s the club's festivities were still being called by German names. The memoirs of Alice Gerstle Levison reveal that, in addition to the gala balls held three or four times a year, the Verein also sponsored *Kranschen*, which translates literally as "wreath," but was used diminutively to describe "little" parties. According to the program — written entirely in German — a dance program for a large winter ball in 1888 was held on *den 1sten Dezember*.

Another factor was perhaps the exclusivity (some prefer to call it snobbishness) of the club. Relationships among the Jewish First Families had become so tightly interwoven by marriage that they felt no need for outsiders. Indeed, outsiders had as much chance of penetrating their closed circles as a weed in a carefully-tended garden. Their club was merely an extension of an increasingly insulated family life; a larger setting — with built-in advantages — in which to entertain the same people. As Mrs. Levison wrote:

"It was a great meeting place for men and girls. We had a lot of good times there and lots of wonderful parties because, being a club, they could go in for it in a big way with costume parties and theatrical things."

"Theatrical things" always played a major role in Verein activities. The presentation in 1892 of "Christopher Columbus: A Romantic Opera in Two Acts and an Interlude," written by club members with music by William Hinz and libretto by Hugo Waldeck, was a typical undertaking.

•        •        •

Like the Concordia Club, the Verein had moved to opulent new quarters before the turn of the century. The New Year's Eve Ball in 1896 was held at the new clubhouse at Post and Leavenworth Streets. Earlier that year, members initiated their luxurious new home with a "Bal Poudre" on March 14. It was a leap year affair and, according to newspaper accounts, "twelve married ladies had entire management of the entertainment."

While the Verein was primarily a men's club for dining and playing cards, the "First Families" were quick to make use of the premises for their private parties. The club's by-laws outlined its conditions for such use: "The Board of Directors may permit the exclusive use of the clubrooms, with the exception of the card, billiard and reading rooms, by members who desire to give private entertainments and shall charge thereof a sum not less than $100 for one day or fraction thereof."

After Alice Gerstle announced her engagement to J.B. Levison, her cousin Louis Greenebaum (the wrestler of gold medal fame) entertained the couple at a theater party for twelve friends and "after the show a supper was served at the San Francisco Verein." And, "Mrs. Marcus Gerstle gave a luncheon on Thursday afternoon in honor of Mrs. Joseph Koshland of Boston, at the San Francisco Verein. Tables with covers for fifteen were decorated in the prettiest of spring blossoms."

Like the Concordia Club, the Verein was also the setting for marriage ceremonies, such as the spring wedding of Miss Olga Adelsdorfer to Sanford Goldstein in March 1898. Dr. Jacob Voorsanger officiated at the ceremony. "Dancing was enjoyed until a late hour, with an intermission for supper served in the banquet hall. Here, as elsewhere, were pretty decorations; the pink color scheme being carried in the silk-shaded candelabra."

With family life so centered around the Verein, no wonder President Hugo Rothschild was amused when a *Morning Call* reporter sought his reaction to a survey question, "Does Club Life Interfere With Home Life?" The reporter recounted his exchange with Rothschild:

" 'Why bless you, our wives are the most enthusiastic friends the Verein has,' the president responded.

"Then he told how he had been a member of the club for twenty years, and had never known of a single instance in which it had created any domestic troubles. 'In the first place,' he said, 'the married men hardly ever visit the clubrooms more than one evening during the week. When they do come, which is mostly on Saturday nights, their object is solely to meet friends, read the European papers on file, play a game of whist, or pass the evening in some other social way.

" 'There is no dissipation nor carousing going on, and our families knew it well that the Verein would not tolerate anything of that kind. Now, why should they object to club life?'

"Of course there was no question as to the sincerity of Mr. Rothschild's opinion, and there was a speedy ending to that interview, but he insisted to be permitted to add that for the single men, the Verein opened a far better opportunity to spend their evenings than the public resorts of the city would if they were compelled to find their amusements around town."

On July 8, 1901 the San Francisco Verein signed papers of reincorporation. Officially, it incorporated on June 19, 1867 (although it had been in existence since 1853), and its incorporating papers should have been valid for fifty years. Reincorporation, which altered nothing, nonetheless was required to comply with the amended Civil Code of the State of California. The papers were signed by directors M.J. Brandenstein, E.S. Heller, John Rothschild, Walter W. Stett-heimer, D.J. Guggenhime, J. Blumlein and Julien Hart.

Three years later, the Verein underwent a momentous change when it shed its German identity to become the Argonaut Club. An article in the *San Francisco Chronicle*, mistakenly referring to it as "the oldest incorporated club of California," explains the reasons for the transformation:

> "The Argonaut Club celebrated its birth last evening with a dinner, followed by a jinks in the clubhouse at the corner of Post and Leaven-worth Streets. The Argonaut, new only in name, is the oldest incorpo-rated club in California. It was incorporated in 1851 (sic) under the name of the San Francisco Verein, and has acquired fame for its splendid hospitality under the old name, entertaining some of the most distin-guished visitors, artists, scientists, travelers, and men and women of world fame. From its modest rooms in the early days at Sacramento and Sansome Streets, (sic) it occupied commodious quarters at Grant and Sutter Streets, until its clubhouse at Post and Leavenworth, one of the finest in the country, was erected some nine years ago.
>
> "It gradually changed from the original German club to a progressive American institution, and the change of name was deemed timely, as the majority of the 220 members are Americans. It took years to overcome the reluctance felt by many members to change the old name, but the majority favored the change, and the new name was adopted one month ago."

The Club took its name not from the Greek legend, but from the sobriquet given to California emigrants at the time of the Gold Rush. Although most of the Verein-Argonauts arrived by ship, mirroring Jason's voyages in the Argo, the Club adopted the symbol of the covered wagon.

●     ●     ●

While the Argonauts merrily drove their wagon full speed into the twentieth century, the Concordians continued to ring out with good times on Van Ness Avenue.

In the spring of 1901, the City anxiously prepared for President William McKinley's visit to San Francisco. Elaborate plans had been made for a parade on Friday, May 17, from the railroad station at Third and Townsend, up Market Street to Van Ness, down Van Ness to the Bay. There the President was scheduled to launch the warship Ohio which was built at San Francisco's Union Iron Works. School children were to be stationed all along Van Ness to welcome McKinley, while students from Lincoln Grammar School were to form an honor guard in front of the Concordia Club.

In anticipation of the parade, Club members festooned the building with red, white and blue bunting and flags a full week in advance of his arrival, which proved fortuitous, since the only time the presidential carriage passed along Van Ness was on Sunday, May 12. Due to his wife's illness, President McKinley cut short his tour of Central California, and made a hasty and unscheduled appearance in the City to be with her. Suffering from what the newspapers called "nervous exhaustion and the results of a felon operation on her hand," she was taken to the palatial home of Republican leader Henry T. Scott, secluded on Clay and Laguna. For a week, as Mrs. McKinley lay near death, celebrations honoring the President were canceled.

While the Club's preparations for the presidential visit were foiled, their planned surprise party for Concordia Club President Simon Newman and his wife on the occasion of their twenty-fifth wedding anniversary in June 1902 was an unqualified success. What had been intended by the pair to be a quiet family dinner at the Club was transformed into a gala celebration by the entire membership.

The morning of the party, Club members sent a "large and magnificent silver vase to the Newman home, accompanied by a silver tablet bearing the good wishes of the members of the Club." Throughout the years, the vase—in actuality a punchbowl surrounded by silver serving dishes—has been loaned by Mrs. S. Walter Newman, Simon's daughter-in-law, to the Club for special occasions. To gauge its value, her grandsons, who delight in polishing the handsome family heirloom, recently weighed it (in 1981) for its silver content and estimated its current worth at upwards of $20,000.

According to a newspaper account, the dinner was served in the Clubhouse parlors, while an orchestra and the Paloma Ladies Quartet entertained the guests.

"Mr. and Mrs. Newman were married in this city twenty-five years ago at the residence of Mrs. Newman's parents, Mr. and Mrs. Louis Straus, on Green Street. Mr. Newman is president of the Simon Newman Co. of Newman, California, and is a member of the firm of Newman Brothers, prominent grain shippers. He is one of the founders of the town of Newman and received many telegrams of congratulations from the residents of that place."

Later that year, the Concordia inaugurated its winter season with a "magnifi-cent Bal Masque . . . under the most auspicious conditions and had a night of unlimited, unstinted revelry continuing until the early morning hours. It was one of the most successful and brilliant affairs in the history of San Francisco," exclaimed the *San Francisco Chronicle* the following morning.

The article described the decor of the ballroom in lavish detail. There were "garlands of greens interspersed with fancy and grotesque faces. The chandeliers were hidden behind the large masks and brilliant incandescents shed light through the colored eyes of the masks . . . . Palms and rows of potted plants transformed the broad foyer and the corridors into veritable parks."

The costumes of the revelers were richly drawn: "Mrs. Will Hochstadter represented the drop curtain of the Tivoli Opera House, with its advertisements of all sorts of wares, which elicited much favorable comment for originality . . . . Mrs. Henry Ahpel represented the queen of the night in a rich costume of black and silver stars . . . . Miss Gertrude Ettlinger was a diminutive shepherdess, while Milton L. Schmitt, dressed in the uniform of a local policeman, made a stunning guardian. Irving Lyon was a rather large baby in infant's white gown, blue sash and baby cap, displaying his toys . . . . M.J. Lyon, dressed as Sousa, was the image of the famous composer."

There were angels, devils and clowns, and "six young ladies in fancy cos-tumes made entirely of crepe tissue of many colors," Crowned heads of Europe and Asia, Chinese maidens, and local and foreign celebrities "all mingled in bewildering profusion until shortly before midnight, when the signal was given to unmask. At midnight a splendid supper was served, lasting until 2 a.m. when dancing was resumed and continued until 4 a.m."

And then, on the morning of April 18, 1906, the "unstinted, unlimited revelry" came to a crashing halt as the Argonaut's wagon swayed, crumbled and burned, and the peal of the Concordia bell was heard no more.

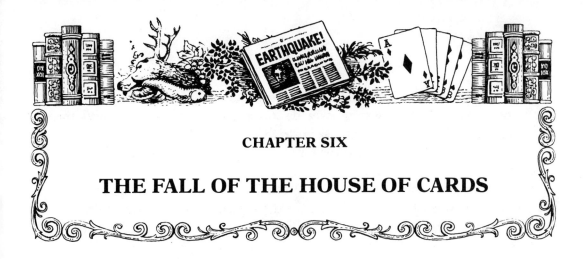

CHAPTER SIX

# THE FALL OF THE HOUSE OF CARDS

 N FRIDAY THE THIRTEENTH of April, subscribers to *The Emanu-El* were reminded that Passover would begin in a week. They also read the story about the death and destruction caused by the eruption of Mt. Vesuvius half a world away. Three weeks later when *The Emanu-El* next appeared, it carried a report of catastrophe at their own doorstep — the earthquake that devastated the City at 5:14 on the morning of April 18, 1906.

"From the ferry to Van Ness, from North Beach to the county line, the City is a melancholy pile of ruins," wrote Dr. Voorsanger on May 4. "In this devastation the Jewish community has probably suffered more than any other. Two thousand Jewish families living south of Market, mostly immigrants, have had their area totally eliminated. Sources of Jewish relief are paralyzed at the present time until all banks are in working order and all safes dug out of the ruins. The Relief Committee cannot cope with providing shelter; it has its hands full just clothing and putting people on their feet . . . ."

The newspaper, taking account of the damage to Jewish institutions, reported that while "Mt. Zion Hospital is a mere frame, a shell," the staff continued to use the building to house the wounded. Temple Sherith Israel, the only synagogue left standing, became the City's courthouse. "The Pacific Hebrew Orphan Asylum on Hayes and Divisadero is heavily damaged . . . 200 children had to be moved, but now a few additional kids have been added whose parents were killed in the earthquake. . . . The following buildings have been totally destroyed: the Russ Street Synagogue, Temple Emanu-El, the new Geary Temple, the B'nai B'rith Hall and library of 15,000 volumes, the O'Farrell Street headquarters of the Eureka Benevolent Society; the Emanu-El Sisterhood School buildings and clinic on Folsom Street, and the plants of the three Anglo-Jewish newspapers. Every building in the Mission is gone.

"The magnificent Concordia Club building on Van Ness, which was the social center of our wealthier co-religionists in the community, is a total wreck."

The story of the Club's destruction still pains the old-timers. Unlike the Argonaut Club, which was quickly destroyed in the fire that followed the earthquake, the Concordia died a slow death.

The quake, having ruptured the City's underground water lines, left the fire department helpless to control the numerous blazes caused by broken gas lines, short-circuits, and collapsed chimneys. When D.T. Sullivan, the Chief of the Fire Department, was killed in the quake, the department was strained to its limits.

The brick exterior of the Concordia Club, fortified with cement strong enough for a military fortress, withstood the earthquake. Although the interior was decimated, the facade remained a mute testimony to the splendor that had been within those walls. No fire could have destroyed that brick exterior. But when the path of the roaring inferno leveled the Downtown and Mission Districts and began to sweep westward, drastic measures were called for. By Thursday afternoon, April 19, while Nob Hill still burned, Mayor Eugene Schmitz and the City's chief of police had made a decision: to save the Western Addition (a tinderbox of frame dwellings) and the Richmond District, they had to check that wall of fire at Van Ness, the broad boulevard crossing the City from north to south. Orders were given for every fire engine in the City to converge at that avenue. Federal troops, the police and an army of workers made one last stand to save what remained of the City.

The artillery was secured. Soon huge cannons, drawn by military horses, thundered up the Avenue to aid the dynamiters in blowing up the mansions of the millionaires which lined Van Ness. Every available pound of dynamite was commandeered, and according to one eye-witness, the sight of the fusillade was both awesome and appalling.

The Concordia Club, its shell still echoing the sounds of happier days, shuddered under the barrage of cannon fire. The bricks crushed the etched-glass portraits of Schiller and Mozart. The remains of the stately building were sacrificed to save the City its builders had loved so well.

A first-hand account of the devastation on Van Ness Avenue is related by Paul Sinsheimer, brother of Henry Sinsheimer. "On our walk, we found the St. Dunstan's Hotel (located at the southeast corner of Van Ness and Sutter Streets) with only a small portion of its roof. The Concordia was a total wreck and it was clear that a frightful disaster had occurred.

"Everyone was alarmed, but there was a great deal of forced joking, each offering to buy real estate from the other. . . . On Van Ness we met a score of friends and tried to make the best of a bad situation, but the humor was strained . . . .

"We made our way through the streets, walking along the car tracks, leaving space on either side for tottering walls to fall. In the streets were great throngs of people talking wildly, terrorized by the enormity of the disaster. Men poured out tales of their private affairs to utter strangers."

•          •          •

The quake, though centered in San Francisco, struck along the Tomales-Portola Fault, and was felt from Point Arena in Mendocino County to Hollister in San Benito County. Edgar (Ned) Kiefer, Daniel Stone, Jr.'s uncle, wrote to relatives in New Orleans describing how he made his way back to San Francisco from Livermore, where he was on business when the earthquake struck.

"We couldn't get to the folks in the City and they couldn't get to us, so there was uneasiness all around. All wires were down. How I ever got there is a wonder to me. The ferry buildings had toppled and were burning when I went through . . . martial law had been declared and no one was allowed in the City, but I did not give up and kept right there with the mob. Finally we succeeded. Well, after walking through fire and smoke, dodging glass and walking up and down hills, I finally came to Rose's house (his sister, Mrs. Edward Livingston), and I found no one there. . . ."

Finding all his family at a relative's house on Broadway, he continues,

"There were about twenty-five of us and each one had a different idea, all so excited, all crazy with fear, but the fire was still many blocks away. I brought some to Livermore, some went to Alameda. The Simon and Phil Anspachers had a place across the bay which was out of danger.

"Two or three hundred thousand people were sleeping on the Presidio grounds and in Golden Gate Park and in every little park throughout the City, in blankets they carried with them. Many did not even have a blanket and very few had anything to eat or drink. One can't imagine what the disaster really is. The earthquake did great damage, the panic did greater damage, and the fire did the greatest damage of all. We only have what clothes are on our backs, that is if our houses are not destroyed by fire. But, I guess what is left in there will be stolen or given away by the relief society. They stand back at nothing.

"I.W. Hellman, the richest man in the West, stood in line for bread, so you can imagine what the situation really is. On top of it all, it poured down rain for twelve hours yesterday after the fire was all out, and the many thousands in the parks, homeless, were drenched. People mailed letters without stamps or envelopes, and the Southern Pacific offered free transportation to all who were destitute. I know of a case where someone

45

wrote a letter on a piece of paper from a tomato can, address and all on the paper, and it reached its destination! Give me yellow fever ten times to the earthquake and fire we had here. . . ."

While banker I.W. Hellman might have stood in line for something to eat, he was also observed doing other things. According to a report in *The Emanu-El*, he was "the first in his field to instill comfort in the public mind. On the first morning of the fire, he telegraphed East for $5 million and notified banks that money was forthcoming for the purpose of aiding the businessmen of the city in the resumption of their work."

J.B. Levison — like Hellman, an Argonaut member — second vice-president of the Fireman's Fund, helped save the City from financial ruin. He proposed the scheme that salvaged the insurance company, which owed more than $4 million in claims — much more money than it had on hand. Rather than liquidate the firm and reincorporate as his superiors proposed, Levison devised a plan to pay half of each claim in cash and the remaining half in company stock. This plan, accepted by the Board of Directors and the policy-holders, not only rescued the Fireman's Fund from financial ruin, but became the standard for insurance reorganization throughout the world.

The spirit in which Concordia and Argonaut members accepted the terrible catastrophe — wiping out not only their homes but their businesses — is expressed in these accounts from the writings of two of the Club members.

"Totally destroyed but not discouraged," was the message of the telegram sent by Edward Livingston, of Livingston Brothers, to a supplier back East. Livingston, in a book published for his family in 1941, entitled, *A Personal History of the San Francisco Earthquake and Fire*, relates how he hired a wagon and loaded it with merchandise he retrieved before the fire engulfed his store. The merchandise was taken to his sister's house on O'Farrell Street and offered for sale.

While the telegram to their suppliers made it clear that Livingston Brothers intended to remain in business, a letter from an amazed customer in Tonopah, Nevada (reproduced in Livingston's book) applauded the store for its uninterrupted service to customers. Sent to the store's post-earthquake location at Geary and Fillmore Streets, and dated July 7, 1906, it read:

"Gentlemen:
    "Am glad that, while you are not 'still doing business *at the same old stand*,' you are still doing business, nevertheless, in San Francisco.
    "Permit me to hand you herewith my check #384, your favor, on Rye & Ormsby County Bank, Tonopah, $47.50, in full, of my personal

a/c with you for silk dress purchased April 17, 1906, at 3:30 p.m. It is a pleasure for me to pay this, as the incident showed the promptness with which you attend your business matters . . . .

"I had naturally thought, when after the shock and smoke cleared away and I had the time to think of the matter, that, this purchase having been made so late in the afternoon of the day before the catastrophe, both the garment that I had charged and the one for which I had at the same time paid had 'gone up in smoke' and flames. Therefore, I thought it nothing strange not to find them here on my return, a week later, nor to receive them thereafter. Imagine my surprise and gratification, when, almost a month later, I came to my office one morning to find the package here containing the garments safe and sound.

"While the contents of this letter are not for publication in any form, I nevertheless take this occasion to extend to your firm the hope that success may attend your effort to face the game anew.

"Very truly, C.H. McIntosh."

Jacob Stern, then president of Levi Strauss and Concordia Club director, shared McIntosh's optimism. Stern was a great patron of the arts. Writing to his friend, the famous painter Toby Rosenthal whose works were among those he collected, Stern said, "My sister, Mrs. Samuel Heller, was hysterical and dazed, but nevertheless gave orders to our servants to save as many pictures as possible from our house. The 'Cardinal' (on permanent loan to the de Young Museum) was one of those saved." Stern was in New York on a business trip at the time of the earthquake while Rosenthal, whose parents were in San Francisco, was living and painting in Munich. After assurances that the paintings were safe, Stern went on to write:

"I was kept in New York longer than I expected. When I left, San Francisco was a prosperous city. When I return it will remind me of Pompeii. Our business (offices) and two city factories are entirely gone. We had a small factory in Oakland, the roof of which fell in. Through a kind act of providence the earthquake occurred before our force of girls that work in the sewing machines had gone to work. We now have our temporary headquarters at this factory.

"Our folks spent the first night in their auto and carriage stationed in front of their houses. The next day they went to the Presidio, and when the cinders and heat became unbearable, they went to the Park. Having brought their blankets and pillows with them, they slept in the grass. The following day they drove their vehicles to the country near San Mateo where they now are and where we will join them . . . .

"I have not lost my faith in San Francisco. Out of the ashes will rise a grander, nobler, stronger city — a city that will inspire the admiration of the world for its beauty and bustle. I am not painting you a fairy tale. I mean all that I say. The weak spots will be improved in every way, and it will not be long before you will hear of the new city."

●     ●     ●

Preparations for construction of that new city began almost at once, and Concordians and Argonauts had a prominent role in building the City's future. Members of both clubs were part of the "Citizen's Committee of Fifty," called by Mayor Schmitz less than ten hours after the disastrous quake struck. The committee met at the Hall of Justice on Kearny and Washington Streets at 3 p.m. on Wednesday, April 18. That select group included H.U. Brandenstein, Alfred Esberg, Mark Gerstle, I.W. Hellman, J.B. Reinstein, David Rich, I. Steinhart, M.C. Sloss, Gustav Sutro, Charles Sutro, Jr. and Rabbi Voorsanger. (I.N. Choyinski, the journalist, was also on the committee).

The "Committee on Feeding the Hungry," which distributed food in many parts of the City, based its operations at the Young Men's Hebrew Association. Stanford University students, many of whom were sons of clubmen, aided the committee's work. They acted as runners canvassing the City to ascertain the wants of the needy.

When the "Committee Of Fifty" completed its work after three weeks, they were succeeded by the "Committee of Forty on the Reconstruction of San Francisco," which began its deliberations on May 4. Hellman served on the Finance Committee; E.S. Heller, on Special Sessions of the Legislature; J.B. Reinstein on Charter Amendments; Gerstle and Heller on the Judiciary Committee. Reinstein also served on Parks, Reservoirs, Boulevards and General Beautification; Gerstle was also on Lighting and Electricity and Reinstein was on yet a third committee, the Library and the Restoration Thereof.

When all the reports were in — recommendations that would indeed lead to the "grander, nobler, stronger city" that Jacob Stern envisioned — one of those recommendations was for the creation of a Civic Center at the junction of Van Ness Avenue and Market Streets, to consist of "a group of buildings surrounding a plaza or open space, instead of one building housing all municipal departments."

The plan was carried out, and the inscription in the Rotunda of the present City Hall, written by Edward Robeson Taylor, Mayor, 1907–1910, reads:

> *"O glorious city of our hearts*
> *that has been tried and not*
> *found wanting go thou with like*
> *spirit to make the future thine."*

Meanwhile, both Concordians and Argonauts were at work rebuilding the Jewish community. Concordian Henry Wangenheim, then president of Temple Emanu-El, worked diligently at the temporary offices of the demolished Temple, set up at 2053 Sutter. Within a month of the catastrophe he was able to announce the complete reorganization of the congregation's records, including a new registry for members and registry books for marriages and deaths. Members of both clubs, including Simon Newman, Marcus Koshland and Lippman Sachs of Concordia, and Julius Jacobs and I.W. Hellman of the Argonaut, sat on the committee to reconstruct the temple.

Having looked to the rebuilding of their homes, their businesses, their City and their temple, the clubmen worked with equal vigor to restore their clubs. The Concordians promptly rented a large private house on Pacific Avenue near Fillmore, belonging to Mary L. Treanor, that was to be their home away from home for the next two years. With only the most momentary pause, the weekly card games and daily lunches continued.

The Argonauts used the beautiful home of Max J. Brandenstein, at 1901 California Street, a brick Victorian which had emerged unscathed by the fire as their meeting place. They continued to meet there for nearly three years.

Throughout the clubs' interim months when talk was not of food or inside straights, conversations centered on the rebuilding.

PART TWO

# NEW PLANS & FAIR PLANNING:
# 1907–1939

## CHAPTER SEVEN

# 1142 VAN NESS . . . AGAIN

Y THE TIME Simon Newman became president of the Concordia Club in 1901, he had accumulated thirty-six years of membership in the Club. From the day the Club organized as the Concordia Society when he was a lad of eighteen, it figured prominently in his life. For Simon and for the other Club members, there was never any question that they would rebuild their Club on the Van Ness Avenue lot, even though the complexion of that once elegant boulevard was changing rapidly. The magnificent mansions were gone; in their place arose hastily constructed frame buildings which, for the next few years, would house the famous downtown retail stores demolished in the catastrophe. The few remaining homes in the area gave way to commercial development.

Simon's son, Edwin Newman, recalls that "promptly after the fire, homes still standing on the west side of Van Ness were converted into businesses. For example, the Emporium opened in the Hecht house on the southwest corner of Van Ness and Post. The Van Ness Theater was rushed up on the corner of Grove, and for a while it was San Francisco's chief playhouse."

By December 1908, the Concordians anticipated the return to their own clubhouse. *The Morning Call* reported on December 7 that:

> "Plans for the rebuilding of the Concordia Club at its former location, Post Street and Van Ness Avenue, are now being considered by the directors. Within a few weeks the directors' ideas will be placed in the hands of the architects.
>
> "The Club will occupy the southern portion of the spacious lot. The corner will be leased. According to the plans of the directors and members, the new building will be one of the most artistic structures in San Francisco. The furnishings will be specially designed and made to order.
>
> "The directors are already preparing a plan for financing the proposed structure, and according to information from authoritative sources, will have the work commenced shortly after the first of the year. Until plans

have been approved by the board of directors, the amount to be expended will not be determined."

The architect chosen for the project was Gustave Albert Lansburgh, the same young man selected to rebuild Temple Emanu-El. Lansburgh, born in Panama, moved with his brother and his mother to San Francisco in 1882 after his father's death. Six years later, following the death of their mother, the two Lansburghs were placed in foster homes. Rabbi Jacob Voorsanger acted as their guardian. G. Albert, as he preferred to be called, received his religious education at Temple Emanu-El, was graduated from Boys' High School and attended the University of California for two years. The young architectural student was encouraged by his patron Moses Gunst to enroll in the Ecole des Beaux Arts in Paris, the leading architectural school of the day. Graduated in 1906, he returned to San Francisco a month after the earthquake. He would later build the Elkan Gunst Building at Geary and Powell for his patron's son; Temple Sinai in Oakland, and the Koshland Building at Market and California. Acclaimed as a master of acoustics, Lansburgh was most renowned as a theater architect, and he designed over fifty theaters of the Orpheum circuit.

Lansburgh was greatly restricted in designing the plans for the new Club. Because funds were tight, he could use only half the lot and provide for only the most essential activities. The new three-story building, its main entrance on Cedar Street, contained card and billiard rooms, lounges and dining facilities — the same amenities that are housed in the south side of the Club today.

Soon the newspapers were reporting resumption of social activities at 1142 Van Ness. The *Emanu-El* of December 17, 1909 heralded the building's reopening inauguration with these words:

"The formal opening of the Concordia Club took place last Saturday (December 11) and will hereafter be the scene of many social functions. Unusually beautiful were the magnificent gowns and the rooms — a very brilliant spectacle."

Some months later, the newspaper reported that "the Concordia Club has become the nucleus of Society for Sunday evening informal dinners."

Reminiscing about those days, Mrs. Justin (Amie) Hoffmann recalls, "When the club reopened, I had just graduated from Girls' High, and, as was the custom in those days, my parents were taking me to Europe for an extended tour. I recalled how I cried and cried that I didn't want to go. My brother, George Siebenhauer, was a member of Concordia, and I kept thinking about all the dances I would be missing. . . ."

The Club was the scene of numerous distinguished dinners, such as the Judicial Banquet given on March 21, 1911 to honor four eminent jurists: Federal

Judge Julian Mack of the U.S. Circuit Court of Connecticut; Judge Henry Melvin, Justice of the Supreme Court of California; and Judge Max C. Sloss and Congressman Julius Kahn of San Francisco. The toastmaster for the occasion was the Club's eloquent attorney, Otto Irving Wise.

In the eyes of the 150 members and guests at the banquet, the most important figure in attendance was Concordia member Julius Kahn. Kahn, born in Germany in 1861, lived in San Francisco from age seven. The son of a modest San Francisco baker, the young Kahn rose each morning to make deliveries with his father's bread wagon.

Later, Kahn launched a promising career as an actor. Traveling extensively throughout the country, he played supporting roles with such famous actors as Edwin Booth, Joseph Jefferson, Clara Morris and Tomasso Salvini. It was his trips to Washington, D.C. that most impressed him. While in the nation's capital, he became friendly with members of Congress, who greatly influenced the actor. Kahn left the stage in 1890 at the age of thirty to take up the study of law. Kahn was ever the actor; throughout his lengthy career in Congress, he became known for flamboyant neckties and his dramatic and masterly elocution.

Kahn was still a law student when elected to the State Assembly in 1892, the only Republican from San Franisco. After serving one term and declining nomina- tion for the State Senate, the young man returned to his law practice. While outside the political arena for several years, Kahn continued to play a prominent role in such civic events as the Midwinter Fair. Then in 1898 Kahn was nomi- nated and elected to the U.S. Congress from California's Fourth District. Re- elected in 1900, he lost his bid for re-election in 1902, recaptured it in 1904, and served continuously thereafter until his death in 1924. He enjoyed such popular- ity that during his last five terms in Congress he faced little or no opposition, receiving the endorsement of all major political parties in California.

●     ●     ●

Congressman Kahn was the man of the hour that March evening in 1911 due to his success in securing federal approval of San Francisco as the site for the upcoming Panama Pacific International Exposition (PPIE), to be held in 1915.

A month before the banquet, the *San Francisco Call* praised Kahn, stating, "Representative Kahn deserves well of his constituency and all his townsmen. On him fell the burden and his was the heat of the day in the fight before Congress for the World's Fair. . . . It is justice to say that to Mr. Kahn more than to any other single influence is due the success of San Francisco in the winning fight before the House of Representatives."

The PPIE was very close to the hearts of Concordia and Argonaut members, many of whom were on the original planning committee when the Exposition was conceived by Reuben Hale in 1904. The young Hale had first proposed the idea to the San Francisco Merchants Association. "The Panama Canal will probably be built," he told the Merchants board. "Is the time not ripe for us to consider a world exposition here in San Francisco?"

The canal's construction had been guaranteed since the cruise of the battleship Oregon. The Oregon, built in a shipyard in San Francisco, was completed in 1896. Two years later, when the United States was embroiled in war with Spain, the Oregon was lying at Bremerton Navy Yard, at Puget Sound. The ship was ordered to San Francisco, then sent to join Admiral Sampson and the Atlantic Fleet in Cuban waters. That 14,000 mile journey around the South American continent took two months to complete. As the ship journeyed alone toward the fleet, the sailors stood at her guns day and night knowing the enemy was near, but not knowing their own fleet's location. Although the Oregon completed her dramatic run without a mishap, that voyage demonstrated an alarming national weakness. It proved that protecting both seaboards without separating the navy into two divisions, each incapable of giving the other support in an emergency was impossible. After the cruise of the Oregon, public opinion was united: the Isthmus of Panama posed strategic problems which the American people would no longer tolerate. "There are few instances in our history when the Government has received so distinct a mandate to do something as this public demand that the Canal be dug," wrote historian Frank Morton Todd.

In addition to alleviating naval vulnerability, the Canal promised to promote economic strength in the West. San Franciscans understood that construction of the Panama Canal would profoundly enhance the City's place on the planet.

In the four decades from 1870 to 1910, the tonnage of cargo transported by nations almost doubled. Initially San Francisco profited little from the expansion of world markets. While China and Japan, previously outside any competitive commercial economy, were awakening to the latent power of their vast labor pool, it was England that benefitted most. The distance to Asian and Australian ports was shorter from Liverpool than from New York. Panama would reverse that. With the canal, goods from the East Coast could be shipped from San Francisco to Asia more quickly. Conversely, San Francisco would be brought nearer to New York by sea, and thus to the great ports of Europe. "It was like shifting the nations on the map; decreeing that one should make way for another giving some advantages that once belonged exclusively and seemingly in perpetuity to another," wrote Todd.

There was no better cause for a world's fair to the merchants of San Francisco than the inception of the Canal, and their enthusiasm for Hale's idea was undiminished by the events of 1906. Many Concordians and Argonauts served on the Ways and Means Committee, which was formed in 1910, including: Jacob Barth, H.U. Brandenstein, M.J. Brandenstein, Albert Castle, A.I. Esberg, M.H. Esberg, Herbert Fleishhacker, Mark Gerstle, W.L. Gerstle, B.A. Goldstein, M.A. Gunst, William Haas, J.K. Hecht, I.W. Hellman, I.W. Hellman, Jr., H.L. Judell, Marcus S. Koshland, J.B. Levison, E.R. Lilienthal, David Livingston, Jules J. Mack, J. Henry Meyer, H. Meyerfeld, Jr., C.F. Michaels, Alfred Meyerstein, Edgar D. Peixotto, Allan Pollock, Robert A. Roos, Lippman Sachs, Louis T. Samuels, Louis Saroni, B.F. Schlesinger, Henry Sinsheimer, Leon Sloss, Louis Sloss, Jacob Stern, Sigmund Stern, Charles Sutro, Edward I. Wolfe, Gustav Wormser and Isadore Zellerbach.

Among the individuals and firms contributing to the PPIE's initial fundraising campaign held at the Merchants' Exchange Building on California Street, April 28, 1910 were Levi Strauss & Co., Leon Sloss, Isaias Hellman, Alaska Packers Association, M.A. Gunst & Co., and M.J. Brandenstein & Co.

PPIE officers and members of the Board of Directors included: Vice presidents I.W. Hellman, Jr., and Leon Sloss; Directors M.J. Brandenstein and A.I. Esberg, and Sub-Directors Herbert Fleishhacker and J.B. Levison.

Thus Concordia members and their guests toasting Congressman Kahn that night in 1911 had a very personal involvement in the exposition legislation he introduced just one month after the earthquake and fire.

The date for the PPIE was to be set when President Taft determined that $5 million in individual and corporate subscriptions to finance the fair had been secured. Raising the money posed few problems, but political difficulties arose when New Orleans began to vie with San Francisco to become the site. Both cities raised the ante. Then, with the outcome still in doubt, San Francisco issued the *coup de grace*: Kahn informed Congress that the City would not ask one dollar from the U.S. Treasury. What San Francisco did want was Federal recognition as the nation's official host of the celebration which was to mark the opening of the Panama Canal. Easing Kahn's task a little, a delegation of lobbyists from San Francisco arrived in Washington bearing gifts. The delegation included California Governor James Gillett; Mayor P.H. McCarthy, Argonaut member William Gerstle, then president of the city's Chamber of Commerce; and Concordian M.A. Gunst. Delivering a bounty of California wines and fruits, the group incurred a freight bill which, alone, totalled $1,900!

But the most persuasive part of the campaign was Kahn's stirring speech before the House of Representatives. Employing all his oratorical skill, Kahn described the valiant efforts his city had made to rebuild itself after the devastating 1906 disaster. Repeatedly interrupted by loud applause, he predicted that San Francisco would raise the money needed to hold the exposition, and concluded with a rousing plea for support. He got it — and the City got its fair.

The site selected for the Exposition was Harbor View. It was no mystery that most San Franciscans had no idea where it was located. Most of the land was under water. Habor View, an area three miles long and a third to a half-mile wide, located between Fort Mason on the east and the Presidio on the west, was, through its middle, either entirely submerged or uninviting swampland. Such an unlikely site was this to those of timid imagination that, when President Taft arrived in October 1911 for the ground breaking, he was ushered off to Golden Gate Park to shovel the first spadeful of dirt.

It was at a luncheon the next day at the Cliff House that President Taft, saluting the indomitable spirit of the City, coined the now familiar cliché, "San Francisco . . . the city that knows how." In this instance, it was a city that knew how to turn that uninviting marsh into an area of exquisite, unforgettable beauty.

It was also called "the university of the world," because of the numerous exciting, innovative exhibits at the 1915 Exposition. The fair introduced wireless telegraphy; demonstrated the transcontinental telephone; exhibited a million-volt electrical transformer; offered the public airplane rides; showed an auto assembly plant in operation; held auto races, and used moving pictures in its exhibits. It was also the first occasion a clothing manufacturing company made a public demonstration of mass production methods. Using the assembly-line technique perfected by Henry Ford to mass produce cars (at a rate of 18 a day), Levi Strauss & Co. re-enacted the large-scale manufacture of overalls. President Jacob Stern watched with great satisfaction as the material was laid out in ninety-six thicknesses, the pattern marked on the top of the heap, and an electrically driven knife, which made 3600 strokes a minute, sawed the cloth into the proper shapes. The pieces then moved down the line to the seamstresses and then to the finishers.

The exhibit of H. Liebes & Co., was equally facinating: a realistic Arctic scene composed of icebergs, seals, voracious looking polar bears, an igloo and Eskimo fishing gear. Some of the best skins of the North were on display, along with finished garments made by the San Francisco furrier.

Only sixty years had transpired since San Francisco had risen from a frontier town to a cosmopolitan city, and less than ten years had elapsed since it had shaken off the ashes and rebuilt itself after the devastation of the 1906 catastrophe. During the course of the Exposition, San Francisco readied to meet and entertain the international elite. Many of these statesmen, academicians, capitalists and artists of world prominence were entertained at the Argonaut and at the newly-enlarged Concordia Club. The talk about adding on had begun soon after that momentous banquet in 1911.

## CHAPTER EIGHT

# THE ANNEX

HE NEW BUILDING was not an unqualified success. The empty lot on the north side of Van Ness was a constant reminder of the constraints which had prohibited the architect from providing all the amenities of a truly luxurious club. Depite all efforts to economize, the existing structure strained the financial limits of the Club. Minutes of Board meetings and reports by President Herbert Rothchild give some indication of the Club's economic woes. In September 1910, initiation fees for men over thirty were raised to $25, and dues were increased by $5 a month.

However, certain expenditures were apparently considered essential. Board minutes of October 1910 note that Fred Seller was authorized "to install a telegraph wire in the Club for election night returns." And in December the Board approved the Entertainment Committee's proposal to host complimentary banquets scheduled for January and March.

By January 1911 the Club's initiation fee was again raised — this time to $50 — and each member was assessed an additional $120. This new policy resulted in dissension within the Club's ranks, as evidenced by the following notes: "February — Members to be notified that resignations after the assessment was announced do not nullify their indebtedness to the Club. . . . May — Several members want to resign without paying the assessment. . . . September — A member is expelled. . . . October — Four members owe a great deal of money to the Club; two to be expelled unless they pay up. . . . November — Men, twenty-one to thirty, do not have to pay any initiation fee; dues lowered $5 per month."

Financial difficulties notwithstanding, one November entry is noteworthy: "Christmas gift to employees — one extra month's salary."

The decision to dismiss initiation fees for men ages twenty-one to thirty was significant: the newly rebuilt Club was no longer attracting young men.

Edwin Newman recalls the deficiencies of the clubhouse from a young man's perspective. "There was nothing for us to do in that building. My father was President when it was in the planning stages. He said he'd like me to bring in quite a few young people. I was then around twenty or twenty-one. I said I'll be very glad to if you put in a swimming pool."

Young Harry Hilp voiced the same complaint. He said, "the facilities were adequate for the older men, but there was nothing in the Club to interest us except good German food and card playing. In 1910 Charles Hirsch was elected president (sic). His son, Arthur Hirsch, belonged to a fraternity of which I was a member. In early 1912 Mr. Hirsch talked to Arthur and me about what we could do to help the Club attract members. We suggested a gymnasium, swimming pool and handball courts for the new addition. Charles Hirsch suggested we contact our friends to see if they would be willing to join the Club with no initiation fee, $5 monthly dues and all the privileges of senior members, until the age of thirty. In early May 1912, before Charles Hirsch's term expired (sic), we held a meeting and thirty-two fellows signed up.

"Louis Schwabacher became president in June 1912. In early November, just before the holidays, a membership meeting was called to present the plans for the new athletic facilities. At the same time a request was made for funds in the form of bonds to be paid off in twenty or twenty-five years. It was a gala occasion and a very able attorney, Otto Irving Wise, gave an outstanding address. It was so impressive that even I pledged $200." It was fortunate that Otto Wise was such a convincing speaker, because the amount of money required to build the "Annex," as it was called, was projected at $90,000.

A photograph of the building during construction of the Annex was spread across four columns of the *San Francisco Examiner*'s Real Estate and Finance Section on Sunday, May 23, 1915. The photo caption read: "Annex that is to be built by Concordia Club to its quarters at Post Street and Van Ness Avenue. It will cost $90,000 and will contain gymnasium, swimming tank, handball courts and other features. It will be ready by August 1. G. Albert Lansburgh is the architect."

Lansburgh was able to add to the existing building with little problem, no doubt due to his foresightedness when the original plans were cut back. The entrance on Cedar Street was sealed, while the former entrance lobby was incorporated into the library and billard rooms, whose windows faced onto Van Ness Avenue. The Annex, with its new entrance on Van Ness, thus formed a graceful addition to the old building.

"The result," according to a story in the *San Francisco Examiner*, in April "makes for one of the handsomest clubs in the City, with all the modern conveniences. . . . Half of the ballroom, a swimming pool twenty-five by seventy-five feet, the gymnasium and a handball court are included in the new parts. The ballroom is now ninety by thirty feet. There is a splendid hydro-therapeutic department, with all modern appliances in the basement.

"Three large dining rooms on the main floor are arranged so they may be converted into one large apartment .... Cardrooms, a woman's lounge, the directors' boardroom and other smaller rooms comprise a harmonious whole of which the members are pardonably proud. The furniture and hangings are notably beautiful and artistic . . . ."

Nearly a thouand members and their friends attended a dinner and ball to formally inaugurate the completed club on April 19, 1916. (The Club had been in use since the fall of 1915.) In a setting of "floral opulence against a background of handsome and rich furnishings," the affair was described as "one of the most elaborate entertainments given by the Club since the fire. Before that time, the Concordia Club balls were events of social consequence and sumptuous decorations. Last night's ball was said by old-time members to have been a revival of the old regime."

Dinner was served in the new gymnasium, latticed for the occasion with "bamboo, palms, ferns and huckleberry so that the walls were entirely concealed. Overhead, from a lattice of bamboo, hung thousands of wisteria blossoms and yellow Japanese lanterns."

Dancing was held in the third-floor ballroom which extended across the entire front of the building from Cedar to Post Streets. At the north end of the ballroom (the present dining room) Lansburgh had constructed a stage which would accommodate generations of Concordia-Argonaut actors. The south side of the third floor, beyond the ballroom, comprised a group of rooms intended as bachelor studios. However, since only three or four members took advantage of the rooms, this practice was discontinued after a short time.

Directly below the ballroom on the second floor, Lansburgh had built a lounging gallery, flanked on either side by four new card rooms, as well as a bar and a barbershop. An inner court, just beyond the entrance lobby on the main floor, extended to the roof three stories above, providing a light and airy atmosphere.

Among those who hosted private parties at the dinner preceding the ball were happy young men such as Harry Hilp and Lansburgh himself, who had become a Concordia member, and the Club's Officers: President Louis A. Schwabacher, Vice President Julius I. Cahn, Treasurer Fredrick Seller, Secretary Max I. Koshland, Assistant Secretary John E. Madocks, and Directors Joseph E. Bein, Herman Frankel, Arnold L. Liebes, Louis J. Newman, Fred Patek, Henry Schussler and Sidney L. Schwartz.

A month after that formal opening, a new slate of officers was announced at the annual Board meeting. Louis Schwabacher continued his tenure as president, but the new line-up of officers included Fred Patek as Vice President, Fred Seller as Treasurer and Max I. Koshland as Secretary. By that time the soaring demand for membership had necessitated a change in the by-laws to raise the number of active members from 400 to "not to exceed 500" seniors and juniors. Senior initiation fees rose to $200 and annual dues had become $120 for seniors and $60 for juniors. A new category of membership — called "Junior Associate" — was devised for young men aged fifteen to twenty-one, the number of Junior Associates not to exceed 100.

The by-laws also made provision for women to utilize the newly-completed clubhouse: "Members may extend to the ladies of their household the privilege of using the Ladies' Dining Room, provided that they be accompanied by a Club member. Ladies visiting the Club as provided above shall not have access to any of the clubrooms excepting the Ladies' Dining Room and the Ladies' Reception Room."

The Club was described as "one of the oldest and most important social organizations among the Jewish people in the West," according to Rabbi Martin Meyer in his book, *Western Jewry*, published in 1916. He wrote that the Club "has been recently enlarged and is as fine and imposing a structure devoted to social purposes as any city can boast of. The clubhouse is three stories in height and contains — besides the features usually found in first-class social institutions — a plunge and baths, a library of carefully selected authors, a gymnasium and similar attractions.

"The aim of the Club from its earliest period has ever been to provide a social home for its members and their families. That it has been eminently successful in this respect is evidenced by the use women and children are making of the gymnasium and numerous other attractions provided for them by a generous membership. The Club is primarily a family institution and is often referred to as the 'House of Concord.' "

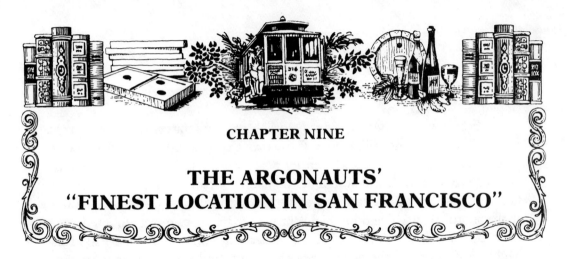

## CHAPTER NINE

# THE ARGONAUTS'
# "FINEST LOCATION IN SAN FRANCISCO"

HE GRACIOUS HOSPITALITY of the Max Brandenstein home notwithstanding, members of the Argonaut Club were as anxious to be back in a clubhouse of their own as the Concordians were. Three years after the devastating earthquake and fire, the Argonauts found what they regarded as the finest location for a men's club that the City could offer: the second and third floors of a newly-completed office building at the corner of Post and Powell Streets. (The building now houses United Airlines.)

Conveniently located in the heart of downtown San Francisco, the building was within walking distance of the Financial District. Its handsomely appointed dining room faced Union Square and conversation at the tables was punctuated by the clanging bells of cable cars climbing Nob Hill. What sound could be more typical of San Francisco?

An article in *The Emanu-El* of January 15, 1909, announced the good news: "The Argonaut Club, of which Mr. Alfred Esberg is president, has just received the completed plans for a new home which will be situated at the corner of Post and Powell Streets. It will be supplied with all the modern conveniences and appliances to accommodate its members."

One year later, on the very night that the Concordia Club opened its doors (December 11, 1909), the Argonauts followed suit. The Jewish community newspaper noted: "The formal opening of the Argonaut Club took place last Saturday and will hereafter be the scene of many social functions. Unusually beautiful were the magnificent gowns and the rooms — a very brilliant spectacle."

"If you belonged to the Argonaut," wrote Ruth Bransten McDougall, in her delightful book, *Coffee, Martinis and San Francisco*, "you belonged to snobbish Jewish society. The members . . . considered themselves as exclusive as the Gentiles who belonged to the Pacific Union Club on Nob Hill."

Mrs. McDougall's father, Manny Brandenstein, a member of that "snobbish Jewish society," served for many years as Argonaut president. According to his daughter, Brandenstein would rather have spent his time writing and directing theatrical productions at the Club than helping direct the family's coffee and rice empire.

In February 1916 Manny staged a delightful show for two successive nights at the Fairmont Hotel. The *San Francisco Examiner* described two of the production numbers — both written by Manny — in glowing detail. One was a one-act play called, "A Rehearsal at the Club," which invited the audience to take a glimpse behind the scenes of a purported dry run of a play to be produced at the annual show. The other highlight was Manny's two-reel motion picture, "The Eye of India, or the Rajah's Gift," filmed partly in Golden Gate Park. Ruth McDougall described the movie her father wrote and produced:

"The swarthiest and fattest member of the club played the part of an Indian rajah. He was called 'Abdullah Seemore,' because he possessed a pair of magic glasses that permitted him to see through the diaphanous robes worn by the harem girls. In this movie, my brother Joe played a Western Union messenger boy. He was a bitter disappointment to Manny. Despite the hours my father spent coaching him, Joe was unable to deliver the telegram with any real drama."

The show was scheduled to run for two nights, Sunday and Monday, at the Fairmont Hotel. However, there was an unexpected incident during Monday night's performance that brought the Club some unusual headlines in the *Examiner*: "Brandenstein's Monkey is Freed — Delay in Part of Argonaut Club Festivities is Explained in Police Court."

The one-act play called for a monkey and an organ grinder. A fellow in red satin trousers had to be slain, but not before the monkey and the organ man delivered their lines. Manny had hired Antonio Canzana, the champion hand organ musician of the Pacific Coast, and Canzana's partner, an intelligent simian named Lily to play the parts. When they failed to show for Monday's performance, Manny made several phone calls and discovered that the organ-grinder and the monkey had been arrested and charged with vagrancy.

Brandenstein called Attorney Richard O'Connor and explained his problem. O'Connor got out of his pajamas, into his trousers, and hustled down to police headquarters, posted bail for Conzana and Lily and escorted them to the Fairmont. Meanwhile, the show went on. But when the audience saw Lily and Conzana accompanied by O'Conner, they applauded so insistently that Manny had to have it played all over again.

McKinley Bissinger, who moved into the Argonaut Club in 1918 and lived there for a year, recalls the "good life" that Club residence offered. "Fabulous," he exclaimed. "Cost about $75 a month. For that you got a beautiful room with fantastic service. I remember we had a Japanese valet named Eddy, who saw that your clothes were always in order. We had maid service, and excellent food.

There was a good sized basement in the Club, and because we knew Prohibition was coming, I remember that I bought a great deal of liquor and kept it in a locker there. The Club was a wonderful place to live for a single fellow."

Roy (Brick) Van Vliet joined the Argonaut Club a few years later. In his Montgomery Street office the spry octogenarian recently talked about the Club's early days. "The Argonaut didn't offer a damn thing except lunch and an annual play, but it was a damn nice club. You could play billiards and cards after lunch or on the weekends. Monday night was always Club night.

"It was small . . . you knew everybody well. About twenty to thirty people came to lunch every day. The members dated back to San Francisco's pioneer days. There were living quarters upstairs on the third floor. The Steinbergers, who later changed their name to Stanton, occasionally lived there. Three sons and the old man. They manufactured Aris gloves. Their business was international — the boys ran the plants in various countries. When they were in town, they lived at the Club with their father."

Edgar Gould, whose father was an Argonaut before him, joined the Club in 1922 and lived there as a permanent resident. Remembering others who lived there at the time, he reminisced: "Bachelors like Brunn Livingston, and a number of doctors like Lionel Prince and Clarence Brunn who had their offices across the street in the Fitzhugh Building, also lived there. The food was good — you could get a full lunch in those days for $1.50."

Gould remembering how the interior of the Argonaut appeared said: "When you got off the elevator on the second floor, there was a reading room to the left of the lobby. Beyond that was the office of Mr. Altmeyer, the manager. Straight ahead was the dining room, facing Powell Street. The game room windows looked out on Post Street. The game room was about the size of the Concordia's Ladies' Lounge. There was a billiard table, and you could also play dominoes in the game room. There were also smaller card rooms. The carpeting throughout was deep red, and the furnishings were subtle but elegant. We had about a hundred members during the time, as I recall. Dues were $12 a month at a time when Concordians were paying $5 to $7.50, and Beresford Country Club (a Jewish country club, now the Peninsula Country Club) was $15."

●     ●     ●

During World War I activities at both clubs were reduced to a minimum. The advantages of German ancestry had begun to diminish; Argonauts and

Concordians with long German names began Anglicizing them: Brandensteins became Branstens; Sinsheimers were called Sintons; Edgar Goldstein became Edgar Gould, and Mr. Steinberger and his sons changed their names to Stanton.

Young men from both clubs were being called into service, or like Walter Haas, they were volunteering. Although he was married and a father, Haas felt it his duty to serve, as did his cousin Daniel Koshland.

Once the armistice was signed, things quickly returned to normal. The two clubs embarked on parallel courses: renovating their buildings; attracting new members, and staging elaborate entertainments.

The Argonauts toasted the Twenties with an extravagant old time minstrel show staged by Manny Bransten in January 1921. Daniel Aronson and Milton Bremer were the "Bones" and Walter Samson and Herbert Shirek were the "Tambos," with Louis C. Greene acting as Mr. Interlocutor, ably assisted by Messrs. Bissinger, Ransohoff, Heller, and Ehrman, among others. The elaborate dinner which preceded the show featured a broad range of international cuisine.

A thorough renovation of the Argonaut clubhouse was started in the spring of 1924. The minutes of the Concordia Club reveal that "a motion was made that Concordia extend to Argonauts all the privileges of our club during the rebuilding of their club." When the work was finished nearly a year later, Argonaut President C. G. Levison sent a letter to Concordia president Herman Waldeck and to the Board of Directors inviting them to dinner and entertainment at the opening of the new clubhouse on April 21, 1925.

That renovation resulted in a fifty percent dues increase effective July 1, 1924. "But they waived the initiation fee to entice us to join," recalls Robert Goldman. "About eight or ten of us joined the Club around 1927. My boss, H.S. Crocker, said, 'Now that you're a member of the Argonaut Club we'll have to give you a raise, I guess, to pay the dues.' As the newest members, we had to put on a show for them. Paul Bissinger directed us in something about the 'Big Game.'"

Bob Levison, another of the young Argonauts, also recalls a "Big Game" story. "There was a party at the Club the night before the game. A guy from Los Angeles got smashed—this was during Prohibition. So he stays overnight in one of the rooms of the Club. The next morning he doesn't know where he is, so he phones the room clerk to find out. The clerk responds, 'There is nobody in that room.'"

Lloyd Liebes was attracted to the Argonaut Club because of its location. "I had just moved back to San Francisco from New York to work in the family store. I liked to go to the Club for lunch because I could check the competition's windows on the way—Ransohoff's, Magnin's, Livingston's. For the first three months after my return, I lived at the Club. During Prohibition they never served liquor in the dining room, although everybody had a bottle in his room."

Liebes also liked playing dominoes at the Club after lunch. "There was always a bridge game and once or twice a year they'd have a special Club night with crap shooting and big gambling. Our regular meeting night was Monday night. I remember Clarence Lindner of the *Examiner* was a member, and Cobbie (Edmond) Coblenz of the *Call Bulletin*, plus a lot of doctors from 490 Post Street. It was a very pleasant club, with excellent food. Yes, it was true that we were considered snobbish. Actually, it was a matter of being very selective. Although Concordia had high standards, too, they were bigger and could take in more people . . . ."

For those who were selected, whether they lived there, lunched there, or partied there, they did it in the "finest location in San Francisco."

## CHAPTER TEN

# THE BULLISH '20s AND THE BAREST '30s

T WAS A BENCHMARK of worldly success when Adrien Falk, a young man still in his thirties, was made a Concordian in 1922. Falk was a self-made man. Son of French immigrant grocers, he began his career as an errand boy at age fourteen. Before long, he had built a business empire called S&W Fine Foods.

Today Concordians admit with pride that it was their Club which provided Falk a place for recreation and relaxation, which sustained him throughout his more than forty years of service to the City. "Mr. San Francisco," as he affectionately was known, served as president of the San Francisco Chamber of Commerce, the State Chamber of Commerce, the San Francisco Board of Education, the San Francisco Community Chest, Mt. Zion Hospital and the San Francisco Board of Trade. Perhaps the most valuable civic contribution he made was as a member of the Bay Area Rapid Transit (BART) Board. Serving for twelve years as a BART director, and eight of those as board president, Falk earned major credit for bringing rapid transit to the Bay Area.

"The Club was a second home to Adrien," said Bert Rabinowitz, a close personal friend and Falk's attorney until the food magnate's death in 1969. "He was a tall, gangling guy, with a marvelous sense of humor and the ability to calm people in heated situations. Put a stove-pipe hat on him, turn his smiling face into a sad one, and you'd have an Abe Lincoln. Adrien wasn't much of a card-player, nor did he use the athletic side of the building very much, but he loved to come to the Club to relax with the fellows and to enter into spirited conversation. He was so well-liked and had such leadership qualities that he was a member for only three years before we made him president."

Marcel Hirsch, describing Falk as "one of the most generous and wise persons I ever knew — he was overgenerous, and gave to everybody, and got very little for himself," explained how Falk became president:

"Uncle Fred Patek was president, and he resigned in a huff because of something he didn't like. They called in Adrien Falk to organize a board of directors, which he did, and we elected him president."

The new president was ready for the challenges facing him in 1925. The clubhouse, nearly ten years old, was badly in need of improvements. The outside of the building needed a coat of paint, and there was a call to move the library to free the area for a new domino room. Then the elevator had to be fixed; there was plumbing work, carpets to be replaced and furniture in need of reconditioning. But the financial condition of the Club was weak. For years the Concordia's net income was sufficient only to cover operating expenses; it was wholly inadequate to support major renovations.

While the Board approved the partial rehabilitation of the first floor; the project increased the indebtedness of the club approximately $36,000. That was just the beginning. The next year Falk told members that, "obviously, to make our Club comfortable and attractive, we will have to make improvements on the second floor and in the dining and billiard rooms, which will cost about $15,000." An assessment of $210 for senior members, $90 for juniors, payable in twelve monthly installments, solved the financing problems.

A year later Falk reported the successful conclusion of the program. "The special assessment enabled us to wipe out our prior indebtedness and to renovate and refurnish the Club. We are now comfortably situated. Our total net worth, according to the book value, is $214,993.59. Of course," he added quickly, articulating what every president both before and after him has thought: "This Club is not conducted for the purpose of making a profit. We are content if we can keep our members happy, pay our current debts, gradually reduce our fixed indebtedness and once in every decade dig in our jeans to put our house in order."

That May, in 1927, when Falk made his announcement, Concordia's roster listed a total of 467 senior and junior members. The Club came to enjoy sound fiscal health under the young president's direction.

Falk's talents weren't confined to his facility as a leader. Because of his great sense of humor, he was called upon to contribute to such Club shows as the one held only a week prior to the stock market crash of 1929. According to the program, the show was the product of "a brain spasm suffered by Emil Belasco Brisacher, saved and agonized by four musical jingles written by Adrien Berlin Falk and a malicious jangle by David Paderewski Zimet . . . ." Thanks were expressed to Paul Bissinger, who "spent an ungodly amount of time in his futile endeavor to make actors out of nincompoops." In addition to writing the lyrics, Falk performed in the show. In a skit entitled, "Strange Intercourse," a spoof on the hit play *Strange Interlude*, he impersonated fellow-club member Hugo Newhouse.

Advertisments adorned the program. There was one display ad with the S&W logo and the words: "If Nature Won't, S&W Swill." There were quips about members. Another, paraphrasing the Lucky Strike ad of the time — "reach for a Lucky instead of a sweet" — portrayed a rotund man attempting to pick up a cigarette from the street. The caption: "I can't reach for a Lucky. That's why I'm fat . . . Dan Stone." An ad headlined "Wanted" requested three beginners at bridge to play with a man "utterly opposed to gambling, but who will play for small stakes — or what-have-you. Apply BIG Harry Levy." *Little* Harry Levy was Concordia's auction bridge champion. So skilled was he, that according to Ben Baum, "we syndicated him and financed his trip back to New York to play in a national tournament. He won."

There were two depictions of contemporary affairs: one displayed a bag of money pumped through a ticker-tape with the caption: "the pump which is used by one of our Club members to make big stock issues out of little assets." The other referred to Harry Hilp, Falk's successor as Club President. "Of course we know he acts like Eppy plays bridge. But then, he's the President of Concordia. What could we do?"

Like Falk, Harry Hilp was outgoing, and fun loving. He sprang from a pioneer family. His father, imigrating west from Cincinnati in the 1860's, settled in Nevada where he married Emma Greenberg of San Francisco. Hilp, born in San Francisco in 1888, married Adelaide Wollenberg, a woman whose family was also among the early waves of settlers. With his extensive ties to the settlement of the West, Hilp maintained a life-long interest in California and Nevada history — particularly the chronicle of the Jews' imigration and development in the new land.

By profession an engineer, Hilp gradated from the California School of Mechanical Arts — now Lick Wilmerding — and the University of California. When he assumed the Concordia presidency, he was a partner in a major general contracting company, Barret & Hilp, the firm which carried out the construction of Temple Emanu-El. Later Hilp's firm achieved fame as one of the prime contractors of both the Golden Gate and San Francisco-Oakland Bay Bridge. Barret & Hilp also won many awards, including one titled the Army-Navy "E" for the firm's 1940s war construction of such projects as Air Force bases and shipyards.

A man with a tremendous zest for life, Hilp was an avid golfer, a violinist who staunchly supported the musical life of the City, an ardent Giants booster, and a devoted family man. He presented his son, Harry Jr., with membership in Concordia when the boy was ten years old. Hilp Jr. was an active member until his death in 1982.

The Club inherited by Hilp in 1928 was in excellent shape, and only later would the full weight of the stock market crash and the Depression be felt.

Meanwhile, Hilp, in his first official act as president, had no trouble a month later (June 20) persuading his board to call a special meeting so that members could decide whether to buy an adjacent piece of property on the south side of Post street. They readily agreed. It was purchased for the sum of $23,000. In his report to the Board of Directors, Hilp boasted that the active membership was the largest in Club history — 472 seniors "with five more pending and with excellent prospects of additional desirable members in the immediate future." Yet as vitaliz-ing as the growth in membership seemed, Hilp noted that "this increase is taxing the existing facilities of the Club, particularly the dining room, billiard room and lounge."

The dining room had troubled Hilp ever since the Annex was built in 1916. "Sure," he reminisced, "we had our athletic facilities which lived up to our expectations, but because the Club was in two sections, the kitchen and the dining room remained on the ground floor in cramped quarters . . . . And the living rooms on the third floor were hardly ever used." The time was ripe to revamp the rooms. Club finances were in excellent condition, and because Hilp believed that "the objective is not primarily to have the Club make more money, but rather to provide you with more comforts and desirable club facilities," he readily got the membership to go along with him. "In August 1930, we had the architects Hyman and Appelton submit plans that would eliminate the living rooms on the third floor, move the kitchen and the dining room to the third floor, and make other changes that would improve the Club."

By January 1931, the Club had a new look. At a cost of $62,418, only slightly exceeding the $60,000 budget, they not only acquired a new dining room and fully-equipped kitchen, but a redesigned first floor. The western extension of the old dining and billiard rooms was combined into one large area, creating the lounge as it existed until the fire of '82. Arches cut into the wall linked the hallway to the lounge, for an even more spacious effect. The rest of the existing dining room was refashioned into a billiard room, and to the left of the lobby, what previously served as the Club's lounge was refurnished as a ladies' waiting room. However, these were not the final renovations. Everyone who has ever redecorated a home or an office knows that the newly revamped areas focus attention on the glaring inadequacies of the old.

In a letter to the general membership, the Board noted that "while the membership is . . . highly pleased beyond all expectations with the beauty of the main floor . . . many have criticized the bareness of the third floor dining room and ball room . . . We believe that it is desirable to carpet the entire third floor, dining room and ball room, and to purchase seven dozen dining room chairs, a more attractive stage curtain, a new piano and radio and to fill in with incidental furniture, some of which is already on the downstairs floor on approval. The purchase of these items will complete the modernization of the Concordia at a cost not to exceed $11,000."

Barrett & Hilp, the general contractors, charged the Concordia only 2% of cost to do the job, providing substantial renovations to the Club for its money. The entire project was undertaken without any assessments or additional charges to members. According to a resolution adopted March 24, 1920, Concordians had been paying an assessment of $2.50 a month for the secured debts owed by the Club. A simple amendment permitted the Club to use the proceeds of that assessment for new debt payments and "thereafter the assessment is to be continued until all of the . . . indebtnesses have been fully paid." Similarly, the $11,000 to purchase the items necessary to complete the renovations came from money borrowed on the Club's open note and was to be repaid out of operating profit.

It soon became apparent that the operating profit was turning into an operating loss. In 1931 Hilp told Club members that "we all realize this year business conditions are worse than in 1930. . . ." They continued to worsen. By 1935 membership, which had reached an all time high of 472 senior members, fell to 396.

In the Juvenile Associates (ages eight to fifteen), and the Junior Associates (ages fifteen to twenty-one), however, membership was increasing. Two factors helped lure members' sons to the Club in large numbers. One was that athletic facilities in the public schools were poor. For example, no school at that time had a swimming pool, and one of the few places one could swim, outside of a private club, was the Fairmont Hotel. The other enticement was the highly popular athletic director, Hoyt Wood.

The annual Father and Son night was the climactic event following a year of competitive sports, an event the kids as well as the dads looked forward to. In anticipation of the 1931 celebration, the juveniles published a humorous four-page newspaper under the banner headline, "Fathers and Sons Battle." The story began:

"Thousands of fathers and sons laid aside the evening paper and homework to attend the annual banquet, now nationally known as Concordia Father and Son night. San Francisco's most notable butchers, painters, card players, wholesalers, building contractors, athletes and merchants drove up to the entrance accompanied by their sons, arrived in Rolls Royces, Chevrolets and, mostly, Cadillacs. The doorman checked each member's status as to the payment of his dues, and only a few were refused admission to the palatial Club, which is world renowned for its cuisine. (Editor's note: For the benefit of those who do not understand the word, 'cuisine' means 'EATS.')

"The most notable arrivals were Mr. Herbert Judah, president of the Eighth National Unknown Bank; Mr. Al Saroni, famous as the Catcher for the Fish and Game Commission; and Mr. Louis Newman, the politician being touted as San Francisco's next Mayor. Mr. Sam Jacobi walked into the Club heard but not seen.

"The elaborate show, which is an important part of the famous dinner, had to be postponed until after the banquet. This was on account of the inability of the actors to perform due to the noise and fighting between the various fathers and sons in their attempts to steal each other's food. This finally reached a climax when the dessert was served, and Mr. Max Frederick, in a quiet and unnoticed manner, stole two macaroons from his son, John Frederick. The son accused the father, who denied the charge, offering to prove his innocence by having his stomach pumped. This angered the son, who addressed the father in Hebrew, and the father, not understanding the foreign language, answered him in Russian. This led to more words, and, finally, all the members within earshot of the argument joined in. It looked like a battle royal was starting when Mr. Adrien Falk, Chairman of the evening, stepped in by placing a riot call to the police department. The police quickly took charge of the situation and brought Law and Order, as well as a couple of detectives with them. They immediately began an investigation and at 1:15 a.m. reported they had completely solved the matter. They found the missing macaroons."

The fathers retaliated with an editorial written by Milton Marks in which he quoted Homer's *Odyssey*.

" 'Few sons attain the praise/Of their great sires, and most their/sires disgrace.'

"Had Homer beheld the fine, stalwart boys who honor us with their presence and whose very being warms the cockles of our hearts, might he not . . . have written:

" 'These sons deserve the praise/Of doting sires in life's stern race.' "

He continued:

"Here, among these sons of ours is no maudlin lamentation concerning 'oppression,' 'persecution' or the usual stock phrases of the professional racial pessimist. To them, in this Club, life is a glowing experience and America a glorious field for endeavor. Here is no more academic, mere bookish attitude toward existence, but rather a sane and balanced admixture of mental effort and physical well-being. Here is the highest form typifying the principle of *'Mens' sana in corpore sano'* — a phrase with which all adult Concordians, from their study of the classics, are on terms of the closest intimacy.

"The Concordia has done no finer work than to furnish these boys with the means for physical development under trained and expert auspices and, realizing that man is a social animal, to provide them with their full need of joy.

"Adult Concordians should not look for vocal thanks. Rather should they hope for that form of appreciation which is more enduring — conduct which creates justifiable pride in our own progeny, and achievement which is the realization of our fondest hope."

Mr. Marks' hopes were justified, not only by the conduct of his own son, later State Senator Milton Marks, Jr., but by that of the rest of those boys who form the backbone of today's leadership in the Club, in the Jewish Community and in the City.

In the program following the banquet President Hilp and "radio announcer" Adrien Falk both spoke. A talk by Babe Hollingbery, coach of the Washington State Football team, came next on the bill preceding a magician. This in turn was followed by a boxing and wrestling exhibition performed by the Juveniles who were billed thusly:

"Contractor (Harry Jr.) Hilp vs. "Wild Red Billy" Zellerbach.
"Fruitcake (Richard) Meyerhoff vs. "Pickle" (Peter) Wangenheim.
"Smiley" (Walter) Newman vs. "Showy" (Dan) Aronson.
"Talkie" (Donald) Bibbero vs. "Fatty" (Robert) Kahn.
"All American" (Eddie) Nathan vs. "Wildeyed" (Robert) Jacobs.

Walter Newman, speaking about that particular night recollected:

"That was the night my self-confidence was born. I was a chubby kid, not too sure of myself, and I was pitted against Danny Aronson, the well-coordinated Club jock, in a wrestling match. It ended in a draw. From that time on, I had it made!"

At the time the boys were equally pleased with themselves as evidenced by the newspaper page entitled, *Juveniles' Role Call.*

"Jimmy Abrahamson: The Club's greatest Cookie Provider. An all around athlete but for the moment has not decided to specialize in any particular sport.

"Harry Hilp, Jr.: Although the President's son — he's still very young — but will grow up — trains hard, works hard at boxing. Says he will need it when he goes into his father's business.

"Bob Jacobs. Here's a tall, skinny, all-around athlete who likes tough competition. We'll give it to him in the 10,000 point contest, although he is favored to win.

"Maurice Knox: Better known as the "Battler" — outside of being a great speech maker, he sure swings a nifty fist — being trained by his father for future Jewish Heavyweight.

"Milton Marks, Jr.: The Club's flea-weight champion wrestler. Many predict a great future if properly trained in the sport by his dad.

"Walter Newman, Jr.: He's the fellow with the personality and the smile. Added to this he is a good all-around athlete in the north side of the club, although the kids say his father is a star on the south side.

"Dick Goldman: Here's a peach of an athlete, but what a slave driver! No rest when he's around. Stars at basketball and is captain of the Eagles.

"William Peiser: Billy is also known as Poky, he has the Club's Gold Cup for being the laziest fellow in the Club. Recently he won the 100 yard dash for Concordia against Stanford — but he says he owes his success to Roll-O-Ball Bearings.

"Edgar Stein (now Stone): Edgar is another one of the nice real fat boys — but don't fail to remember him, as he is an up-and-coming swimmer. You'll hear from him in a couple of years.

"Eddie Zelinsky: Developing nicely at boxing, at which sport he is devoting most of his time. The balance of his time at the Club is spent painting new keyholes on the juvenile lockers.

"Bob Zelinsky: Bob is the dark horse of the entire outfit. You never can tell when Bob will walk away with the whole race. Bob should be a politician. A good athlete and thank goodness a nice quiet one.

"William Zellerbach: Billy is red-headed and improving in sports every day. He forgot to dive in his first swimming race, but now he is our real prospect for All-American."

•     •     •

Despite the erosion of membership due to worsening economic conditions, the good times at the Club continued and the shows went on. Messrs. Falk and Marks were thanked by the 1931 Board "for the splendid entertainment which you furnished the Club . . . We feel that this show was one of the most successful events in the history of the Club . . . We have incorporated these thoughts into the minutes of our meeting of November 4, 1931 so that future generations of Concordians may be reminded of what may be accomplished . . . by such loyal members as yourselves."

During the following two years, although dining room receipts dwindled along with membership, the Club maintained its complete program of such enter-tainment as the complimentary Thanksgiving Eve Buffet, Christmas Dinner, Father and Son Night, New Year's Dinner and the Assembly Dance. The seventieth anniversary of the Concordia Club was celebrated in 1934, the year the Depression bore down on San Francisco with full weight, and violence erupted along the Waterfront. In the spring the International Longshoremen's Association led by Harry Bridges walked off the docks when their contract demands for higher wages and better working conditions were rejected. Other unions joining in the strike helped bring the waterfront to a standstill. When employers attempted to break the boycott by bringing in non-union workers, the Embarcadero exploded into a battle ground. The violent climax of the strikebreak-ing effort was "Bloody Thursday" when clashes between police and strikers resulted in two deaths and more than one hundred injuries. In response, San Francisco workers declared a general strike, honored by 140,000 union members, which virtually paraylzed the City for three days. Finally, three months after the initial walkout, the employers and union leaders agreed to mediate their differ-ences, and in October the longshoremen, having gained most of their objectives, returned to work. Peace was restored.

In November, as things slowly normalized in San Francisco, Concordians permitted themselves a modest celebration to mark the Club's seven decades. The affair was held on two successive evenings, and though food and entertainment met the Club's highest standards, the event lost money. Entertainment Chairman Adrien Falk submitted the cost breakdown to the Board with his analysis of the losses: "Cost of entertainment for two evenings: $1,434. Cost of Food: $978. Income for the two evenings was $1,178. From the foregoing figures you will notice that all but $200 of our income was spent for food and service, which merely proves that our charge of $1.50 per person for the first evening, and $2.00 per person for the second was totally inadequate. . . ."

●        ●        ●

In 1935 a doctor came to the rescue of the ailing Club as its new President. He was not just any doctor, but the Chief of Staff of Mt. Zion Hospital, the renowned, autocratic — some said dictatorial — Dr. Franklin Harris.

In a humorous speech to the Board of Directors, Dr. Harris gave his own diagnosis of the Club's ailments: "What ails Concordia? It possesses a low mental metabolism, and as a result, its intercourse is definitely anaemic. Its blood is impoverished . . . there being an excess of the white or socialite corpuscles and a paucity of the red or Ishmaelite (commonly known as McAllister Street) corpuscles. There is some infection in the intestinal tract, no doubt due to unbalanced diet and overindulgence. Analysis of the stool proves that everything is not kosher. . . . Its genitals appear to function normally, but the enlarged and inflamed condition of the left testis connotes unnatural usage and it is my deduction that they are employed excessively for retaliatory or 'lehachlis' copulation."

The doctor, prescribing a program for the hospitalization of the Club, opined: "The Consultants who form our Election Board should prepare to receive additional red-blooded patients. The facilities of our operating rooms, formerly known as card rooms, must be enlarged under the supervision of our anaesthetist (club manager) Mr. Kelk. . . . Patients will be properly segregated. All kibitzers will be isolated because it is recognized that their chutzpah is contagious. . . . Winning card players will be permanently separated from losers, and both groups will be graded according to their blood pressure. . . . Gastronomic patients will be divided into three classes, viz., common fressers, gluttons, and diabetics. One rule will be strictly enforced in the gastronomic department: enemas will not be given during meal hours. We will distinguish between the inebriates who shake to drink and those who shake from drink. We will split the athletic ward, protecting patients who suffer from simple attacks of impetigo and erysipelas from those who are chronically afficted with pes-planus extremis, which is the medical term for congenital Jewish flatfeet. . . .

"One more thing. We must do our part to help solve the social problems that are now engaging the attention of the President, Congress, the State Legislature and the genius of our learned Board of Supervisors. Concordia must not lag when it comes to participating in the division of the wealth. It is a subject close to our hearts and for which most of our members possess a complete and inherent sympathy. Fortunately, several of our members bear a name illustrious in the annals of social and political reform, that of Karl Marx, the founder of modern State Socialism. I am taking the advantage of that circumstance to appoint a committee to work out the details of the proper division of wealth among our members. The committee will consist of the following: Sonny Marx, chairman, and the four Marx brothers, Milton, William, Asch and Kelsey."

When the laughs subsided, Dr. Harris and the Board got down to business. A report prepared by Sylvan Lisberger, Club treasurer, showed that the Sinking Fund was sinking rapidly, that dues had decreased, and sales in the food and beverage department had dropped off as well. "The results could be summed up by saying that the overall expenses have been increasing while the revenue has been falling. From 1933 to 1935, the loss per member has increased from $2 to $9." Lisberger recommended that all committees reduce expenditures to a minimum; that no expenses over $50 for repairs, renewals or special purchases be undertaken by any committee without the recommendation of the Finance Committee; and that the Finance Committee "deal effectively" with delinquent members. In addition, both the House and Athletic Committees were given strict instructions to cut their expenses and make no improvements "no matter how trivial these expenses seem" without the full recommendation of the Board.

The following month, the cost-conscious Board was delighted when Vice President Carl Plaut announced that "a saving from $85 to $100 per month can be made on the telephone bill by charging members five cents a call." The policy actually resulted in a yearly savings of $1100. Great as the savings were, they were insufficient to bail out the Club. Thus, Finance Committee Chairman Fred Patek developed more substantial plans. He and his committee arranged to mortgage both the Club premises and the Post Street property and, finally, to renew an open note bank loan for $22,000.

The Argonaut Club was also experiencing its share of financial problems. Parking in the downtown section had become intolerable. By the mid-thirties, third floor Club rooms were no longer used. And as the old-timers died, there were few young men with the necessary credentials to replace them. In the midst of such a crisis, Harry Hilp, a member of both clubs, brought up the subject of a merger.

"I took it up with the Concordia Directors," he reminisced, "and we addressed the letter to Argonaut President Phil Bush. We informed them that we would like to discuss with them the matter of combining the two clubs . . . . But it appeared that Bush and the Directors were sitting on a pinnacle and wanted us to submit a proposal which they might consider, and I said, 'To hell with it.' " The subject would come up again, five years later.

The financial picture of the Club in the '30s was grim, but it had little impact on the vitality of life within Concordia's walls. Bert Rabinowitz, a struggling young lawyer and a bachelor who lived at home with his parents at the time, reflected, "In the early years, when you were young and ambitious and you worked in your office at night, you came by the Club at 9:30 and there was a big fire in the fireplace and a half a dozen people sitting around . . . and you'd have a drink, and some of the senior members would chat with you. It was a second home . . . a friendly place, and you knew most of the members your own age. It was open every night."

A senior member recalled with particular fondness by Rabinowitz was Henry Schussler. "He was in the jewelry business, and stone deaf. He used to sit at the table and say, 'This deafness is not a total curse. I am undoubtedly missing an awful lot of – – – –!' He was everybody's friend. And he smoked cigars prodigiously — every pocket of his coat was filled with cigars. He was generous in giving them to you, but he gave them according to his estimate of your worth. I got tired of getting lousy cigars from him. So one day I went out and bought a box of the most expensive cigars I could find and gave it to him. 'You think you're fooling me,' he said, 'You think you'll get better cigars in the future. You'll get 'em when you earn 'em!'

"It wasn't until I was older that I discovered the Club had a second and third floor. For the first few years I was a member I never knew there was anything but a swimming pool, a gym and handball courts. I would swim there every day. It got to the point that when I was in my locker room I could hear the swimmers' strokes — I knew Mat Tobriner's stroke — he was a wonderful swimmer — and I could tell without looking through the door which good swimmers, like Jack Strauss and Kurt Stein, were in the pool. And there was the unmistakable plop, plop of Abe Gump as he walked to the diving board, climbed up and jumped in. Although he was blind, he knew exactly where he was going.

"It was a salt water tank in those days and much more fun. A round trip was 50 yards, and you built up to doing a mile — this was *after* a game of handball. The same people played handball and swam. There were two handball courts, one singles and one doubles. I once got into the handball finals. Most of the players were third rate. We had one member, Dr. Herb Friedenberg, though, who really was first rate. He had been national doubles champion.

"Afterwards, before dinner, we used to shake dice with Abe Gump for drinks. Gump would shake, and we would tell him what he threw and somehow or other, we would arrange for him to win most of the time. He would wail over his bar bill."

Rabinowitz, who held a variety of high offices in the Club in the years that followed, recalls being on the Membership Committee in the mid-thirties. "It was about that time that the Club was beginning to open up — both as to the origins of applicants and to their business and professional occupations. It was moving away from the stictly German-American club where everybody lived on Washington, Pacific and Broadway, and everyone's occupation was in some way connected with wholesale merchandising. Now we were getting members whose home addresses were in the avenues, and whose business addresses were spread from the Mission to North Beach. Yet, while the base broadened, it still had the same high quality of membership."

What helped broaden the base of the Club — to attract the "red corpuscles" Dr. Harris mentioned — was that in 1935 the initiation fee of $200 was dropped. In spite of this, and despite the fact that twenty-one senior members were admitted to the Club the expansion was offset by the resignation of sixteen members and the loss by death of seven — leading to a net decrease in Concordia membership. The loss was countered by the juvenile and junior associate divisions which gained twenty-nine new members to a total of 116. Although membership did not increase as planned, another bright note was struck when Club members began patronizing the Concordia more than in the preceding year.

If spirits were brighter in the dining room, they merely reflected the mood of excitement throughout the city: a fifty year dream was about to be fulfilled with the completion of the San Francisco Bay and the Golden Gate bridges. For four days in November 1936, the whole Bay Area celebrated the realization of the first of those two monumental engineering feats. "San Francisco Bay is bridged!" read the jubilant Official Souvenir Program. "Traffic flows over a great ribbon of steel and concrete eight and one-quarter miles long! . . . San Francisco celebrates! The rejoicing is more than a tribute to the brains and brawn that went into this vast undertaking. It is more than a tribute to the engineering wonder of this decade. We celebrate a monument to the indomitable and undying spirit of the West."

Four days of parades and demonstrations on land, sea and air, plus banquets and ceremonies marked the event. Into those days were crowded "all the glamour and all the joyful anticipation of what the bridge will mean to the future — the future well founded on a brilliant past.

"Hospitality and festivity strike the keynote of the week. Clubs and lodges declare open house. . . ."

Concordians had a personal reason to celebrate at their open house. It was their past president, Harry Hilp, whose firm, Barrett and Hilp, was one of the principal contractors on the construction of that bridge and for the one that would be completed across the Golden Gate the following year.

●     ●     ●

Conditions may have been looking up in the dining room, but there were strong undercurrents of displeasure in the pool. Before long the Great Salt Water Controversy erupted.

Ever since the swimming pool had opened in 1916, it had been fed with salt water right from the Pacific Ocean through the Olympic Salt Water Company. This company was set up in 1892 when the Olympic Club got a franchise from the Board of Supervisors to pipe water from the ocean into their swimming pool. Demand from other clubs for the same rights led to the formation of the Olympic Salt Water Company and the project, Operation Salt Water, was born. An eleven-inch cast-iron suction pipe, which stretched from the ocean under the Great Highway to a pump house, was the heart of the operation. Each of its three pumps was capable of carrying up to 85,000 gallons of salt water per hour. There was a storage reservoir at Geary and Masonic Streets and fifteen miles of pipeline carried the salt water downtown. The main line, travelling along Geary to Taylor, had one arm which branched off Van Ness to Sutter, then from Larkin to Post Streets. This line supplied the Concordia Club pool, Lurline Baths, Neptune Baths, the YMCA, the YWCA, the Women's Athletic Club and two smaller bath houses. Barber shops also subscribed to the service because they found it useful for quick brining in the back rooms.

By 1936, however, the Olympic Salt Water Company was in financial trouble: bath houses had closed down and many private clubs had switched to fresh water because of salt water's tendency to corrode expensive carrying equipment, leaving deteriorated pipes in its wake. Since it had fewer and fewer customers on its rolls, the Olympic Salt Water Company was forced that year to dramatically raise its rates in order to remain in business. This posed a dilemma for the Concordia Club. Marcel Hirsch, House Committee chairman, faced not only the soaring rate hike, but the prospect of replacing the Club's rapidly corroding pipes.

Club members favored the salt water. Not only did it make swimmers buoyant but pool users found it healthful and invigorating. Consequently, there was great resistance to switching to fresh water. Hirsch and his committee studied several alternatives before arriving at a decision. For example, Alfred Fisher investigated the "Synthetic Salt System," which called for a heavy concentration of chlorine. Another alternative was named the "Silver Plan," popular in the East, which was available on sixty-day trial period. The Committee surveyed the membership to determine how many actually used the pool. Then as a last ditch effort, Benny Lowry tried to negotiate a more favorable permanent rate with the Olympic Salt Water Company.

Two months later, when Lowry and Fisher made their reports, the Club's course of action was obvious. The Salt Water Company was unwilling to alter its rates, and alternate plans were unworkable. Yet the cost of installing the new filtration system necessary to make the switch from salt water would total $1,571; this course would save the Club approximately $2,500 a year.

Toward the end of 1936, Hirsch reported that the installation of the new filter tank had been completed. But this was by no means the end of the Great Salt Water Controversy. Four months later a petition, signed by 120 members of the Club requesting that salt water be returned, was read to the Board of Directors. The Board responded with a letter to the membership outlining the problem and offering that the matter be submitted for discussion at the Club's annual meeting the following month.

At the annual meeting, Emanuel Lewis made a motion, promptly seconded, asking for the reinstatement of salt water. Dan Stone responded with an amendment, also seconded, that in the event the reinstatement of salt water resulted in increased expense to the Club, the money should be raised by an increase in dues. Stone's amendment lost. After much heated discussion, the matter was left up to the Board of Directors, which with reluctance, approved continued use of salt water.

It was nearly two decades before the Great Salt Water Controversy flared up again. In 1954, Everett ("Whit") Whitney, Athletic Director, made note in his monthly reports of the swimming pool's deteriorating plumbing. In May he reported: "The return line from the pool to the filters has again failed to operate . . . another series of small holes have developed in the pipe. This will have to be replaced with some type of pipe that will resist the action of the salt water."

Two months later, Whitney wrote: "The water in the pool has been drained and filled with fresh water. At first a few men made vigorous protests against this action, but for the past two weeks things have been rather quiet in this regard. Many other men have pointed out how much more they enjoy the fresh water; they, along with the boys who like it, add up to a large number in favor of the change.

"Your director has also noted that high amounts of residual chlorine in the water up to over one part per million have not resulted in any sore eyes. This is a decided improvement over salt water. When a residual amount of .3 ppm was present, we had some men who just could not stand the water in their eyes."

But the salt water enthusiasts did not remain quiet for long. In January 1955 Adolph Meyer presented a petition to the directors signed by thirty-three swimmers who declared: "we have given fresh water what we consider a fair trial. It has proven unsatisfactory and undesirable to us. We do not get the same pleasure or stimulation from our evening swims."

The protest prompted some of the non-athletes on the north side of the Club to respond with a petition of their own on the subject of whether the matzos served daily should be changed from square to round!

Finally, the Board of Directors was spared the decision when the Olympic Salt Water Company went bankrupt, making a return to salt water impossible. The matzohs, however, remained square.

When the controversy of salt water versus fresh first surfaced, Marcel Hirsch was House Committee Chairman. He was elevated to the presidency in 1938, a time of high expectations. While the City anxiously awaited the Golden Gate International Exposition, scheduled to open the following year, the Club's financial picture was looking a great deal brighter. Only the shadow of war clouds darkening Europe marred the happy picture.

Franklin Delano Roosevelt, in a visit to San Francisco the month following Hirsch's installation, voiced the thoughts uppermost in everyone's minds. He spoke in the Administration Building on Treasure Island at a luncheon before one thousand civic, business, labor and political figures who had gathered to celebrate the half-way point in the construction of the Exposition.

"The year 1939 would go down in history not only as a year of two great American fairs, but would be a year of world-wide rejoicing if it could also make definite steps toward permanent world peace," he said. "This is the hope and prayer of an overwhelming number of men, women and children in the world today."

In the audience listening to the President's words were Concordia and Argonaut members who had been working since 1936 to make a reality of "The Pageant of the Pacific," theme of the world fair. On the Board of Directors were Harold Berliner, Jacob Blumlein, Sidney Ehrman, Alfred Esberg, Herbert Fleischhacker, Walter Haas, E.H. Heller, Harry Hilp, Samuel Kohn, J.B. Levison, Nat Schmulowitz, R.S. Shainwald, Judge M.C. Sloss and Max Sobel. Paul Bissinger served on the Special Events committee, and Lloyd Dinkelspiel and Walter Heller were on the Sports committee.

It was a time of high hopes — and crossed fingers.

## CHAPTER ELEVEN

# HONORARY CONCORDIAN
# MARCEL HIRSCH

HEN MARCEL HIRSCH left office in 1948, after serving the longest term of any president in the Club's history, he was awarded the title of "Honorary Member of Concordia-Argonaut," a distinction which has yet to be bestowed on another member. The Club continued to be a vital part of Hirsch's life until his death in 1980. A member for sixty years, he had become a bridge from the past to the future, a keeper of traditions. In many ways, Marcel personified the essential nature of the Concordia.

Hirsch was attracted to the Club because he perceived it as a place where men of means could enjoy each other's company in gracious surroundings. When Marcel joined the Club in 1919, the twenty-four-year-old was already well on his way to becoming a man of means. He joined along with fourteen of his close friends, all of whom had been in the Sigma Kappa Phi fraternity since their days at Lowell High School. The group included Dan Stone, Richard Stone, Leon Blum, Allison Reyman, Erwin Hirschfelder and Esmond Schapiro, among others. Like his fraternity brothers, who were all self-made men, Hirsch neither inherited money nor stepped into a family business. What he inherited—and readily accepted—was the support of his mother and sister. From the time of his father's death, when Marcel was sixteen, the young man made his own way in the business world. He began as a traveling salesman and later improved and developed a highly successful business in industrial soaps and chemicals.

Two years after his admittance to the Club, Marcel was appointed chairman of the Athletic Committee by President Fred Patek, (who later became Hirsch's uncle by marriage). A short man, Marcel made up in bulldog courage what he lacked in stature. It was no surprise that the scrappy little player soon became captain of the unmarried men's football team. Years later he related a story about those days:

"Merv Cowen was captain of the married men's team. We played at Ewing Field, and we needed suits for the players, so we went to Babe Hollingberry, who was coach of the Olympic Club team. We gave him a few dollars, and he gave us twenty-two suits. We carried them up to the roof of the Olympic Club and threw them over the roof into the lot, which is now occupied by the parking station. We packed them into two automobiles and took them to Ewing Field so we could dress our players."

This youthful prank was probably Hirsch's only deviation from a rigid code of ethics he abided by throughout his life. "He did not bend the law in any shape or form," said Bert Rabinowitz, a friend since Hamilton Grammar School days who later became Marcel's business attorney as well. "His business reputation was super. He would not send out a product that he wasn't satisfied with, even though he could sell it and even though there was a request for it. He wouldn't make it; he wouldn't send it."

Hirsch's uncompromising honor was not always appreciated by Concordia Chef Steve Blumenthal. "During World War II, food was hard to come by," Steve said. "Mr. Hirsch told me, 'Steve, whatever you do, don't buy anything on the black market — if we get caught, it will become a reflection on the Jews.' His insistence made it very hard for me because I could only serve so many meals with what little food we got."

Like most Concordia members, Marcel came from a pioneer San Francisco family and was well-connected to other members, either by birth or through marriage. Six years after he joined the Club, Hirsch married Grace Patek Jacobi. Both his father-in-law, Alex Jacobi, and Alex's brother Sam, as well as Grace's uncle, Fred Patek were active in the Club. Uncle Fred's daughter, Anita Newman, (Grace's cousin), was the wife of S. Walter Newman. A few years later, Marcel became a brother-in-law of his close friend, Dan Stone, when Stone married Marcel's sister Helen. That marriage made him the step-uncle of Dan Stone, Jr.

"Related to all those families, Marcel carried a lot of weight around the Club," said former Club Manager Tony Pels. "Everyone knew what he represented, and they also knew that if Marcel didn't get his way, he could get awfully mad. He didn't have too much patience at times, especially with the young people. He was very conservative and insistant that the Club preserve its traditional elegant style.

"Marcel was a Napoleon," said Ben Baum, Dan Stone's partner in the brokerage house of Stone & Youngberg. "Marcel and I didn't hit it off in the early years. He was a very pompous, opinionated man who was also very successful. If there were three opinions, there was one right one: his. He came up the hard way and put Patek & Company on the map. He was very positive in whatever he did."

Baum, who became Club President in the late 1960's, recounts a typical Marcel anecdote:

"Dan Stone and I had our own table at the Club. I was perhaps 30 years old at the time. I was sitting with Dan; the table was full and we were eating. Marcel walked over and said, 'Would you mind getting up and moving to another table? I'd like to sit next to Dan.' I said 'yes, I would mind. Why don't you sit at another table?' That's the kind of man he was.

"But he was a very qualified guy and a good president. He put a lot of effort into the job. And to be a good president you have to be a dictator — a Napolean — to a greater rather than to a lesser degree."

Another typical Marcel anecdote illustrates his stubbornness. Dan Stone, Jr. relates it: "Marcel once proposed a man for the Club when I was on the Election Board. It was very hard to turn down somebody who Marcel had proposed, but in this case the Election Board did. Throughout different terms on the Board I had never seen such an outpouring of letters and telephone calls. People were being collared in the corridor and told, 'you *must* accept this man.' Whether the people who objected were right or wrong I don't know, but there was enough opposition to the man that the Election Board did not pass him. Somehow I was given the task of telling Marcel that his nominee did not make it. Marcel simply stopped talking to me.

"Well, Marcel and my father, in addition to being brothers-in-law, also shared the same birthday, although Marcel was two years older. For a number of years we celebrated their birthday's first at one house and then the other. After three or four years of the silent treatment from Marcel — even in his home — I was obviously extremely uncomfortable. One day I called him and asked if we couldn't have a talk. He grumbled, 'yes', and we met over lunch and came to a very amicable agreement. I think he had been as uncomfortable as I was during those three or four years when conversation ceased between us. But when you have two stubborn people, neither of whom was wrong . . . well, somebody had to take the initative. As the years went on, we became extremely close."

There was an occasion when Marcel wanted a membership application rejected. The applicant was a Los Angeles man who was moving to San Francisco and had friends who were Concordia members. In his letter to the Election Board, Marcel wrote:

"While I do not know him personally, I have heard enough about him to make me wonder if his is the type of person who deserves membership in Concordia-Argonaut and I question whether he can contribute anything to the club. I met his son, who was the guest of his father-in-law. The young man made statements which made me feel he is definitely unfit to be a member of any responsible organization.

" I bring this up for a very good reason. I realize that it is the father, not the son, being considered. However, it usually follows that when one member of a family is elected then there are attempts to bring in other members. Presently, there are two of our members who were elected only by the skin of their teeth and have been attempting to admit relatives of theirs. Despite denials, they are still at it. I believe the Board should make an objective evaluation before voting."

The Board did, and despite Hirsch's opposition, the man was admitted.

"True, Marcel was very conservative; that just indicates what the Club was," said Jack Lipman, a protegé of Hirsch's who became Club president in the early 1970s. "But with youth, and with changes—and we constantly had both—he was the easiest guy to go with changes. Oh, he didn't give in right away. For example, when I first served on the Board the question of admitting women to lunch in the main dining room was raised. That had been absolutely unheard of, but by the time I left the Board, we already had women in the dining room. These things have to be done gradually. And Marcel exemplified that. He was able to accept change when the time came, but he fought it until the very end. He really didn't like change."

One change that Marcel absolutely would not tolerate was any deviation from the dress code. A dapper man himself, always stylishly attired in well-tailored dark suits, he insisted on rigorous enforcement of the house rules. The rules still state: "Members and their guests are expected to dress in a manner befitting their presence in the social rooms, lobbies, dining rooms and other departments of the Club. Women should dress accordingly. Members are required to wear coats and neckties when using the Club's facilities."

The rules were not always convenient, not even for Marcel. In his later years he remarked that, "When Fred, my grandson in Sacramento, comes to town, he phones me and says, "Grandpa, take me to lunch.' I always ask, 'Well, how are you dressed?' so I'll know where to take him. He's usually dressed like a slob. I can't take him to the Concordia-Argonaut because you have to dress well. But I like to see him and talk to him, so I take him to some place on Geary Street."

Marcel typified the "old guard." To some, like Richard Goldman, it seemed the old guard was selfish about the Club. "When I was a kid it was a kind of German Jewish hangout. But I've seen it broaden the base a lot. . . . Some people get into leadership and they want to retain the Club for themselves. Some of them—good friends of mine who were really of the old school—are no longer at the Club. Marcel Hirsch, Dan Stone, Newton Stern—these fellows didn't want to let outlanders in. . . ."

Whether Marcel wanted to maintain the leadership for himself is debatable. Said Jack Lipman, "For a man to be president as long as he was — nearly eleven years — depends on many things. First is the question of timing. Sometimes you are there when no one else wants to be president, and then you're stuck. On the other hand, sometimes you have to contend with the political ambitions of several people dying to run for office. During those eleven years I'm sure there was a little of both. Marcel was able to handle the job any way he wanted to. He could have been president for as long as he wanted.

"The years of his presidency were bad ones, starting with the Depression and on into the war years," said Bert Rabinowitz. "Marcel was no figurehead. As in anything he undertook, he had to know all there was to know. He was thorough. He knew both the main lines and the detours. I don't know how he found the time. He headed a business dealing with chemicals and laundry supplies in a semi-technical field. He stopped at the Club before he went to the office each day and he returned to the Club every evening. He oversaw all the departments and the kitchen, as well as the mechanics of the place. He was on friendly terms with the older group of members, who respected his ability."

When the war was over, Hirsch became even friendlier with the younger men, who had also come to respect his ability. They knew it was only because of his dogged determination to keep the Club going that they had a place to come home to.

Marcel Hirsch, the little man who was big enough to preside over the combined clubs, typified what Concordia-Argonaut has come to signify. He recognized that the desire to preserve tradition must be matched by the ability to adapt to change, and that one of the measures of a man is his commitment to his community, a hallmark of Concordia-Argonaut leaders since Levi Strauss, Simon Newman, and Dr. Jacob Regensburger.

In Marcel's case, his leadership in the Jewish community included serving as president of the *Jewish Community Bulletin*; the Jewish Family Services; the Federation of Jewish Charities, and the Western Region of the Council of Jewish Federations, as well as chairmanship of Jewish Welfare Federation campaigns. Hirsch was a founding member and national officer of the American Jewish Committee and the recipient of its Western Region Human Relations Award in 1977. He also volunteered his services to the Community Chest, University of San Francisco fund-raising drives, the St. Vincent de Paul Society, and the Columbia Park Boys' Club.

Hirsch believed that a gentleman would conduct himself in his Club in the same manner as he would at home or in the business world. He believed that old-fashioned courtesy, integrity and morality, the distinguishing features of past members, should be the guidelines for present and future members as well.

"Marcel was stubborn in his beliefs," said his life-long friend Sylvia Stone. "He hated things or people that were false and tawdry. His belief in goodness and truth will always be an inspiration to those who knew him."

Hirsch's commitment to the Club remained steadfast to the end of his life — and beyond. At the suggestion of then Vice President and House Committee Chairman Adrian Scharlach, Marcel undertook in his later years to establish an Endowment Foundation as a source of supplemental Club funds. In his will, Marcel Hirsch left the first — and to date, the only — bequest to that Endowment Foundation.

## CHAPTER TWELVE

# THE MERGER

MERGED THE Concordia Club and the Argonaut with Argonaut President Stanley Sinton. We were both drunk," said Marcel Hirsch. According to Hirsch, it came about in the summer of 1939 at Cal-Neva Lodge, Lake Tahoe, where he and Sinton were vacationing. Whether he and Sinton deserve all the credit for the oft-discussed merger which was finally consummated the following December is debatable. Certainly it was an idea whose time had come. Four years had passed since talk of a merger first arose and now the Concordia Club was negotiating from a stronger position. The Argonaut was in a far more precarious one, no longer "up there on a pedestal."

Any former Argonaut Club member, asked why the merger took place will say, "We lost our lease." That is part of the story.

United Airlines, in a plan to expand its operations, reclaimed the second floor of the building for office space. Since there was also a shortage of hotel space due to the Golden Gate International Exposition, the airline decided to appropriate the third floor Club rooms as well. These rooms enabled the company to give first class accommodations to their pilots and crew members during their lay overs in San Francisco.

"The reason for the merger was purely financial," says Lucille Bush, widow of former Argonaut President, Philip Bush. "They couldn't take in new members. They were the biggest snobs in the world. Individually they were all fine men, but as a club, the Argonauts were the biggest snobs in the world." Ruth Bransten McDougall wrote, "The members considered themselves as exclusive as the Gentiles who belonged to the Pacific Union Club on Nob Hill."

The Argonaut Club, flourishing during the 1910s and 1920s had by the '30s run out of new blood with old money.

"The Depression helped to put it out of business, plus the club was too snooty," said Robert Goldman. "I'm sure that if I hadn't joined in 1927 I never would have joined in 1934. It was an unnecessary Club, because there was nothing but eating. But it was a delightful place to eat lunch!"

Edward Bransten joined the club in the '30s, and so continued a family tradition. "We kids coming out of college were taken in for a very small amount of dues. I don't know how big the membership was then — not very big. The Club broke up for the same reasons the Beresford Country Club did: what happened was that it was so exclusive at both places that it reduced itself to an absurdity . . . ."

Despite the loss of their lease and their dwindling membership, the Argonauts were divided over merging with Concordia.

"I voted against it," said Lloyd Liebes. "About 40% of us did. The only other option was to rent a suite in a hotel. That option was presented to the membership and the reason the proposal lost was that the move was too expensive."

Over on Van Ness Avenue, meanwhile, the merger was being explored from the Concordia's end. After that informal discussion between Hirsch and Sinton, Marcel came back and promptly appointed his close friend, Adrien Falk, as chairman of an Ad Hoc committee to study the merger and work out specific plans. By September 20th, Falk's report had been approved by the Board of Directors. Two weeks later, it went to the general membership at a special meeting, where it was unanimously agreed that "the Board of Directors be authorized to accept into Concordia the membership of the Argonaut Club . . . and it be further resolved that all members of the Argonaut Club in good standing as of December 1, 1939, . . . are hereby elected members of the Concordia as of December 1, 1939 . . . and it be resolved that Article I of the Articles of Incorporation be . . . amended to read as follows: 'That the name of the said corporation shall be 'Concordia-Argonaut.' "

The news appeared in the press a month later, when *The Emanu-El* ran the following story in its November 10 edition:

"If all goes well, the Concordia and Argonaut Clubs will be amalgamated December 1 under the name, Concordia-Argonaut. A new directorate will be formed and members will meet at the Concordia Club's present building at Van Ness and Post Streets.

"In speaking of the consolidation of the two Clubs, Stanley Sinton, president of the Argonauts, stated, 'It is for the benefit of the entire community that the consolidation was effected. Today the average businessman has time to attend but one organization of a social nature. The membership was unanimous in its decision to amalgamate.'

"Marcel Hirsch, president of Concordia, voiced Mr. Sinton's sentiments.

"The history of the Concordia Club dates back to the days of the Alemanian Club. It was organized June 10, 1865 [sic]. Among the first members were William Scholle, David Stern, Levi Strauss, Israel Steinhart, Martin Heller, Sol Wangenheim, Emil Wangenheim, William Herman, Felix Steiner, David Bachman, J. Rosenbaum and M. Kahn.

"Organized for social purposes, the membership comprises men en- gaged in professional, civic and social endeavor. The club is primarily a family institution and is often referred to as the 'House of Concord.' "

Although there are no records to indicate what Argonaut members were elected to that "new directorate" formed by the merger, much is known about some of the new members who were added to the roster. For example there was Walter Haas, president of Levi Strauss & Co., whose dedicaton to the Jewish civic and cultural communities earned him the City's highest accolades. Haas' cousin, brother-in-law, and close business associate, Daniel Koshland became legend for his philanthropic activities. Daniel's brother, Robert Koshland, and Joseph Bransten, also fit the mold of what is the "San Francisco tradition." Richard Sloss, A. S. Glikbarg and Paul Bissinger were the gifted trio who gave the Club some of its most memorable evenings of entertainment. Others included Morgan Gunst, Max Frederick, Milton Salz, Raymond Anixter, and Roy Van Vliet. Among those still active in the Club are: Robert Levison, John Dinkelspiel, McKinley Bissinger, Edward and William Bransten, Robert Goldman, Lloyd Liebes and Edgar Sinton.

The Argonaut Club, in addition to expanding Concordia's membership ros- ter, also added to the ranks of the Club's employees. "They brought with them two waiters, their manager, Mr. Altmeyer, and Andy, their Club Secretary," recalls Concordia Club Chef, Steve Blumenthal. "So I asked to have another cook, too. And our manager said, 'Oh, no, there won't be more than fifteen of them coming up for lunch. We don't need to have an extra cook. But instead of fifteen, there were forty who came up every day. They sat at their own round tables — they didn't mix much with the others — and they were the easiest people to take care of. Seldom did they order anything special or extra — they ordered what was on the bill of fare."

"At first, going to lunch at the Concordia seemed like going all the way to the beach," said Liebes.

Except for the rich carpeting from the second floor, which was used for ten years at 1142 Van Ness, they brought none of their Club's furnishings to the Concordia. "They sold off all the furnishings," recalls Lucille Bush. "I bought two beautiful ginger jars from Al Beanfield. I gave them to my granddaughter."

"They kept pretty much to themselves," recalls Bert Rabinowitz. "And they kept to their own traditions. They didn't come to the regular Wednesday night meetings because their households — their cooks and their wives — were adjusted to their not being home on Monday night. They would have had to reform their households as well as themselves. So they carried on their Monday Club night at the Concordia. In the dining room, there were about three tables of them, and when my brothers and I were at the Club, I would automatically go to the table with the fellows I associated with, and Leo and Ralph would go to the table over there to the men with whom they ate every day. Just like horses going to the trough."

And what happened to the Argonaut's old home? "When I was discharged from the Air Force in 1947, I moved to San Francisco," recalls Concordian Sam Camhi. "I had difficulty finding a nice place to live. I saw this ad in the paper about 'beautiful rooms' to rent at 421 Powell Street, a place called the Carleton Club. I went up to the third floor, through wide halls covered with heavy burgundy carpeting. I was shown a room which I rented immediately. It was large, about twelve by eighteen feet, and had a huge closet and private bath, tiled from floor to ceiling. The plumbing fixtures were the finest, but old-fashioned — about vintage 1920. My room overlooked Union Square and the St. Francis Hotel's Post Street entrance. Each night I'd go to sleep lulled by the sounds of the cable cars."

Camhi lived at the Carleton Club for the three and a half years before it closed. "There were about eighteen or nineteen rooms. United Airlines pilots occupied a few of them, and the rest were leased to Lillian Campell who managed them. She also ran the Guest House around the corner on Taylor near Cosmo Place. I'd go over there for breakfast and dinner occasionally. I never knew the Carleton had been a Jewish club until years later. When I joined Concordia, Roger Coffee, with whom I was associated at New York Life, told me about the merger of Concordia with the Argonauts, who had had their club house at 421 Powell. I told him I had lived there. From then on, he introduced me as the 'last former resident of the Argonaut Club!'"

## PART THREE

# CONCORDIA-ARGONAUT:
# 1940–1980

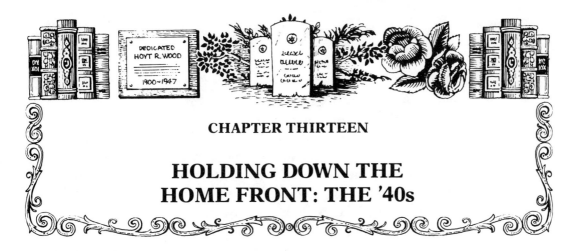

## CHAPTER THIRTEEN

# HOLDING DOWN THE
# HOME FRONT: THE '40s

 HILE THERE WERE NO SPECIAL FESTIVITIES to mark the entry of the Argonauts into the Concordia, their first collaboration — production of "The Little Foxes," presented in the spring of 1941 — was one that inaugurated nearly three decades of delightful Sloss-Glikbarg-Bissinger theatrical entertainment.

Sam Glikbarg's book was a spoof on life at 1142 Van Ness. He lampooned the temperature in the steam room, Sonny Marx's betting and Louis Lurie's Hollywood connections. Glikbarg suggested the Club's cuisine was so impressive it could be offered as leverage to negotiate a truce in wartime.

The musical's lyrics, adapted to current popular songs, were superbly parodied by Richard Sloss. One memorable number, sung by Marcel Hirsch to the tune of "God Bless America," concluded "From the gambler at his table/ to the athlete in his tub/ God Bless Concordia/ One great, strong club.'

Nine months following the final curtain call, the "great strong club," like every other American institution, was shaken by the war.

"The war years were very tough here," reminisces Steve the cook. "I even had my wife and sister-in-law coming down to wash dishes, because in the mornings you never knew if the help were coming in or not. Most of them went to the shipyards. During the war we didn't close the dining room for even a single day. First they told me: 'At least have a couple of cold plates,' Well, I said, 'No one is going to be satisfied with that for very long.' Sure enough, after a few days we had to start serving a few hot dishes that were easy to make. We also had to cook for members on special diets, like Mr. Lilienthal and Mr. Triest. But then, at that time, we didn't have a big membership. . . ."

(Many of the clubmen were on Military Service Membership, fighting the war in distant parts of the world. At least three members would never return: John Meier, who died in Europe; Ernie Fleishman, who died in Alaska; and pilot Jack Jordan.)

Keeping the kitchen stocked with food was very difficult for two reasons: the strict rationing of meat, and the strict orders of Marcel Hirsch not to buy anything on the black market. The chef's irritation with Jimmy Ransohoff led to an incident which has since become a Club classic. "Mr. Ransohoff loved nice cars," recalls Steve. "He had just bought a new convertible before they stopped making cars during the war. Ransohoff would always park his car in the alley near the delivery entrance. Each day the butcher came by with what little meat he had, but if he couldn't park he would just keep on going. I was up in the kitchen waiting for the meat with nothing to cook. I talked to the cops and they said it was no use giving the guy a ticket because he always got them fixed. He never had to pay, so they just stopped giving him tickets.

"One day I was so furious — I was angry and a nervous wreck — as I watched the butcher truck drive away without stopping, I took a box of garbage, opened the window, and dumped it out into his open convertible below. It took a couple of hours before it was discovered and then Ransohoff was up in arms. The manager, Mr. Hartman, came up to the kitchen and asked, 'Who in hell threw that grease down?' I said I did it. And he said, 'You dirty s.o.b.' Then Ransohoff said to Dan Stone, who was House Committee Chairman, 'If you don't fire that s.o.b., I'll resign.' Stone said, 'Jimmy, we surely don't want you to resign, but we can still find members easier than we can a chef!' "

Procuring supplies and keeping the kitchen help happy weren't the only problems with which Marcel had to contend. There was the problem of the Club manager.

Since the early '20s, for more than two decades, Norman Kelk had managed the Club. He endeared himself to its members not only for his efficiency but for the personal attention he gave them. With Steve in the kitchen and Kelk in the dining room, Marcel felt he had most problems under control as he made his daily rounds at the Club. Then, early in 1944, Kelk suffered a heart attack and died. "After that we had a string of managers from back East, and they were each what you would call a 'flop,' " said Steve.

Throughout the hirings and the firings, Marcel would appear twice a day, determined to do whatever had to be done to sustain the Club.

It was open and operating during the eventful week of April 1945 when the eyes of the entire world were focused on San Francisco as its leaders met to form the United Nations. High on the agenda was the plight of the tiny enclave of Jews surviving in Europe. Two representatives were invited to speak for American Jews: Henry Monsky, of the American Jewish Conference, and Judge Joseph Proskauer, on behalf of the American Jewish Committee. Both speakers were agreed on most of the Jewish agenda, each advocating an International Bill of Rights; each sought the restoration of political and civil rights to Jews and urged the abrogation of the British White Paper. Both Monsky and Proskauer sought measures to ensure the rehabilitation and resettlement of Jews in liberated European countries, the restoration of confiscated properties, and the punishment of war crimes. The two men differed only on the question of Palestine. While the American Jewish Conference called for Palestine to become a Jewish commonwealth, the American Jewish Committee favored the establishment of an international trusteeship in the mandated territory.

Both views had supporters among the members of the Concordia-Argonaut. Spirited discussions took place around dining tables as members entertained visitors and delegates.

On Friday night, April 20, of that momentous week, two thouand people crowded into Temple Sherith Israel for Sabbath services. Hundreds more lined California Street outside. The congregation heard Rabbi Elliot Burstein, president of the Northern California Board of Rabbis, call for "One God, One Humanity."

Rabbi Morris Goldstein prayed that "the beauties of the Golden Gate and the graciousness of San Francisco tradition contribute to inspire the delegates with vision, spirit and courage . . . that they may establish the foundation of a just and enduring peace."

Shortly after the conference, with the fate of a Jewish homeland as yet undecided, San Francisco received another visitor. David Ben-Gurion, the man who later became the first Prime Minister of the State of Israel, was in the City on a fund-raising mission to the United States in his role as chairman of the Jewish Agency. Attorney Leo Rabinowitz, president of the San Francisco chapter of the Zionist Organization of America, invited Ben-Gurion to the Club for lunch.

"Leo took Mr. Ben-Gurion in tow, but no one paid very much attention to him," recalls Edgar Sinton.

Although Rabinowitz and his guest ended up eating alone, accompanied only by the two Club Zionists, Judge Isadore Golden and Dr. Henry Harris, Ben-Gurion's mission was not a complete failure.

"I met him the next night at Philip Lilienthal's house," continued Sinton. "He had a letter to Ruth Lilienthal, who invited some of us to hear him speak. He was out raising money, which he hated to do. But he did all right."

●     ●     ●

By the following year, most of the Concordia-Argonaut members in the military had returned home. A partial list of names transferred from the Service List to the regular membership roster included: Dr. A. Lincoln Brown, Dr.

Ruben Gold, Dr. Harold Rosenblum, Richard Sussman, Carl Foorman, Jr., Sam Ziegler, Jr., Maurice Knox, Jr., Alan Marks, William Zellerbach, Stuart Erlanger, Jay Hamerslag, Jr., Ed Zelinsky, Phil Ehrlich, Jr., Richard Guggenhime, Don Bibbero, Robert Jacobs, Richard Goldman, Edgar Stone, Harmon Shragge, and Walter Newman.

The Club, which had opened its Athletic Department, lounge and billiard room to the military throughout the war, officially closed its doors to members of the Armed Forces by June 1946.

The war was over and the boys were back. It seemed a proper time to restore the condition of the Club, which had declined during the war years. Accordingly, Hirsch appointed a Building Committee comprised of Newton Stern, Sylvan Lisberger and M.G. Zelinsky, to direct the rehabilitation of the Club in line with a two-year General Plan. Money for the work was to come from a Voluntary Contribution Plan. A total of nearly $140,000 was spent (about $4,000 more than anticipated). Most of the money was spent on refurbishing projects; for such things as refinishing stairways and replacing stair carpets; rebuilding the men's showers; providing new steps for the swimming pool; replacing the circulating filter system in the pool; refinishing floors in the gym and handball courts; upgrading the lockers, and so on. In addition some changes were made. The third floor dining room was completely rebuilt and the stage altered to conform to the new architectural treatment of the room. On the second floor, a new bar was installed with modern fixtures and seats, and all the small card rooms were given a face-lift.

All this just scratched the surface of the needed repairs. At the conclusion of its report, the Building Committee noted that "the front and sides of the main building need attention; the metal cornice is badly deteriorated, the concrete ornamentation over the doors, windows and columns is breaking away and is a hazard to which our insurance companies have directed our attention . . . the hot water pipes are about to go and all the rest of the Club cries out for repainting and repairs."

●　　　●　　　●

December 1947 was a sad time at the Club, particularly for the younger members. They lost a man they idolized, Hoyt Wood, the director of the Athletic Department, who died that month in the Club gym.

Richard Goldman, the former captain of the Eagles basketball team, expressed the members' affection for Wood. "Hoyt was a person we all admired. He was a real leader, not only in the Club; he used to plan all sorts of activities for us outside the Club. For example, I remember we had Saturday visits to manufacturing plants . . . . We'd travel on the bus or the street car and go to a cookie factory where they'd give us samples. He'd always choose a place that would have an intrigue for kids. Then we'd take a bag lunch and go to the park to play a little touch football, or whatever. We all looked forward to those outings. I guess we were between eight and twelve years old at the time, because I started at the Concordia at age eight.

"Hoyt was so dedicated to us. He could be stern, but he was kind. I remember the way he taught some of us, including me, how to swim. I was afraid of the water, so he'd get me to go in the deep water with a rope he tied around my waist. He insisted that I swim with him while he held onto the rope, and then slowly he'd let go. That's how I overcame my original fear. Later there were a number of us who liked to swim. We used to compete among ourselves and then we joined our school swimming teams. I was on the Galileo team and played some water polo at Berkeley.

"Several of us continued swimming during college: Danny and Steve Aronson, for Cal; Bill Zellerbach, for Stanford; and Louis Saroni, for USC. There was great competition to hold a Club record. We had all kinds of events. One fellow, Bill Peiser, held the underwater swim record. He could swim two laps without coming up for air. We'd also swim relays at different weight levels — 110 pounds up to a category called 'unlimited'. Hoyt loved to get a group together, let us practice a little and then time us to see if we could break the Club record. And that was a big, big deal!

"Hoyt sponsored athletic competition within the Club — intramural events. Then, just after World War II, he organized a basketball team for inter-organization competition. I can't recall exactly where we played the night that he died. But I remember it was a game that started around seven and ended about nine. After each of the games, Hoyt would take all the equipment back to the Club on his way home. He lived over in Alameda with his wife and two daughters. On that particular night, he went into the Club, and as he was walking with all the equipment along the balcony above the pool, he had a heart attack and died."

Richad Goldman's sense of loss was shared by the rest of his contemporaries. They formed a committee, chaired by Donald Modlin to collect donations, and soon sent the following letter to the Board of Directors:

"We, acting for the Junior Members of the Concordia-Argonaut Club (sic), request that the Club accept as a gift, a bronze plaque in memory of Hoyt R. Wood, to be hung on the wall in the gymnasium of the Club. . . ." The letter was signed by Goldman, Modlin, Stuart Erlanger, Philip Damner, Jr., Sherman Selix, Harold B. Getz, Jr., and John Greenberg.

The plaque reads, "Hoyt R. Wood, 1900–1947. In sincere appreciation of his lifelong dedication and loyalty as a moulder of character and builder of men. In the hearts of 'his boys' he will live forever."

The Senior members also honored the dedicated Athletic Director. After paying funeral expenses, the Board of Directors sent Wood's widow a check for one half of his regular salary each month for a year. Meanwhile, Club counsel Bert Rabinowitz represented Mrs. Wood in her claim before the Industrial Accident Commission, and in October 1949 she was awarded a settlement.

●　　　●　　　●

A concerted membership drive, which was inaugurated in 1947, attracted a substantial number of young men to the Concordia-Argonaut. Among them was Jack Lipman, who became Club president in 1973. Like most of the others in the group, Jack had recently returned from the war and was single. "I spent an awful lot of my time at the Club. I played cards on Saturday afternoon and Sunday. On Monday night the old Argonaut gang used to come in and I would play cards with them. Tuesday night there was a young group — a little younger than I, and they made it their night. They weren't married yet, and I'd come in for their games. And Wednesday was Club night and I'd play bridge again. There was a group of us bachelors who'd come in and have dinner at the Club every night of the week.

"The Club was open for brunch — oh, that was the greatest — on Sundays only. What a fine meal! But women were only allowed to dine at the Club in the evenings. I remember taking Ruth, my future wife, for dinner at the Club on Saturday nights. It would be almost empty, but it was great. Joe, the bartender, would see Ruth coming and he'd make her a stem martini. . . .

"In those days a lot of people used the Club as much as I. Men didn't get married as young, or if they were married they went out, certainly on Wednesday nights. Men were there every night of the week."

The parking problem, as bothersome then as it is now, prompted the following suggestion to the Board by member Albert Haas:

"With the present congestion of automobiles on all streets of the City, and which condition will probably always prevail, it is my idea that, if feasible, a large automobile elevator might be installed in our Club to take members' cars to the roof.

"While the question of financing would naturally be given consideration, my thought in this regard is that the costs of such expense would be defrayed by assessing the members a regular parking charge, until such time as the cost would be returned to the Club, and thereafter such parking would be free of charge."

If somebody had taken Haas seriously, members at least until the fire of 1982 could have enjoyed free parking privileges, while laughing all the way to the roof.

The laughter in 1947 was aroused by the second of the Sloss-Glikbarg-Bissinger collaborations, "Dream Boy," a spoof on Marcel Hirsch's longevity as Club president. Based on the Broadway smash, "Of Thee I Sing," the hit number of the musical was a parody of "Wintergreen for President," entitled, "Marcel Hirsch for President." The setting of the first scene, which purported to show a meeting of the nominating committee, was a room with four chairs, each occupied by a Newton Stern. As expected, each of the committee members nominated Marcel Hirsch. After futile attempts by "a small, insignificant-looking man" to nominate someone else, the four Sterns closed the nominations singing "I Run the Works." An elaborate nominating speech was made by Nat Schmulowitz, who was famous for his use of polysyllabic words.

After appointing a cabinet comprised of Roy Van Vliet as Secretary of Treasury; Fred Ganz, Secretary of War, ("The best secretary of war since Alexander Hamilton," who was never Secretary of War), Hirsch offered the following suggestion for members of the Supreme Court: "All retailers — two Liebeses, two Ransohoffs, two Livingstons, one Newbauer and two girls from the Emporium basement."

When it appeared that Hirsch was to be indicted for his cabinet's scandalous conduct, he turned to Newton Stern for help, saying, "You're the big fixer." But the helpless Stern replied, "I can't fix this. You're indicted . . ." Whereupon, the chorus sang, "I Got Plenty of Newton."

A critical review of the show, expressed by Louis J. Newman in a letter to the Board of Directors, read in part: ". . . to my way of thinking it was by far the best show ever given, and it proves that a good, clean performance is more successful than the smutty ones put on in past years . . ."

Marcel Hirsch stepped down from the presidency a year later, in May 1948, "with pleasure and regret. Regret because over the many years that you have honored me with this office it has become a part of me, and it has been a real satisfaction to know that in some slight way, particularly during the trying war years, I may have been of some help in keeping things normal. On the other hand, it is a pleasure to be relieved of the responsibility . . . ."

When Hirsch stepped down, he left the Club in a healthy condition. Senior membership stood at 555, up from the 526 it had been the year before. The overall roster was 636. On the advice of Treasurer Sylvan Lisberger, dues were raised for the first time in many years, to ensure the Club money needed for maintenance costs and refinishing the building's exterior. The officious Mr. Hartman was replaced by a new manager, Mr. Fletcher, who, according to Marcel, "is receiving the complete cooperation of the entire staff of employees, a matter of no small importance."

The long tenure of Marcel Hirsch had come to an end. All that remained was for the gifted attorney, Lawrence Livingston, to proffer the gratitude of the membership in a witty, graceful speech. At the conclusion of his remarks, a resolution was made and seconded recognizing Hirsch's outstanding leadership, devotion and consideration for the welfare of the Club throughout his eleven years as President, and designating him an "Honorary Concordian."

## CHAPTER FOURTEEN

# DEBENTURES & DESEGREGATION: THE '50s

IKE HIS FRIEND Marcel Hirsch, Abe Shragge was a self-made man. His was a typical American success story. Born in Odessa, Russia in 1887, spending his childhood in Canada, he arrived in San Francisco in his early teens. Founder and president of the Federal Outfitting Company, with twenty-two stores throughout California and one in Reno, Nevada, Shragge joined the Concordia Club in 1935, at the time the Club seemed to be emerging from the depression doldrums. Two decades later, when it went into a decline again, Abe Shragge was able to rescue it from oblivion.

"I saw the club almost die," recalls Richard Goldman. "Abe Shragge saved it. He was the one that initiated the plan where people would make a loan to the club — the debenture plan. Most people turned them in as gifts ultimately. But the money that was raised from those debentures rehabilitated the club and really, I think, gave it the lift that resurrected it."

There were many reasons for the financial bind in which the club found itself in 1954. When Sylvan Lisberger took over as president from Dan Stone, whose wife's illness forced him to resign, Lisberger itemized the problem with his usual precision. Membership, which had been on a downward spiral since 1952, was at a new low with 438 seniors and a total of 643 members. The Club's net income from operations was $540, hardly enough to meet the $8,400 yearly improvement costs, and it seemed that projections for the coming year were no better. In fact they were worse. The elevator had broken down and a new automatic one had to be installed. The Club's payroll increased by $10,000 after the City's clubs negotiated a revised agreement with the unions and Social Security taxes were raised one-half percent. The Club was in no position to conduct a membership drive. The carpeting, most of which was acquired in the Argonaut merger, was in shreds. The furniture was badly worn and dirty, and the swimming pool and locker room hadn't been painted in fourteen years. Another sure sign of the sorry state of affairs was the dining room: no one could boast about how much money it was losing as in past years, because so few people were coming in to be served.

Drastic measures were called for. First the Board investigated the possibility of selling 1142 Van Ness and leasing other premises. There were no buyers. Then Sylvan Lisberger devised a plan to lease the main floor of the Club to two firms that would use it for office purposes. It was approved by the Board of Directors. All that was necessary to accommodate the firms was to build two new entrances to the office space, one on Post Street and one on Cedar. This would have done away with all the Club's facilities on the main floor.

In a letter to the general membership on January 18, 1954 Secretary Maurice Knox gave a detailed explanation of the plan. "From our own front entrance, members will go directly upstairs. The billiard room will be done away with, the lounge and the domino room will be moved to the second floor and the present music room will be converted to office space." As compensation, the Club would receive $27,000 annually from the tenancy, and with this new-found income could begin rearranging, refurnishing and redecorating at least parts of the remaining space. Because the tenants were eager to move in, members were given only four days in which to vote. The alternatives to the plan were grim. If members were faced with an assessment in order to keep their building but did nothing to rehabilitate the Club, its physical condition would worsen. Or, if the membership assessed itself for the purpose of refurbishing the Club, it was still faced with the problem of meeting operating expenses and paying off the loan. Four days later, January 22, the votes were in and counted: the plan to lease the building had passed by a more than a two-to-one margin. But fate intervened. Before the contracts could be signed, the tenant interested in the larger area of the ground floor withdrew his offer. The whole deal fell through.

With little delay, Abe Shragge stepped forward with his debenture plan. The Club might be financially stressed he reasoned, but the *members* weren't. The Club meant so much to him and others; how much a part of their lives it was! To men like Judge Milt Shapiro, or Samuel Jacobson, honored by the Club for his achievements in the Jewish community; to Newton Stern, whose long service with the Club was commemorated at a testimonial dinner on his seventieth birthday; or to men like Marcel Hirsch, it's importance was great.

Hirsch, who acted that year as Building Chairman, assessed the cost of improving the facilities of the Concordia-Argonaut. The aim, as President Sylvan Lisberger described it, was to create "not the fanciest club in San Francisco, but quarters that are clean, attractive and comfortable." Hirsch estimated the capital outlay would be $250,000 including retiring the burdensome $75,000 mortgage. Assessments or debentures were the only means of raising a quarter of a million dollars. In either case, the average amount per senior member would be $600.

Shragge explained the merits of the debenture plan. First, it permitted those members unable to subscribe in full to continue their membership in the Club at no added cost. Second, if all the debentures were sold, the entire Club debt would be carried by the members, maintaining the possibility of placing a mortgage on the property if that became necessary. The most advantageous aspect was that, third, the sale of debentures was not subject to luxury tax, unlike assessed funds. Thus the full amount of the pledge would be made available to the Club.

Members voted on Shragge's plan at the Club's Annual Meeting in May 1955, the same occasion he stepped in as president of the Concordia-Argonaut. The debenture plan was debated and approved. Translating that vote of confidence into concrete action took months, but in September Shragge was able to report to the membership that "we have subscriptions amounting to over 40% of our goal, and we feel that the Special Committee, consisting of Ernest Blum, Joe Blumenfeld, Sonny Marx, Harold Simon, Dan Stone, Joe Tonkin, Sanford Treguboff and William Zellerbach, is doing a wonderful job." By November 80% of the debentures had been sold.

That same month the tentative plans of the Rehabilitation Committee, headed by Joe Blumenfeld, were approved and finalized. Wrote Shragge to the membership, "Several decorators have been interviewed . . . There will, of course, be competitive bids for everything selected for the Club." After final approval from the Building Committee, the Board awarded a joint contract to the firms of Hilp & Rhodes, and Rothschild, Raffin and Weirick. Construction began April 4, 1955. The next month Shragge announced that all but $7,000 in debentures had been sold, and a committee would soon be visiting the forty-seven senior members who had not as yet subscribed.

As a cushion against cost over-run, President Shragge asked for and received permission to sell the Club's Post Street property. The value of the real estate, which cost $23,500 in 1928, had risen, and given 1955 market values, Shragge estimated, "we believe it can be sold for between $25,000 and $30,000."

In return for their pledges, the members were to get a completely repainted clubhouse, a refurbished lobby with new doors, carpeting, and ceiling and the addition of a ladies lounge. The card rooms and the bar on the second floor would be repainted, recarpeted and fitted with new lighting fixtures. But the biggest change was slated for the third floor. The dining room would be redone, and a private dining room, to seat forty-five to fifty people, south of the existing main dining entrance was planned. And, finally, a most needed item, a third floor bar would be added.

Shragge appointed his friend, Sylvan Lisberger, to take charge of both the Rehabilitation and Refurnishing Committees. "Without him," Shragge later stressed to the membership, "I don't know what we would have done. Syl deserves the thanks of every member of our Club, and you will realize how much we owe him when the job is completed."

Sylvan Lisberger was a pragmatist. An electrical engineer who worked most of his professional life for the Pacific Gas and Electric Company (PG&E), he was a Chief Power Engineer when he retired. He later became a consultant to other municipalities on power needs. After his retirement from PG&E in the late Forties, he devoted much of his time and skill to making his Club more secure both financially and structurally. "Sylvan, who was born in Virginia, was a true Southern gentleman," said Sanford Treguboff, a close friend, who, as Executive Vice President of the Jewish Welfare Federation, also worked with Lisberger when Sylvan was JWF president. "He was not interested in decorating the Club, but in seeing that it was structurally sound."

When the dust settled, and members had a chance to see Lisberger's accomplishments, they held a testimonial dinner in his honor January 22, 1957. The program read:

> . . .A friend of all;
>
> . . .A man whose shoulders carried the full responsibility for the masterful job of rehabilitating our club;
>
> . . .A man who has carried out countless assignments on our behalf for many years, without stint of time and with consummate skill;
>
> . . .A man of whom we are justly proud, for his administration as our President, for his services on many committees as well as his numerous community activities;
>
> . . .A man we all hold in the highest esteem and respect and in whose honor we are assembled here to pay him the tribute he so justly deserves.

A. J. Shragge, President<br>For the Officers and Board of Directors

And that night, the private dining room was named the Sylvan Room to honor permanently the Southern gentleman who worked so hard for his Club, his Jewish community and the City he adopted and served so wholeheartedly.

●       ●       ●

The second major issue of the Fifties was the admission of Gentiles to Club membership. The doors to what once had been a German-Jewish enclave had been opened to Jews from other parts of Europe for only two decades. In the mid-thirties, Bert Rabinowitz, a San Franciscan of Russian parents, and Abe Shragge, born in Russia, were among the first to break the all-German tradition. In 1950, Frank Heggblade became the first Gentile proposed for membership.

Heggblade was the business partner in a produce packing corporation of Club member Joseph Marguleas, and lunched at the Concordia-Argonaut with his associate everyday. It seemed only natural that Heggblade be proposed for membership, especially in view of the exemplary man he had proven to be. At one time Heggblade had nominated Marguleas for membership at his club, the California Golf Club. When Marguleas was turned down, Heggblade, a past president of the association, promptly resigned and joined another golf club. Harry Hilp thought it a good idea to propose Heggblade and did. Melville Marx promptly seconded the nomination. This was followed by a great deal of unresolved debate among past presidents of Concordia, and the matter eventually was dropped. But it came up again shortly. This time Heggblade was voted in. One of the compelling arguments was that the Club already had a Gentile member — the husband of a woman who was descended from the "First Families."

Harold Dobbs, who was on the Election Board at the time, recalls the stir caused by that application. "Someone asked, 'Well, is he Jewish?' and the reply was, 'He's married to a Jewess.' I remember saying that kind of reasoning is a lot of nonsense. Either we have a clear cut policy that states we let in Gentiles or we don't. I was in favor of letting them in."

So was Richard Goldman. "I was upset about the short-sightedness and the intolerance of some of the members of the Board. I was younger than some of my fellow board members, and I sometimes felt it was a bit presumptuous, but I argued strongly, as did a number of us, for it. The rest were worried — the old cliche: 'Let one in and they'll take over your Club.' I think the Club's come a long way since then. I don't know what percent of the Club is non-Jewish, but it certainly hasn't upset anything. I think it's too bad that some people think it's an all-Jewish club, because I don't think anything should be all Jewish or all Gentile."

Also favoring Heggblade's admittance was Philip Diller, then a young man who had been a member only a short time when the matter arose. Diller came from a long tradition of observant Jews. His grandfather, Bernard Diller, was known as the "dean of Orthodox Jewry in San Francisco." He was the founder of the Talmud Torah Association, predecessor to the Jewish Education Society; and the Chevra Kadisha, predecessor to the Sinai Memorial Chapel. When the chapel opened in 1938, he was its first president, and was also an early member of the Hebrew Free Loan Association. Phil, who would follow his grandfather on all these boards, and become the first president of the combined Congregation Beth Isreal-Judea, a unique merger of a Conservative and a Reform synagogue, had this comment: "I didn't object because I thought a Jewish organization should not discriminate. Besides, I couldn't envision large numbers of Gentiles leaving the Olympic Club or the Bohemian Club and flocking to join Concordia. . . ."

The other compelling reason for admitting Heggblade, that which set the policy for opening the door to Gentiles, was voiced by Edgar Sinton. "We did it so that we could not complain that other clubs did not admit Jews. I was Chairman of the American Jewish Committee at the time, and I felt that not to do so was completely contrary to our principles, that there should be no discrimination. There was some opposition . . . this was a family kind of club where everyone was intimate. People probably wouldn't have felt as comfortable as they had before, and I understood the reasonableness of that. But I felt the other thing was overriding. We couldn't be restrictive and not have other clubs be restrictive too."

Bert Rabinowitz, was one of the members against the admission of Gentiles. "Milton Shapiro was president at the time, and he was a Superior Court Judge and a very fair-minded man. I was a member of the Board. Philosophically I was not in favor of broadening the membership base.

"It was a fact that most rabbis were made honorary members of the Club, and I don't believe the Archbishop was ever made an honorary member. Had the membership decided to open to non-Jews I would not have resigned. Oh, I wouldn't have felt as free at the dinner table to say that the rabbi gave a terrible sermon last week, because somebody at the table might not have any interest in the subject . . . .

"But technically I felt that the Board, which consisted of eleven people, should not take it upon itself to set such policy. I felt such a decision should be made by the membership at a special meeting. If we were going to have an assessment we'd have a special meeting of the membership. This was a radical change. There was nothing in the constitution or the bylaws which covered it."

Dan Stone and Ben Baum took strong stands for the admission of non-Jews. Baum recalls that, "One of the arguments we got was that the only non-Jews we'd get in Concordia were people who could not get into other clubs. This was not the case. We started with six non-Jewish members, in addition to Heggblade and his predecessor. The first man admitted was Harvey Franklin, then Senior Vice President of Merrill Lynch. Another one was one of the top six or seven holders of Merrill Lynch stock, Ferdinand Smith. Then there was George Herrington, of Orrick, Dahlquist and Herrington, a leading law firm of the city. Tommy Dahlquist of that firm, also joined, and Alan K. Browne who was vice president in charge of the entire investment portfolio of Bank of America. And Ferd Smith, Tommy Dahlquist and Alan Browne were all members of the Pacific Union Club.

"Their reasons for joining the Concordia? They were friends of ours. And every Friday we had a domino game in the bar and we'd have a wonderful time. So the first non-Jewish people were the top of the non-Jewish world."

Said Renny Colvin, "There is no question that the character of the Club was Jewish in terms of its membership. I don't think that any violence is done to that by the admission of non-Jewish members. I think their admission is more of a problem to them than it is to us. I don't see any early prospect of the Club's changing its character to a large extent."

The exact number of non-Jewish members in the Club today is not known, since nothing on the membership form indicates religion. None of the original group is still on the roster, mainly due to death, retirement or incapacitating illness. But the best estimate is twenty-five members. Like the first group, they are all men of high caliber. One of them is Dr. Frank Passantino, currently a member of the Board of Directors — the first Gentile elected to the board — as well as vice chairman of the Food and Beverage Committee.

"I have a great deal of Jewish friends and a great many connections at Mt. Zion Hospital," said Dr. Passantino, a dentist, explaining why he became a member in 1973. "I would go to the Club frequently, and then I was asked to join. Ed Sugarman, Dick Newman and Bob Gordon proposed my name." Passantino, a very gregarious man, belongs to such organizations as the Masons, Shriners, and the Italian Men's Club. He was also an honorary member of the Jewish dental fraternity, Alpha Omega. The Concordia-Argonaut is important to him not only personally, but also for business entertaining. "I bring a host of organizations there for dinner — the Dental Society, the University Club Board. I happen to be a director of a Savings and Loan Association and we gave a very successful gourmet dinner there not too long ago for about fifty people."

"My concern for the Club is great because it is such a prestigious club and such an old club — to me that adds up to the history of San Francisco — and I am very interested in its future.".

## CHAPTER FIFTEEN

# FRENCH CUISINE AND
# FOREIGN CORRESPONDENTS: THE '60s

N THE EARLY SIXTIES, Roger Coffee succeeded Abe Shragge as president of Concordia-Argonaut and wanted someone to pep up the Club's entertainment program. He appointed Walter New-man as the new Entertainment Committee Chairman.

"The Club was in the doldrums," recalls Newman. "I was elected to the Board at the behest of some of the older members, principally Marcel Hirsch, who sensed the Club needed leadership with more drive and excitement. They wanted the energies of a younger person and they asked me if I would work my way through the chairs. The first thing I was asked to do was to head the Entertain-ment Committee, which was sorely lacking."

Coffee had made a wise choice in selecting Newman. He himself was an insurance broker with New York Life, the son of a distinguished rabbi, who served as a chaplain at San Quentin State Penitentiary. As a result of his upbring-ing, Coffee was a straight-laced, conservative man with a strict sense of discipline. It was said that one could tell time by his arrival at the Club each afternoon and set one's watch by the moment he emerged from the pool. Coffee was a great nature-lover, and he and his wife were fond of spending their vacations on photographic safaris in Africa. According to his friend Dick Oser, on one of his trips Coffee had to change planes in Paris. "Although Roger had never been to Paris, he just took the next available plane to Africa because he said there wasn't anything of interest to him in Paris!"

Coffee was a most competent president (it was during his administration that a Club pension plan for salaried employees was passed, with Ted Euphrat han-dling the financial and actuarial matters and Club counsel Henry Robinson, the legal aspects). Throughout his tenure membership continued to gradually rise. Nevertheless, the entertainment programs needed stimulation. True, there were the usual number of testimonial dinners, such as the one honoring Abe Shragge for his devoted work for the Club, and the one for J.D. Zellerbach, in recognition of his service as United States Ambassador to Italy. But there was little else by way of festivities outside of the Club's regularly scheduled events like Thanksgiving Dinner, Big Game Brunch and so on. In an attempt to garner inspiration from the membership, Coffee installed a "suggestion box" on the library shelf. He received only one idea, which, he admitted in his President's Annual Report of 1963, he "rejected forthwith. I did not even mention it to the Board, feeling that a large segment of the membership would not have approved it. The suggestion was: 'Vote Democratic.' "

It was during Coffee's third term, 1962–1963, that he appointed Walter Newman as Entertainment Committee Chairman. Newman, a tall, cheerful man brimming with energy and creativity, was then Vice President of the Joseph Magnin Company, in charge of personnel. Imbued with a deep sense of commitment to his community, he was, and has continued to be a leader in the City's civic and cultural life. (As president of the City's Fine Arts Museums, Newman, along with his father-in-law Cyril Magnin, was responsible for bringing the King Tut exhibition to San Francisco in 1979 after the two traveled to Egypt and personally persuaded Anwar Sadat to permit its showing here.)

Walter was the grandson of Simon Newman, who, at age eighteen, was one of the original founders of Concordia. Like his father, he grew up in the Club.

"It's more than a second home to me," says Newman. "It's one of the very important parts of my life. Most of my best friendships were formed there and what athletic ability I have I learned there — swimming, wrestling and boxing. I think I really became a man through the athletic programs. My friendships revolved around the Club — it was a very natural, relaxed place for me to go. It's where I like to entertain people because I have roots and pleasant associations there."

"Under the superb guidance and inspiration of Walter S. Newman, the Entertainment Committee more than doubled its usual number of activities," Coffee wrote in his annual report for 1962–1963. The year began with a Spring Dance, followed a few nights later by a dinner banquet featuring guest speaker Richard Nixon, who was then a candidate for governor of California. Newman had known Nixon from the time he worked on Nixon's senatorial campaign.

John Rothmann remembers Nixon's non-partisan speech very well. "I was just a kid at the time, about thirteen years old. He addressed his remarks to me and to my generation, speaking about the need for young people to be informed about politics and to become involved in political affairs. He also said that in all his world travels, 'the best food I have ever eaten was here tonight.' " Rothmann has a copy of Nixon's book, *Six Crises*, which he was autographing that night. In it Nixon wrote: "To John Rothmann with appreciation for his support from Dick Nixon."

Festivities continued throughout the summer, including a Parents' Night Exhibition, a Club Picnic and a Father's Day dinner. The first big fall affair was a dinner honoring the Justices of the Supreme Court of California, and particularly the Club member who had just been appointed to that august body, Justice Mathew O. Tobriner.

The banquet was followed five days later by a "Giants Night," at which the team members were guests at the Club. On that occasion the star of the team, Willie Mays, got his first look at the Club.

Under Newman' direction, the Sunday night movies were also updated. Through the courtesy of NASA, a movie entitled "Mastery of Space" was shown in September, and the following month Club member Edgar Stone, who was then president of the City's Zoological Society, narrated a film entitled, "Search for the Living Fossil."

The big innovation of the year, one that started a new tradition, was the premiere of Gourmet Dinners.

Several factors contributed to make the Gourmet Dinners the success they were but the primary one was the fact that the Club had hired its first French chef.

"Steve was retiring and we were looking for a new chef," recalls Newman. "We were very concerned about getting someone who would be good enough. My mother's dressmaker for many years was Marie Poumorou. Marie's husband, Theodore, was one of the most noted chefs in San Francisco. I had become acquainted with him both through my mother and because he was the executive chef in the El Prado Room of the Plaza Hotel. He had also been the chef at the Family Club, and maybe even the Pacific Union Club. But he was looking to make a change. I approached Theodore to ask him if he'd come to work for the Club. He said, 'I will come only if I can work with you,' and I replied, 'okay, you've got a deal.'

"And that's when the wine and food really gained importance. Steve is a fine chef, but his dishes were the old German-style food. Theodore was really a great, great chef. So, for the first time, we were able to put on gourmet dinners, only because Theodore knew how to do it and would cooperate."

Another big factor in the success of the Gourmet Dinners was the cooperation not only between Newman and Theodore, but between the Entertainment Committee and the House Committee, headed by Ted Euphrat. The extensive remodeling of the dining room and the first floor had finally been completed and the new dinners offered a perfect vehicle for the House Committee to show the new facilities in action.

Jack Lipman, who in the '70s would carry the Gourmet Dinners to even greater heights, described what that first gourmet series was like. "There were four of them, because only thirty people could be accommodated at each one. We had our cocktails or apéritifs downstairs in the main lounge of the Club. It was quite elegant: ladies in long gowns; men in black tie; the waiters wearing white gloves. Hors d'oeuvres consisted of such delicacies as mushroom caps stuffed with escargot, oysters, and so forth. Then we went upstairs to the Sylvan Room for dinner at one huge round table. We began with a fish course accompanied by a fine '59 Hottenheimer wine. Then we proceeded through several more courses, all with the appropriate wines. It was an excellent dinner with a high ratio of help to guests."

A week after the last of the Gourmet Dinner series came the Centennial Ball in January 1963. "Although the 'centennial' title was a bit premature, it was given that name in order to give us a reason to have a good party," said Newman. "It was super. The theme of the evening was crystal. The redecorated dining room had beautiful new crystal chandeliers; it made for a pretty glamorous affair."

Walter's wife Ellen, a career woman who could draw from her diverse volun-teer experience on City social committees, helped to create the glamorous setting. Silver candelabra illuminated each table, while a revolving overhead mirrored ball in the center of the room cast soft prisms of light on the exquisite floral arrangements.

When the year was over, Walter Newman found he did not have to "go through the chairs," as Marcel Hirsch had advised. The Board of Directors elected him the new Club President.

During Newman's first term, the tradition of Gourmet Dinners, along with other entertainment programs, was carried on by Dr. Stanley Reich. Membership continued to grow and nearly $34,000 was expended that year for Northside improvements to the athletic facilities in response to a national focus on physical fitness.

•     •     •

San Francisco was to be the site of the 1964 Republican convention. To accommodate the anticipated influx of visitors from the East who would enjoy using the Club's facilities, Walter arranged with Hugh Dryfoos, president of the Harmonie Club of New York City, to extend reciprocal privileges to members of the two clubs. It was the first such arrangement to which the prestigious Har-monie Club was a party. The arrangement is still in effect, presumably to the enjoyment of members on each coast. (Concordia-Argonaut also enjoys reciproc-ity with the Concordia Club of Pittsburgh, the Locust-Mid-City Club of Philadelphia, the City Athletic Club of New York City and the historic Ingomar Club of Eureka, California.)

Several major events occurred during Newman's second term. For the first time in its history, the Club established a waiting list for Senior Members. According to the Club by-laws, the maximum number of Seniors was set at 525. With 529 names on the roster, a short waiting list had to be instituted. Total membership that year also reached the all-time high of 737.

It was also the year that inaugurated a series of wine appreciation courses. Said Newman, "I've always had a fundamental interest in wine. I went to U.C. Davis, which was then primarily an agricultural university, and there I learned a great deal about oenology."

Jack Lipman, whose own interest in wine had been steadily growing since his first trip to the French provinces in 1960, recalls the original Wine Appreciation Dinner.

"We had the top wine connoisseurs involved. Marcel Hirsch was instrumental in choosing them, because they were all good friends of his. We had Jimmy Blumin one night; Henry Vandevoort another; Maynard Amerine, who at that time was head of the School of Oenology at U.C. Davis, and George Selleck. The experts were invited to work out their own menus with Theodore and they selected the wines."

"The wine tasting dinners were held in the Sylvan Room, and limited to thirty people, including wives. The table was decorated with grapes. The guest speaker would have all the wines in front of him.

"The most exciting of the speakers was George Selleck, who had a tasting of nothing but Chateau Lafitte Rothschild. At that time Selleck, a retired dentist, was perhaps the most famous amateur chef in the world. He'd been twice decorated by France. Amerine spoke very technically. He had just returned from judging a Yugoslavian wine tasting and he brought some of the entries with him. I almost hit him over the head with them. I was quite critical of anybody who served us bad wine, because I know what bad wines are without any help! That's why I enjoyed George so well. We had the same idea: to go all the way and have a good time. But we could afford those wines at the time. They were a lot cheaper then. Today, a Lafitte tasting would cost over $200 a head to sit down."

In addition to the Gourmet Dinners and the Wine Appreciation Dinners, another event is always mentioned by members in recalling the highlights of the Sixties: the yearly visits of the ABC-TV correspondents, a tradition that began with a deal between Walter Newman and David Sachs.

"David, a member of the Club, was head of ABC in San Francisco. He was trying to give ABC exposure and I was looking for good program material. He originated the suggestion, that made for a fabulous evening. Some of the ABC crew at the time are now among their top-flight people throughout the world, people like John Scali, and Peter Jennings.

"First we had a reception, where we met the guests. Then we went up to dinner. After dinner, the correspondents would move to the stage. There were usually four or five of them representing different regions of the world. Each would talk for perhaps fifteen minutes about what was happening in his part of the world. Then we'd have a question-and-answer period for maybe an hour, followed by discussions over cocktails.

"They returned for five years in a row, saying it was one of the best stops on their swing around the country. They always looked forward to the wonderful dinners at the Concordia Club. Those events became the biggest program of the year and always sold out immediately. We were sorry when Sachs moved away and the policy of bringing the correspondents home was discontinued."

Harold Dobbs recalls the second ABC Correspondents' visit, in 1966. "Nobody wanted to break up the discussions, so I invited them all back to my house where the talks lasted into the wee hours of the morning." Dobbs' young son Greg was home at the time. Whether or not the ABC correspondents had any influence on the boy's choice of a career is uncertain, but it is a fact that a decade later Greg Dobbs became one of ABC's leading foreign correspondents.

## CHAPTER SIXTEEN

# THE WILLIE MAYS AFFAIR

N THE 1960s Giants baseball star Willie Mays was nominated for Club membership, and the social upheaval of the decade entered the life of Concordia-Argonaut. Harold Dobbs, attorney, well-known political figure and Club president at the time, recalled how it came about.

"Jake Shemano cornered me one Wednesday night at the bar of the Club and said, 'Harold, I want to propose Willie Mays for membership. I understand there's going to be a lot of hell about it. I just want to know how you feel.' I said, 'Propose him. If he's a decent man and compares in that sense to any other person, then the fact that he's a Negro — we didn't say black then — doesn't make a damn bit of difference to me.' Which kind of surprised him because I guess he assumed that because I am a Republican I would be more conservative or something.

"When I was asked by other members, I said the same thing and they didn't like it. I could tell trouble was brewing. Well, when the application was filed, you'd think it was the most important event in the history of San Francisco. It wasn't really. He was the first black proposed. I think the excuse by those opposed was — and this was said to me by so many members — 'Harold, it's not a case of being opposed to Willie Mays because he's a Negro, but this is a private club. We have a right to choose anyone we like. And we don't think it's a good idea!' "

Walter Newman, who also objected, explained:

"We had never had a black member. But that in itself was not the critical issue. The issue was that here was Willie Mays, a celebrity, and he was trading on his name to become a member, rather than on his qualities as an eminent person. There was an awful lot of agonizing about it, about how it should be handled. It got out in the press. Herb Caen wrote about it. I think Shemano tipped him off to put the Club through fire. Some of these people thought we were a bunch of stuffed shirts, and they wanted to get the Club into a little more modern mode. But we felt this way, truly, that we didn't object to black members at all. The whole situation of minority rights and so forth was becoming quite evident, and we could not hold ourselves out as being a restricted kind of membership. In fact, we tried to recruit Cecil Poole, who was a federal judge at that time, to see if he would like to become a member, and he didn't want to . . . And there were other blacks we asked to join and they didn't want to. But here was Willie Mays who was nothing more than a baseball player — a very good one — who wanted to become a member of our Club when he really belonged at the Olympic Club."

Other past presidents met with Dobbs to offer similar reasoning. Ben Baum recalled "Dan Stone, Marcel Hirsch, Syl Lisberger and Newton Stern discussed with Mr. Dobbs that they had no objection to blacks becoming members of the Club, but they felt, as I did, that the background and the compatibility of an individual with the existing members both socially and educationally was very important. They asked him to withdraw the application. Had the Board come up with a Dr. Gooseby, for example, who is a dentist here and had been on the board of the School District, had they come up with a Wilson Riles — people who would have been socially, culturally or educationally compatible, that's one thing. But because a man happens to have a baseball record . . . ."

Although every effort was made to persuade Dobbs to table the application, it backfired. "It made me determined not to let Willie Mays be used as a guinea pig," he said. "The Board at that time was very gutless, frankly, with a few exceptions. They were afraid to take a stand. So I proposed — and nobody objected — appointing a special committee to study the application and to make its recommendation to the Board. It was a three-man committee. I purposely picked a man I knew would be opposed to Willie Mays, and one I knew would be receptive. Then I tried to find someone who was impartial, and I found him very easily: Bert Levit, a strong personality. I knew Bert would call it any way he saw it, and it wouldn't be because he like or disliked Willie Mays, or whether he was black, white or purple.

"The three met with Mays, and I remember what he told Bert and the others who spent some time with him. Mays' point was that he was a man of considerable means, and he said, 'I have a son, I travel a lot. The one thing my son loves to do is to go swimming, the one thing I can do with him when I'm here. I'll have a place to go.' At that time he didn't have a home with a pool. He lived in the City. That was what he wanted: he wanted to use the Club with his son.

"So after the special committee met with Mays they recommended to the Board that he be admitted. But there was terrible feeling in the Club."

"Before the election," said Newman, "there were petitions signed by a number of people stating that if Mays did not get in they were going to resign.

And others told us that if he *did* get in they would resign. We were between a rock and a hard place."

Ben Baum has his own theories about why Mays' name was submitted for membership. "In my opinion it was a political maneuver, not Concordia politics but San Francisco politics. Why do I say that? Number One: His name was put up by Jake Shemano. Shemano was president of the Golden Gate Bank. He was Mays' financial manager. He was trying to cater to the blacks. Number Two: Dobbs, who seconded the application proposal, was in partnership at that time with Mel Weiss. They had drive-ins and the Red Chimney restaurant on California Street. He was closed down because he did not hire blacks; he was picketed for that reason. So here is an issue and he can reply, 'Who says I don't like blacks?' I truly believe that if it hadn't been for these two people — Shemano and Dobbs — the name would never have come up."

When the recommendation to accept Mays came before the Board of Directors, the debate continued. "There were eleven people on the Board," said Baum. "Of that eleven, I'd say that probably only three or four would have been inclined to vote 'yes.' Seven of the board said, 'We do not feel that this is necessarily in the best interest of the Club, but we will concur with the Election Board's decision because of the fact that we ourselves are a minority group. We are primarily a Jewish club, and we would be looked down upon if we, as a minority, refrained from admitting a member of another minority into the Club.'

"Then I got up — and I happen to be an outspoken kind of guy — and I said, I am in agreement with the opening statement of the previous seven people, however I have no 'buts'.' I said; 'I feel very strongly that he should not be admitted.' And I gave my reasons why, whereupon Harold got up and made the statement that the reason I took the stand I did was that Mays was black. And I said, to the contrary. I was a member with Dan Stone who fought to open the Club to all religions, races and creeds. I said, 'I will put the ball in your court and say to you that if he *hadn't* been black he wouldn't have been proposed.' And I went on to say that if they proposed blacks who were socially and educationally compatible, I would have voted yes. I would have deemed it a privilege and an honor to admit a man we could associate with."

"Despite how valid our objections to Mays were, the public would only see it as a black-white thing, so we elected him to membership," said Newman. "And nothing happened after that — nobody ever resigned."

Nobody that is, but Harold Dobbs, who resigned from his office as President. Shortly after Mays was admitted, Dobbs chose a committee to nominate the new Board members for the coming year, a president's normal prerogative. "I got up to make the routine announcement concerning the committee meetings, and Baum interrupted to say he had another slate to propose. That had never been done before. It was pretty obvious they were going to teach me a lesson. They were going to put in their own Board so that this would never happen again. I felt they were cutting my legs out from under me, that I was going to be a president in name only. So I resigned from the presidency."

Ted Euphrat, the Vice President, finished the six weeks in Dobbs' term. In his report at the conclusion of that stormy year, Euphrat summed up the experience this way:

"This had been a good year for the Club, albeit not a smooth one. We have learned how to overcome potential dissension by compromise. We have succeeded in reconciling different points of view on various matters by considering the good of the Club and taking that course of action which has improved its strength and vitality. If controversy breeds strength, we are stronger now than ever in the past."

That, indeed, appeared to be the case. While Dobbs may have resigned from the presidency, he certainly did not withdraw from active participation in the Club. The following year he was back on the Board of Directors, along with Sanford Treguboff, who had protested the opposition to Mays by resigning his seat on the Board. Serving along with them was Ben Baum, previously their adversary.

But what about Willie Mays? Did he now go on to become a Club regular? "After he became a member, I don't believe Mays, in the three or four years that followed, ever attended the Club more than three times *total*," said Baum. "And in the third year — I believe I was President then — we received a letter from his manager requesting that he be given an honorary membership. We wrote a nice reply explaining we had no such thing. However, we appreciated the fact that he traveled a great deal and he wouldn't have full use of the Club. So we would give him an out-of-town membership, which was 50% of whatever the rate was at the time. The man that handled the matter was Henry Robinson, the Club attorney.

"We received no letter back, and Henry tried to get together with Willie Mays so they could meet and talk about it, but there was never a mutually agreed date. Some time passed, and then we received a letter with his resignation, which we accepted. All of a sudden Henry brought to our attention the fact that you can't resign from the Club unless you are a member in good standing, and there were still some IOU's out. So we wrote him back saying we'd accept his resignation when he put his affairs in shape. He paid up and we accepted his resignation, and that was the end of the Willie Mays affair. . . ."

•     •     •

Five years after Mays' resignation, another black man applied for membership, Noah Griffin. This time there was no dissension and the application was routinely processed. There was no question about Griffin's social or educational compatability with Club members. Born in San Francisco, he had gone to school with many of the young men in the Club, first at Lafayette Grammar School, then at Presidio Junior High and later at George Washington High School. After attending Fisk College, a black university, he was graduated from Harvard Law School. Both his parents were educators.

"After graduating from law school and coming back to San Francisco, I became the guest at the Club of three of my friends: Mike Burke, Bob Maddox and George Link. We used to play racquetball, in circumvention of the rules, I'm afraid. There is a limit to how often you can bring the same guest to the Club. I captained both my high school and college tennis teams and found you could get a good workout in racquetball in a short space of time. After a few months I said, 'there's no need to circumvent the rules, why don't I just join?' They said, 'fine.' I filled in an application and it went right through.

"It surprised a lot of people that I would attempt to join, and surprised a lot more that the application went through without any problems. The press didn't pick it up — didn't really want to. It just happened. I didn't want any trumpets or hoopla. I didn't feel I was breaking any major ground. . . ."

But, Griffin said, "the first time I brought black guests to dinner it was a little strange and people were looking at us. It was a matter of something new that people weren't accustomed to. There was never anything said to me, but as Mr. Pels, the manager, said, you could cut the tension with a knife. Then, after a while people got used to the idea and I feel as at ease here as I do any place.

"My brother had a real reluctance to come here. For the first time in the seven years I have been a member, he came on my mother's birthday. He really enjoyed it. He's very much stayed within the black community. All his friendships are there, and he rarely gets out of the community at all. But once he came he enjoyed it. He brought his wife and two kids, my nephews. My mother always loves it at the Club. She adores cheesecake, and the waiters always see that she gets it. My mother has a bridge club and she has had a lovely affair here. I am only sorry that my dad didn't ever see the Club. He died just after I joined."

Griffin's main interest in becoming a member was to use the athletic facilities. Explaining why he chose the Concordia over the Olympic Club, the young man, who had connections around City Hall, (he was a Coro intern, an aid to Supervisor Dianne Feinstein and was once himself a candidate for Supervisor) said,

"When I returned from law school in '71, my Harvard classmate came over to Concordia to use the facilities while he was waiting to join the Olympic Club — he was not Jewish. When he joined the Olympic Club (after a two year's wait) he invited me there one day. While I was in the gym with him, they questioned his membership. When I went in the pool, they stopped the swimming lesson. And when I was still swimming and George was showering, they asked him, 'Why did you let that nigger in the club?' These were people in government I would see at City Hall, or who would speak to me regularly on the streets, but who did not know me in that environment."

Griffin, who currently hosts a radio talk show, is also a professional singer. About membership in the Bohemian Club, he noted:

"There's only one black member in the Bohemian Club — Vernon Ally. There's a certain kind of membership you get if you are an artist — and that's what he is. He plays the bass there on Thursday night. I don't want a 'Thursday night' membership. I want to be a full-time member, and I am here. I don't happen to sing on Thursday nights.

"If prejudice is a function of ignorance, then there is a lot of ignorance in men's clubs. You find a higher level of intellectualism at this Club, and I think that helps to eradicate prejudice born of ignorance. Sure, I know there were a few people who were reluctant to accept me when I first joined, but no one had the ill-grace to say anything. I have never had one incident at this Club where anyone has said anything to me or to anyone who was with me. We take each other on an equal basis at the Club. There may be people who don't like me as a person — that's fine. But they don't dislike me because of the ethnic group I represent. I don't find that here."

Asked if the black community feels he has deserted them, Griffin replied:

"Oh, they may make remarks like, 'What are you doing over there? You sold out?' But that's because people don't know what exists here, and it is easy to build up a fantasy about it. No, I didn't follow in my father's footsteps. But I think I am able to do as much good shaping opinion on a talk show that reaches Alaska, Western Canada and nine states at night and actively gets callers, as I would doing a lot of other things.

"I think there are two ways of battling something. One is in a quiet kind of way where you get things done. And the other way is headline grabbing and attention seeking. The second way may show more solidarity with those people in the community who don't know how change really comes about. They'll say, 'Noah's a martyr. He's in the forefront.' But Noah can do more by picking up the phone to talk to Douwe the Club manager and saying, 'Look, I'd like to make reservations for a cocktail party here to get together those backers of Doris Ward (San Francisco Supervisor) who want to raise money to cover her deficit.' That's the quiet way. I'm more comfortable doing that than knocking on doors at some place like the Olympic Club and saying, 'We can't go there — Why?'"

"It's been seven years since I joined. I think the gains here have been solid ones, ones that will set the way for someone else. You always have to look at that — who's going to come behind you and how they are going to be viewed based upon what you did. Especially if you are a member of an ethnic group."

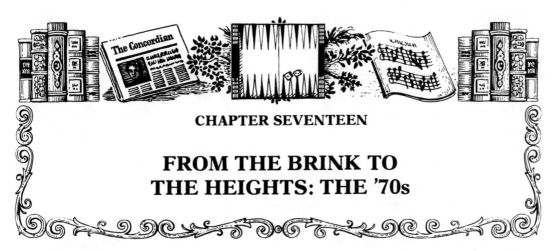

## CHAPTER SEVENTEEN

# FROM THE BRINK TO THE HEIGHTS: THE '70s

HEN LARRY NESTEL ASSUMED THE PRESIDENCY in the mid-Seventies, he was told that "changing lifestyles have made city clubs obsolete, and the best I could hope for was to delay the Club's demise as long as possible." By the end of his term, Nestel's administration had challenged that idea in such a way that the Club had actually become an essential expression of those changing lifestyles. Instead of facing gradual demise, the rejuvenated Concordia-Argonaut took a new, vigorous lease on life.

Nestel, typical of the new membership that joined the Club following World War II, was not a native-born San Franciscan. He was born in Brooklyn. A naval officer stationed in San Francisco during the war, he met his future wife, Harriet Block, in the City. Her father, Charlie Block, took the young man to the Club. "I loved the place — the food, the atmosphere, everything," recalls Nestel. "I was a CPA at the time, and I went to law school at night after I married. I was too busy struggling with work and school and making a living to think of joining." But by 1950 Nestel had become a member.

"The first thing I did, soon after I joined, was to bring Bingo nights to the Club. I still had my contacts with the Naval Supply Centers and I could get great premiums. Bingo was a big moneymaker for the Club; the kids loved it. As for myself, I loved going there to play volleyball on Monday and Thursday nights."

Nestel began ascending the ladder of Club leadership when he compiled a list of suggestions for improving dining room operations and submitted it to Gene Buenzly, then maitre d', who turned his ideas over to a member of the Board. Nestel was soon asked to the Election Board, then to the Board of Directors, and eventually, to the Vice Presidency under Jack Lipman.

The Club that Nestel inherited as president in 1975 was a victim of the times. Social clubs across the country were having difficulty attracting and retaining members. The previous administrations had done admirable jobs — remarkable jobs — but the deck was stacked against them. Dr. Stanley Reich, president from

1967 to 1969, was beset with the problems of maintaining a building nearly sixty years old. He appointed a committee to determine the foreseeable needs of the Club over the next five years. They predicted it would cost $200,000 for the most necessary improvements alone. An assessment of $360 per senior member, with commensurate increases for the other groups, was instituted.

The following year, when Ben Baum became president, the first phase of the Five-Year Plan was underway. $100,000 was spent on such practical needs as boiler repairs, filter pumps, bathroom plumbing, etc. In 1970, after an additional $100,000 had been spent on kitchen renovations, the expansion of the mezzanine into the pool area, and new lockers, dues were raised from $36 to $40 for seniors, with smaller increases down the line for the younger members. The membership, which had remained steady until that point, began to decline. Despite the wide assortment of entertainment activities, people were not using the Club facilities. A public relations committee was formed, under the chairmanship of Dick Sloss, to provide publicity for events. Plans for a club newspaper were in the works.

By 1971 Baum could report to the membership that the second floor had new lighting and air-conditioning and that carpets and draperies had been replaced as needed on both the first and second floors. But membership was still going down. Baum made a discrete pitch for new members by stating in his annual report that "because of a higher number of deaths this year along with the usual resignation rate, there are a few openings to be filled."

Donald Magnin, who became president in 1972, was faced with not only the cost of Year Four of the Five-Year Plan, but also with a 25% rise in the Club's labor costs. The Board of Directors' only recourse was to refinance the mortgage and to raise monthly dues $5 for seniors, with lesser increases down the line.

In 1973 Magnin, with his background in merchandising, got the Board's approval for a plan to attract new members.

"I was a retailer then and I thought, why don't we have a sale? Why not cut the initiation fees in half? They were $1000 at the time, so I suggested we put them on sale for $500, without cutting the monthly dues. That way, we could pick up the difference from what the new members spent in the Club each month. The Board went for it. Rick Colsky undertook the development of the program, and it worked fine. We took in so many new people we had to amend the by-laws on the ceiling for senior members. We were below 500 when we started. The new ceiling was fixed at 575."

During Jack Lipman's first year in office (1973 – 74), there was no loss of membership, but neither was there any gain. Under the enthusiastic leadership of Stanley Diamond in his third year as Entertainment Chairman, assisted by Co-Chairman Allan E. Sommer, the Entertainment Committee originated no less than forty major social events, the largest number in the Club's history. A fashion show, introduced the year before and continued under the guidance of furrier Richard Friedman, was fast becoming a Club tradition, along with the Gourmet Dinners and Wine Tastings. A dinner was held to honor three Past Presidents: Dan Stone, Harry Hilp and Marcel Hirsch. Other events included Polynesian and Japanese nights, museum tours, an evening with the Oakland Metropolitan Museum, as well as an exhibit of members' photographic works, a bridge tournament and backgammon lessons.

An unforeseen expense occurred that year when laundry costs doubled. To avoid an additional annual expense of $10,000 the Club decided to install its own laundry facilities. Complete commercial equipment, plus towels, was purchased for $11,000. It was a blessing in disguise, because the laundry paid for itself within two years.

The five-year renovating plan was completed, but it brought no dramatic change in the number of members. In his annual report of April 1974, Lipman spoke enthusiastically about the fine shape the Club was in. "We know our dining room is equal to any in the country. We have two attractive bars and our card rooms are newly furnished, well-lit and beautifully decorated. We have an excellent swimming pool, sauna, steam bath, gymnasium, handball and paddleball courts. We have a masseur, barber and manicurist constantly available to serve you. Social events average close to one each week. The facilities are here. Members, take advantage of your Club."

There was no overwhelming response; the use of facilites, particularly the daily dining facilities, did not rise, and membership in all categories continued on a slow downward spiral. Meanwhile, external forces were beginning to make an impact on Concordia-Argonaut. There was the women's movement for equal rights, which led to certain changes in the Club's dining facilities, as well as the national focus on physical fitness, which created new demands on the Club's athletic department. Modern lifestyles were reflected in a new informality in dress.

The Club needed an administration which could bring these transitions into focus, and make the changes necessary to transform the Club from a victim to a beneficiary of the times. Larry Nestel, who had served as Vice President and Finance Committee Chairman under Jack Lipman, was prepared to take on the challenge.

"I was concerned with the usage the members were making of the Club as well as its financial condition." He began by reorganizing the Club's committees. "I think committees are extremely important. For one thing, an active member will feel like an important part of a club; secondly, you find out about a man's

131

leadership potential by the way he serves on a committee; thirdly, there was a lot of unused talent in the Club; and lastly, committees decentralize authority."

The House Committee was the first to be decentralized. "It formerly consisted of twenty-five to thirty members," said Nestel. "It functioned as a Food and Beverage Committee, a Building Repairs Committee and a Rules and Conduct Committee. Because the committee rarely met, its chairman assumed an important role. He, along with the Club president, ran Concordia-Argonaut.

"The Athletic Committee met only once a year. We had no Budget Committee and the Finance Committee rarely met. I asked Tony Pels, who was then manager, to go through the roster and pick members whom he felt could fill certain slots. We spent a month sifting names. When we called upon them, people unanimously agreed to serve. We then divided the House Committee into three parts, each with its own chairman."

Adrian Scharlach became Co-Chairman of the new Food and Beverage Committee (along with Jack Lipman). Scharlach, who headed a corporation which owned a string of hotels, had been president of the East Bay Hotel Association for two terms in the late 1960s. He had first-hand experience in managing hotel dining rooms, and as a former member of the Club's Operations Committee created to aid the staff, he was equally familiar with the day-to-day operations of Concordia-Argonaut.

"When Larry asked me to serve on the Food and Beverage Committee, there was quite a deficit in that department. He asked me if it were at all possible to increase revenues or decrease losses by $20,000 that fiscal year. While some clubs are organized to make money on their food departments, ours is not. We expect to lose money on the food. People are paying their dues primarily for the use of the Food Department and Athletic Department. But our losses were far, far too great.

"I had a very good committee comprised of people with a great deal of expertise. We investigated and found that the dining room, open nightly Sunday through Thursday, was doing poorly on Monday and Tuesday nights. In a food operation, you must have a certain number of people in the kitchen and a maitre d' out front whether you are serving one or 100 customers. You can regulate the number of waiters and busboys — if you know how many are coming in to dine. On Mondays and Tuesdays there'd be about six or eight people in the dining room. People would look in, see so few people — it was like a morgue — and go elsewhere.

"We looked at what the help was costing — and a lot of that was overtime — and we decided to close on Monday nights. There was a lot of grumbling, but the Board voted for it and that's what we did.

"Having closed on Mondays, we wanted to build up the number of people coming in on Tuesdays. We instituted a Tuesday night mini-buffet, cutting out a number of expensive items and offering the dinner at a cheap price — I think it was $6.75 then. We included a glass of wine."

"The mini-buffets served another purpose," said Nestel. "We had been getting from twenty to twenty-five resignations each year. I did a survey to find out why and the main reason was, 'I don't use the Club.' This Tuesday night special was a way of getting the members there. On Tuesday nights we began having as many as 200 people."

Dining room losses were significantly decreased by the mini-buffet, the elimination of Monday night service, and a cutback in kitchen staff. But Scharlach and his committee didn't stop there.

"Thursday night, 'maid's night out,' and Sunday night were generally money makers for the Club," Scharlach continued, "but even those nights weren't all that well received at the time. We wanted to get volume. We had to have the same amount of help, and with more people, your food costs come down. So we inaugurated a Beefeater's Special, offering prime rib on Thursday nights. And to even off the costs — we didn't make any money on the prime rib — we also put hamburger on the menu at the same price. It worked well because a lot of the older people, especially women, didn't want the prime rib and would order hamburger. Wine came with that dinner, too. We featured the Beefeater's Special for a long time. As business picked up, we adjusted our prices."

The Rules and Conduct Committee, the second component of the new three-part House Committee, worked on a more contemporary dress code. "Wednesday night is Club night and the dining room is open only to men," Nestel said. "The younger guys used to come to meetings *after* dinner because they objected to wearing jackets and ties in the dining room. They'd work out in the gym, run across the street for a sandwich at Tommy's Joynt and then come back to the Club. So we made two changes. First, we extended the dining room hours for Wednesday night until nine o'clock so the members wouldn't have to cut their time short in the gym. Then we relaxed the dress code for that night. At first it was badly abused; some men wore jeans, and so forth. But people soon conformed to the Club."

The third facet of the House Committee was the Building and Maintenance sub-committee, led by co-chairmen Myron Zimmerman and Jerold Rosenberg. The Committee undertook a comprehensive study of the long range equipment and building replacement requirements of the Club. "Max Garcia, a member who is an architect, prepared specific recommendations as to a timetable for replacing equipment. Previously, we had no system for replacements and therefore no budget provision for it," said Nestel.

Nestel, with his background as a certified public accountant, then turned his attention to cost analysis. Under the guidance of Chairman Edgar Stone, the

Finance Committee instituted a system of budgetary control, even over meat portions. "We also worked with Manager Tony Pels and Club accountant Bill Layton and took them to training seminars."

Dining room changes, a relaxation of the dress code and more realistic cost analysis having been accomplished, Nestel turned his attention to the Athletic Department. It was chaired by Richard Colsky, who had grown up on the Northside of the Club.

"Things began to change in the Athletic Department in the mid-Seventies," said Colsky. "Both the number of people down there and the composition of the department shifted. You used to know everybody in the Athletic Department. When we reduced the initiation fee in 1973 and took in so many new members, the floodgates were opened. You'd look around down there and not know half the people. That was the first indication to me that something was changing.

"Today there is a raised level of consciousness about the benefits of jogging, exercising, and so forth. As a result, people began to come more regularly. Someone like Steve Horn, for example, plays basketball every day. Basketball used to be just on Wednesdays, but now there's a game every night of the week and every Saturday. We started to get crowded. Instead of one or two people in the steam room there might be four or five and when you went to the pool there were four or five fellows swimming laps. That had been unheard of . . . so I came up with the idea of installing lanes to make it more comfortable for people to swim."

The Athletic Committee also conducted a comprehensive survey of the membership to determine their interest in the athletic facilities, including programs for the younger members, the hours the department should remain open, and the types of equipment members would like.

"Until then, the Athletic Department had been considered a second-class citizen." said Colsky. "It was difficult to get the Board of Directors, the people who control the purse strings, to allocate significant funds. Because a lot of them didn't use the facilities, they expended minimal effort to maintain it or introduce innovations. But a lot can be accomplished if somebody takes the lead. Nestel was instrumental because he was a president who was down here working out every day. He started the ball rolling."

The ball actually started rolling in 1975, when Jack Lipman was president and Nestel vice president. It was in that year that operations first showed a profit, since the Club began laundering towels, sheets and gym clothing on the premises. In 1975 Athletic Department Chairman Stu Seiler finally began construction of the whirlpool the men had so long requested. The fact that it took nearly six years before it could be used was another matter!

The survey determined the direction of the Athletic Department in the next few years. A Universal weight machine with nine exercise stations was purchased. It quickly became one of the Club's most popular pieces of equipment. By 1979 Athletic Department Chairman Marv Nathan proudly unveiled the machine's new home in the weight and exercise room. The red carpeted, beige walled room, designed with the help of architect members Howard Fine and Max Garcia, had formerly served as two card rooms used only once a year for the overflow of players on Stag Night. The fact that members were willing to relinquish the card rooms at all was an indication of the growing importance the Club as a whole was placing on the Northside facilities.

A plaque in the weight room designated it as the Everett Whitney Weight Room, in honor of "Whit," who had been the department's athletic director for twenty-five years when he retired in 1975.

When Nestel left office in 1977, he reported that "with the present number of membership applications under consideration, it is likely that the total membership of this Club will shortly be equal to the highest level in its history." A membership profile taken the year before showed the average age of members to be forty-six, compared with an average age of fifty-five a few years earlier. The report also showed that the volume of activity in the dining room was the largest in the Club's history, both in dollars and numbers.

Although he warned members not to be complacent about the progress of Concordia-Argonaut, Nestel told members that "a great utilization of the dining room and Athletic Department, an increase in membership, a healthy balance sheet and a decrease in the average age of members all help to demonstrate that, should the present progress continue, the Club's future is assured."

•          •          •

As the Club moved toward a new decade its future looked even more secure. Because of spiraling inflation, in 1977 President Herbert Leland and his Board increased initiation fees to an unprecedented $1500 — only four years after they had been cut in half, to $500, to attract new members — and raised the monthly dues. They didn't anticipate that the fee increases would be accompanied by an increase in membership.

"Not only was there an unprecedented number of applications in the month prior to the increases, but we also found that every month thereafter, we'd receive an average of half a dozen new applications," said Leland.

As the number of senior members rose to its authorized limit of 575, the Board was faced with a decision either to raise the ceiling or institute a waiting list. Only an unfortunate development, namely the unusually high mortality rate among members (twice the normal rate), postponed that decision for another year.

Credit for the Club's resurgence does not belong exclusively to Nestel or the changes that his administration made, substantial though they were. Other factors — and other people — contributed to the renaissance. The Club that Herb Leland inherited was, indeed, a beneficiary of the times. Men in a position to join a luxury club were suddenly discovering what Concordia-Argonaut had to offer. "If you want to attract members," joked Renny Colvin, "just start a waiting list to keep them out."

Concordia-Argonaut had all the basic ingredients for success. Young professionals, looking for a prestigious place to relax, began knocking at the door for admittance. They found a club with all the advantages of a first-class facility without the disadvantages of a huge, impersonal operation.

One of the things that helped to give the Club a more personal feeling was the publication of *The Concordian*, the club newspaper. Rick Colsky started the paper in 1979 and Stanley Diamond, one of the men most responsible for it's success, took over the editorship two years later.

Diamond, a retired Army colonel with a background in agricultural economics, served on the staff of Senator S.I. Hayakawa, who had once been his professor of semantics at San Francisco State University. Diamond, who said he "dearly loves" his Club, explained why he felt an obligation to serve:

"Since I was going to the Club five or six times a week, I thought I should take responsibility for its functioning and operation, rather than only using what it had to offer me. In the late Sixties and early Seventies, the Club was facing serious questions of survival."

Diamond, with a master's degree in semantics, wanted to integrate members into the Club. "There are a lot of people who have relatives or friends here and they drift in and out without any feeling that this is 'My Club.'"

Diamond proceeded to instill that feeling in several ways. He began with entertainment: "With quality, stylish entertainment they couldn't get in other parts of the City, or in a private setting." Diamond then involved the membership in the process of selecting the directors of the Club. "We established a check list of criteria for the nomination of members as directors. This was very important, because the directors choose the Club's officers from their ranks."

However, Diamond accomplished the "My Club" feeling mainly through *The Concordian*, with its profiles of prominent members, such as Walter Haas, Daniel Koshland and Harold Zellerbach, and its breezy, informal updates on the activities of the various departments. For example, he wrote about the Thursday lunch group that has eaten together for fifty years, the volleyball game that has continued for three decades and the poker game that has been played non-stop since 1938. Diamond would preview upcoming events and reminisce about the milestones of the Club's long history.

"Our purpose was to pull the Club together and to produce a high-quality publication that, hopefully, members would want to read."

At the same time, Adrian Scharlach, then Vice President and House Committee Chairman, contributed to the "My Club" feeling by inaugurating such things as a blood bank account at Irwin Memorial Blood Bank to which members steadily contribute." People like Ben Blum, who passed away recently, were very grateful for it," Scharlach said.

Adrian also secured a medical insurance plan for the Club. "We found through surveys that quite a few members did not belong to group plans and did not have the coverage they needed. We contacted every insurance broker in the Club—it was a hot potato—and finally established a very fine policy through Cliff Barbanell."

Scharlach also appointed a sub-committee, the Hospitality Committee, to set up a program of Wednesday night dinners at which Board members would meet with newcomers and introduce them to their fellow clubmen. Cards were sent to members on their birthdays entitling them to a free dinner (although this practice was later discontinued when food costs skyrocketed). The committee's new policy of inviting the members to a free dinner before the Annual Meeting, a way of ensuring a good turnout, has been retained. Recognition has been given to retiring Board members by presenting them with plaques at the conclusion of their terms; paperweights inscribed with the names of Election Board members are given to those who serve on that committee.

"I, for one, feel that any 'extras' you can give to the members is not a luxury, but a necessity," concluded Scharlach.

The Club, struggling for survival in 1973, was four years later grappling with the growing list of people clamoring for admission. The transition was accomplished first by Don Magnin's decision to cut the initiation fees early in the seventies, which brought in a throng of younger members. Second it was the result of Larry Nestel's ability to recognize and encourage the changes necessary to revitalize the Club in the face of changing lifestyles and the membership's willingness to support, both financially and philosophically, those changes. Third, it was due to the success of Stanley Diamond and Adrian Scharlach in personalizing the Club. And finally, it was due to the staff of the Club. Without an efficient, highly skilled staff performing smoothly behind the scenes, no club could exist as long as the Concordia-Argonaut.

These diverse factors worked to bring Concordia-Argonaut to the forefront at a time when, once again, there was a demand for the kind of excellence the Club had to offer.

The influx of young new members in 1977 not only brought the average age of Concordians down still further, but also placed greater strains on the Club's athletic facilities.

President Leland appointed Larry Nestel and Ted Euphrat to head a Long-Range Planning Committee to determine, as Leland put it, "where we should be ten years down the road . . . forever down the road. What should the Club's future be? Should we remain on Post Street? Should the Club accommodate only a total of 625 members? (It had already exceeded that number soon after the committee began its deliberations. Club Manager Tony Pels thought the Club should be as big as anybody wanted to make it.) Should we acquire a new building somewhere else, perhaps the Elks Club Building? Should we buy a lot and build another building, since we can get a lot of money for the present building? All that was discussed, as well as how we could enlarge the present building. Could we buy the building next door on Post Street, that we once owned or buy the building across the alley and put a bridge across it?"

While half of the Long-Range Plan entailed finding answers to those questions, another group was studying needed improvements to the existing Club in the interim.

"The group was split over whether we should stay where we were, or make long-range plans for another locale. It was only the matter of finances that made the decision for us," Leland continued. "While we were deliberating about building a new facility, inflationary costs went through the roof and we found we were talking about building costs ranging from $3 to $4 million. Then the question arose: where could you buy land in the City?"

By 1979, when Leland, as past president, became chairman of the committee, it was unanimously agreed that the only viable course of action was to proceed with improvements at 1142 Van Ness Avenue. The committee was renamed the 1142 Committee, and plans were made to consult an architect.

However, even before a decision could be made to hire an architect, or design remodeling plans, there were two areas in the Club which required immediate attention: the kitchen and the Athletic Department.

•     •     •

As Concordia-Argonaut entered the 1980s, it did so with a kitchen that had just undergone a major renovation, comprising $50,000 worth of improvements. And the Athletic Department, much to the delight of President Richard Colsky, once the Club's Junior Athlete of the Year, had a working whirlpool, an improved steam room, and a cooling off room twice its former size. Additionally, money had been allocated to transform the old handball courts into two regulation-sized racquetball courts with a glass-enclosed viewing area.

Shortly after Colsky took office, the long-expected waiting list for Club membership became a reality. With the full complement of 625 members over the age of twenty-five immediately met, measures were necessary to prevent overcrowding in the Athletic Department and contend with the scarcity of lockers, which members are required to have in order to use the facilities. Applicants for membership, age twenty-five and over, were put in a holding pattern.

Colsky, who conceived the idea of the waiting list, explained his reasons for it:

"The thing that made the Concordia Club different from other clubs was the availability of its facilities. Members could come down and do whatever they felt like, without a reservation and without waiting. At any other club you'd have to wait to swim, to play basketball, or you'd go to lunch and have to make a reservation. Everything entails a wait, or a hassle. But not at this Club — that's what sets it apart from the others. I felt it was important for our membership to be aware that the current leadership was dedicated to the protection and the preservation of the quality standards we have come to cherish and enjoy. So the question I brought to the Board was, 'Do you want to have a fewer number of people in the Club and have them bear an increased financial burden? We know that costs are going to rise, and we will be required to raise more money to sustain the sort of club we've always had. Or do you want to actively attempt to get more members?' The Board opted for a raise in dues and fees and a waiting list for members."

Despite the price increases and an initiation fee of $2,000, by April 1979 there were twenty-five men on the waiting list waiting an average of six months to get in. By 1980, with initiation fees at $3,000, the number grew substantially, with a year's wait for entrance.

The waiting list brought about a significant change in admission standards. "Where formerly," said Colsky, "the main focus was on the absence of negative factors which might exclude an applicant, we are now primarily concerned with the positive aspects of the man, as well as his potential use of our facilities."

Several Concordia leaders, including Renny Colvin, Harold Dobbs and Richard Goldman, thought those "positive aspects" should be defined to include the applicant's relationship — both financial and otherwise — to community activities, such as the Jewish Community Federation, or, in the case of Gentile applicants, the United Way, or similar organizations.

Said Colvin shortly before he died, "The proposition that because we are a social club we are not interested in civic responsibility is a regrettable one. It assumes that we can make a judgment as to the quality and the character of a man without taking into consideration what contribution he makes to his community outside the Club."

The "positive aspects" suggestion has since been incorporated into the list of criteria determining the order in which an applicant is admitted from the waiting list into active membership.

Colvin's contribution to the community had been exemplary, and in the highest tradition of Concordia leaders. The attorney who successfully defended Allan Bakke before the U.S. Supreme Court in the landmark "reverse discrimination" case, Colvin was president of the San Francisco Board of Education in 1966, and a two-term member of the Board of Governors of the San Francisco Community College District. In the Jewish community, Colvin was president of Temple Emanu-El for two terms; chairman of the Bay Area Chapter of the American Jewish Committee; chairman of the Jewish Community Relations Council, and founding chairman of the statewide Jewish Public Affairs Committee of California.

Another suggestion Colvin hoped to see acted upon was to include events of a more intellectual nature in the Club program.

"To a certain extent the Club prides itself on its low-brow approach. I think we can foster another kind of atmosphere. While we do bring in politicians and athletes and bingo players and a lot of fancy gourmets, we rarely bring in someone because he's a scholar or intellectual. The ABC Correspondents Nights were as close as we've come to that sort of thing. I would like to see an attempt made to take a shot at programs that have some intellectual content."

*Dashaway Hall, 212 Sutter. The Concordia Club's second home, in 1868.*

*The Hoffman Building, O'Farrell and Stockton Streets. The third home of Concordia, 1873. The Club occupied two floors. Note the twin domes of Temple Emanu-El in the background.*

*President William McKinley passes in front of the Concordia Club on Van Ness Avenue, September 21, 1901.*

*New Year's Eve of 1897 at Concordia.*

*Interior of one of the Club's four cardrooms.*

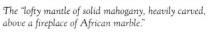

*The "lofty mantle of solid mahogany, heavily carved, above a fireplace of African marble."*

*Concordia's Grand Staircase with "heavy newel posts and elaborate banisters, all of clear mahogany."*

*The Ladies Bowling Team.*

*Concordia in ruins after the 1906 earthquake and fire.*

*Union Square in 1909. The Argonaut Club occupied two floors in building at right.*

*Scenes from Manny Brandenstein's Argonaut film, "The Eye of India." Top: Maurice Liebman (recipient of the Rajah's Gift, the All-Seeing Eye) displays the recovered loot to the police inspector. Bottom: Four gentlemen play cards in the Argonaut Club bar.*

*Costume Party in a private dining room at Concordia, 1921. Seated (left to right): Al Reyman, Jack Goldman, Marcel Hirsch, Leon Blum, Ed Gundelfinger, Al Lobree and Jack Goldberg. Standing (left to right): Jack Lewin, Dick Stone, Charlie Weinshank, Jr., Harold Silverman, Esmond Schapiro, Dan Stone, Sr. and Sanford Stein.*

*The Hawaiian Party, in the Main Dining Room, 1950.*

*Afternoon swim class, circa 1958.*

*"Whit" referees a basketball game in the afternoon gym class, circa 1960.*

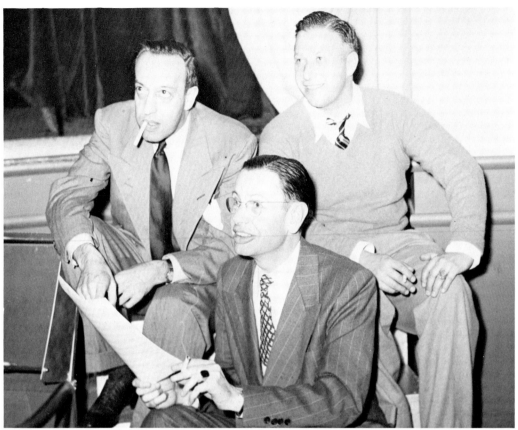

"The Big Three": Front: *Dick Sloss;* rear, *Sam Glikbarg and Paul Bissinger.*

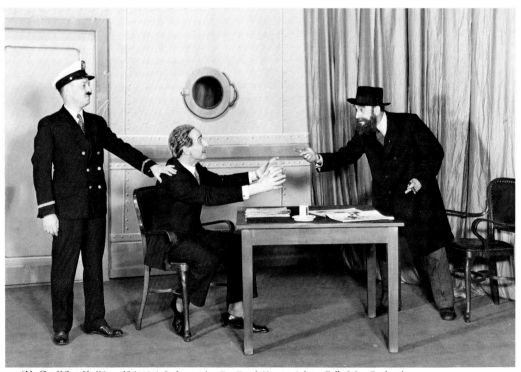

"He Got What He Wanted," (1931). Left to right: *Dr. Frank Harris, Adrien Falk, Max Frederick.*

*"Midwinter Madness," (1949).* Left to right: *Jay Hamerslag, Sidney Kahn, Albert Samuels, Jr., Dr. Bill Auslen, Dr. Albert Cohn, Dr. Harold Rosenblum, Dr. Don Trauner and Walter Miller.*

*"Valley Forgery," (1951).* Rear, left to right: *Jay Hamerslag, Buddy Lees, Percy Barker and Bob Knox.* Front: *Herb Ross, Walter Miller, Albert Samuels, Jr. and Albert Cohn.*

"Me and Trygve," (1957). Left to right: Jacob Voorsanger, Paul Klein, Allen Meier, Herbert Ross, Jack Davis and Herbert Jackson.

"Three to Get Ready," (1957). Front, left to right: Harold Kroloff, Lou Freehof, Joel Horowitz. Rear: Dan Stone, Sr., Dan Stone, Jr.

"Three to Get Ready." Arthur Simon (center) stops the show. Chorus, left to right: Larry Nestel, Allen Meier, Stu Erlanger, John Meyer, Dan Stone, Jr., Neville Rich, Jr., Herb Jackson, Charles Weinshank III, Howard Miller and Joe Kushner.

*"A Real Good Scout," (1966). Tommy Harris (left, rear) admires the "ladies," (left to right) Joel Horowitz, Pierre Granburg, Ed Berkowitz, Mel Lichtman and Stanley Diamond.*

*"Four Founding Fathers," (1963). Choristers perform on the expanded stage.*

*Concordia-Argonaut, 1939.*

*Concordia-Argonaut, 1949.*

*The Sylvan Room before the 1982 fire.*

*The Newman Epergne with Walter S. Newman and Mrs. S. Walter Newman.*

*The Main Lounge, looking east, before the 1982 fire.*

*Concordia-Argonaut in flames, 1982.*

*The Sylvan Room immediately after the fire.*

*Architect's rendering of the rebuilt Main Dining Room.*

*Architect's rendering of the new Second Floor Bar.*

*The Thursday night volley ball group is back in the beautifully refinished gym.*

*The pool and whirlpool get a final inspection as the Athletic area reopens on February 27, 1983.*

*Members work out in the new Weight Room . . . double the size of the pre-fire facility.*

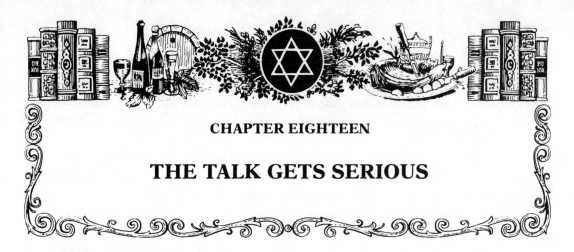

## CHAPTER EIGHTEEN

# THE TALK GETS SERIOUS

E WANTED TO PROVOKE interest in the issues of the turbulent '70s, to bring the world into the Club," said John Rothmann, descendant of Argonaut founders Joseph Brandenstein and William Haas. Rothmann believed strongly that some kind of intellectual content was needed in club programming. Just back from college in Southern California, the young Rothmann was appointed in 1973 to chair a sub-committee of the Entertainment Committee called the Forum Committee.

The Middle East was the topic at the Club with the first forum guest, Rabbi Joseph P. Sternstein, the national president of the Zionist Organization of America, who spoke on the need for American support for Israel.

It may have seemed odd that a member of one of the "First Families" chose a Zionist to be the initial Forum speaker, but sympathies were shifting. As Sanford Treguboff explained:

"If the attitude changed — and it did — it changed because the thinking of the membership changed, the thinking of the Jewish community in San Francisco changed. At one time, a group of people who disapproved of Israel and Israelis were very important and very vocal in San Francisco. Some were important members of the Club. But that didn't mean we did not have Zionists even in the early days — life-long, dedicated Zionists like Leo Rabinowitz and Isadore Raffin. They were respected men in the Club. So if an evolution took place in the Club, it is because there was an evolution in the Jewish community. Since the membership is a cross-section in one way or another of the Jewish community, it obviously spilled over here."

In 1975 Rothmann was asked to continue as chairman by Bertram Tonkin, Entertainment Committe chairman. Tonkin, who headed that committee either as chairman or co-chairman for the next four years, was ideally suited to the post. It was an extension of what he did professionally as head of Western Exhibitors, Inc., an organization which stages trade shows and conventions. Although Tonkin was born and reared in Portland, Oregon, he was no stranger to San Francisco and the Club. His cousin, the late Joseph Tonkin, was a long-time member of Concordia-Argonaut. His wife, the former Mary Ann Brown, was the daughter of Argonaut member Dr. A. Lincoln Brown, and the grand-daughter of Manny Brandenstein.

In May 1975 Menachem Begin, then leader of the opposition in the Knesset, spoke at the Club, and received a far different reception than did David Ben-Gurion thirty years earlier. According to Rothmann and Tonkin, there was one of the largest turnouts in Club history for Mr. Begin's speech on the step-by-step peace attempts by U.S. Secretary of State Kissinger.

Alger Hiss was another of the speakers that year. Club member Dr. Meyer A. Zeligs, a psychiatrist, and author of the book about the relationship between Hiss and Whittaker Chambers, *Friendship and Fratricide*, introduced him. John Rothmann recalls: "Hiss spoke mostly about his New Deal days and provided us with a wonderful glimpse of Roosevelt at Yalta. He told us about a conversation he had had with FDR following an afternoon session between the President and Churchill and Stalin. 'Suddenly,' said Hiss, 'in the midst of our conversation, I saw the President slump, and his head fall on his chest. To cover my embarrass-ment, I pretended I hadn't noticed and went on talking. I asked him a question about Stalin and the talks that afternoon. The president, his head still lowered, opened his eyes and responded with a brilliant and penetrating analysis of what had transpired.'"

Other speakers that year included, Charles Breyer, special government prose-cutor of the Watergate case, introduced by his proud father, Club member Irving Breyer, William Buckley, talking about his U.N. experiences, and the Club's own nationally renowned economist, Dr. Maurice Mann.

•     •     •

Rothmann viewed the Forums as a vehicle for bringing leading world figures to the Club. In January 1976, he invited Senator Frank Church, then widely regarded as a Democratic presidential hopeful, to speak. Since Club rules prohibit campaign pitches on the premises, Church talked about American intelligence and foreign policy after being introduced by Madeleine Haas Russell, an ardent Church supporter.

In 1977 James Roosevelt, oldest son of FDR, gave Club members yet another poignant glimpse of the President. Rothmann recalls: "We didn't have such a large turnout — only eighty people showed up — but those of us there will never forget the moving account of how Jimmy accompanied his father to the podium at the Democratic Convention in 1924, the first time FDR made a public appearance following his polio attack. He said 'It was as if everyone was holding his breath as we made the long walk to the speaker's platform, and then, when Dad waved his arm, there was this thunderous ovation.' "

The forums also created a focal point for the City's mayoral campaigns. "It has now become a tradition that the first 'candidates night' for Mayor is held at Concordia-Argonaut," said Rothmann after the Club hosted two very successful occasions in 1975 and 1979.

In addition to the evening Forum dinners, the committee also inaugurated the Friday Forum luncheons. Initially they were held weekly and alternated speakers from within the Club and from without. Club members who spoke included then Port Commissioner Richard Goldman on the Port Commission; Reynold Colvin on the implications of the Bakke case, John Bolles who discussed San Francisco architecture and Police Commissioner Sam Ladar on police problems. Outside speakers included Robert Alioto, superintendent of San Francisco Schools, and David Dalin, historian and political scientist, on Jews in San Francisco politics.

"We intended the Friday Forums to provide intellectual stimulation. But the attendance began to drop and it was apparent that the two-hour lunches once a week were too much. Now we are doing selected forums at the noon hour which have great interest for members," said Rothmann, "such as the one we held December 1980 on Jewish authors. Participating were Frances Rothmann, author of *The Haas Sisters of Franklin Street, a Look Back With Love*; Ruth McDougall, who wrote, *Coffee, Martinis and San Francisco*; David Dalin, author of *Jews in Politics in San Francisco*, and Fred Rosenbaum, who wrote, *Architects of Reform*, about Temple Emanu-El. It was a great success."

# CHAPTER NINETEEN

# THE PRIVILEGES OF WOMEN

HE QUESTION OF ALLOWING women into the Concordia-Argonaut's all-male sanctuary arose long before the mid-Seventies. The first incident on record occurred back in 1920. The *San Francisco Chronicle* of October 1 ran a story head-lined: "Move to Restrict Women Club Visitors."

The report read, "By official action of 350 of the 500 members of the Concordia Club, taken at a fiery meeting Wednesday, its portals opening on Van Ness Avenue may not be passed by members of the female set except on Sunday evenings. The reason assigned for the restriction was the rapidly growing membership and the consequent need for all available space in the clubrooms."

Mention of the "female set" first appears in the Club's minutes in October 1936. Wives of members were put on notice to respect the sanctity of Wednesday nights as meeting nights. The minutes declared: "It seems that too many social functions are given on Wednesday nights by the wives of members who should give consideration to the Club, as in the case of the Meyerhoff dinner of last week, when some fifteen members were entertained there instead of at the Club."

The plight of widows of Club members was considered in December 1952, when Article II of the By-laws was amended to say: "In the event of the death of a member in good standing, the widow of such member shall have privileges of using the facilities of the Club to the same extent and in the same manner as if the member were living. An annual charge in the amount of $15, payable in advance, shall be made and shall be revoked at the pleasure of the Board of Directors."

"To the extent and in the same manner" meant she could continue to dine at the Club on Tuesday, Thursday and Sunday nights, the nights she had formerly been allowed to accompany her husband, and she could still use the Ladies' Lounge for her women's parties.

While the price of the widows' membership has gone up over the years, the policy has remained the same. The only time that policy was challenged was when one widow remarried a non-Concordia member and insisted on her right to bring her husband to the Club as her guest. The policy was hastily amended to clarify that a widow's rights applied only as long as the woman remained a widow!

The policy of the Club toward women in general came under a much greater challenge in 1974. With the women's liberation movement gaining momentum, and with the passage by California of the Equal Rights Amendment in 1972, it naturally followed that attempts would be made to pry open social clubs which discriminated against women.

The attempt at Concordia-Argonaut was modest enough. All that Mrs. Bertram Feinstein wanted in May 1974, in a move she described as "one small step for personkind," was to be allowed the privilege of eating lunch in the Club's main dining room.

Dianne Feinstein was then President of the San Francisco Board of Supervisors, the first woman to have attained that position. In her official capacity, and because the Club was so close to City Hall, she thought it would be "an ideal location for a relaxed opportunity to meet with leaders of other cities and other countries," she said.

Since a separate membership for her was not possible, she made inquiries, as a member's wife, to see about a possible change in Club policy to allow her to invite guests in for lunch. Ruth Jacobs had made similar inquiries which went unanswered. With the support of Dr. Feinstein, the women decided to test the waters themselves. They received an icy reception.

On the day in question, Dr. Feinstein made a reservation for four: himself, his wife, Ruth Jacobs and Dorothy von Beroldingen, another member of the Board of Supervisors. At the last minute, the doctor was detained in surgery. The women decided to go ahead with their plans.

Quiet pandemonium ensued. Douwe Drayer, the maître d', was very apologetic but he could not seat them, he said, because there was no member to sign the tab. Mrs. Jacobs responded that since the Club bills incurred by her husband were paid from their joint community property, she had the right to sign the luncheon check herself. Drayer turned to Tony Pels, the Club manager. Pels, also very discreet, supported Drayer and explained that Club policy would not permit them to be seated. By that time, every man in the room was staring at the intruders. The impasse was broken by Alexander Anolik's entrance. He gallantly invited the ladies to sit with him, telling Pels he would pick up the tab.

"My offices at the time were in the Jack Tar Hotel across the street, and three of my associates were women," Anolik said, explaining his actions. "They were always needling me about why they couldn't ever eat at the Club. I'd come back from lunch raving about the wonderful buffet, and they'd come back from their daily sandwich at Tommy's Joynt. So when I saw Dianne, who was a political friend, and Dorothy and Ruth, who were neighbors of mine across the hall in the Jack Tar, I decided I had to take a stand."

Anolik was reprimanded for his action. "I got a phone call the next morning from the President, reminding me of the Club's rules regarding women's privileges. Paul Jacobs and Bert Feinstein got letters more or less telling them to keep their wives in line. I guess the letters generated some steam, and the whole incident wound up in Herb Caen's column."

Publicity of any kind — good or bad — is anathema to the Club. There is a strict rule against it. Following the publicity in the wake of the Willie Mays affair, the Board passed a resolution that "it is considered improper for a Club member or any employee to discuss or disclose internal Club information with the hope or intent of publication by commercial news media." The resolution was passed at the Annual Meeting of May 18, 1966.

Actually, the Club was in the process of addressing women's privileges in its own quiet manner at the same time that Supervisor Feinstein tried to liberate the dining room. Two weeks prior to the incident, at the Annual Meeting, LeRoy Hersh had proposed that women be allowed to dine with the men during the luncheon period. Hersh, another attorney with offices in the Jack Tar building, acted from both personal conviction and paternal motivation. He was in partner-ship with his daughter Nancy and his other daughter Jill was an associate in their law firm. Ruth Jacobs and Dorothy Von Beroldingen shared office space with the Hersh group.

"My daughters and my associates wanted to be able to come to the Club for lunch and to entertain clients there. I agreed completely. So I brought the matter up." Hersh's suggestion engendered some heated reaction.

"Roger Coffee stopped speaking to me. At first I thought he hadn't seen me, so I made a point of greeting him. No response. Finally he said, 'I don't speak to radicals.' "

Dan Stone, Jr. and several other members suggested a novel solution. "If women are to be allowed in the dining room," they said, "let's rehire the waiter who was recently fired for gross incompetence. After he spills food or hot beverages on them, the women won't be likely to come back."

"The arguments about having women at lunch," continued Hersh, "seemed based on such complaints as 'if we have women here, I'll constantly have to get up and sit down whenever someone I know comes in.' Or, and this was deemed far more of a threat, 'I don't want women around to see me play cards after lunch and report back to my wife.' "

(When women were finally admitted, Concordians agreed that the inconvenience of demonstrating their innate good breeding was more than offset by the
pleasant sight of pretty faces in the dining room. As for potential card-spying,
that was neatly handled by a sign in the elevator expressly stating "No Women
Are Allowed On The Second Floor," where the card rooms are located.)

President Jack Lipman responded to Hersh's proposal by appointing House
Committee Chairman Lloyd Sankowich as chairman of an ad hoc committee to
study the matter of women's privileges in the Club. Three meetings were held
and members' opinions were heard. Then a questionnaire was circulated among
the membership. More than half who responded favored more privileges for
women — but not the privilege of having lunch in the dining room. There were
lots of suggestions about what could or should be done, but the committee gave
serious attention only to the luncheon issue.

At its Annual Meeting in 1975, the ad hoc committee recommended to the
membership that women be allowed to accompany members as guests providing
they were seated in the Sylvan Room. The Board vetoed the idea on two
grounds: first, that outside organizations in the Jewish community were using that
room for private affairs which would have to be suspended; and second, that it
could cause embarrassment.

It certainly did. In a sense, women had already been using the Sylvan Room
for lunch. Shortly after that room was opened in 1956, Abe Shragge, then
president, suggested the room be rented to Jewish organizations for their luncheon
board meetings. Some of those boards contained women, but economic considerations prevailed over policy and it was decided that women would be admitted
into the Sylvan Room under those conditions. Shragge's precedent setting step
was hailed in song by lyricist Richard Sloss, in a number from the 1957 show,
"Three to Get Ready." The verse, set to the melody of "With a Little Bit of
Luck" from "My Fair Lady," went in part:

> *"Concordia used to segregate its ladies*
> *As if they suffered from a foul disease;*
> *Concordia used to segregate its ladies, but*
> *With a President like Abe,*
> *With a President like Abe,*
> *Integration joins the he's and she's."*

Not quite. But for some twenty years thereafter, women were content to
enter those all-male portals at noontime, to be ushered quickly into the seclusion
of the Sylvan Room and to be whisked out afterwards, their presence hardly
noticeable to the rest of the Club.

While the gradual two-year process opened the Club to women merely to the extent that they were admitted to the dining room as guests of male members, nevertheless many members, particularly the "old-liners," feared the step represented an opening wedge that could not be stopped until women forced their way into full admittance as Club members.

The majority, however, did not see any danger of that happening. They pointed to the practical limits of the Club — an Athletic Department that is being used beyond capacity and a two-year waiting list for membership — and they shrug. "It's silly to talk about taking in more members when we can't take care of them even if they were to join." Besides, they point out, there are many valid reasons for a men's club and no legal prohibition against it.

Herb Leland, Club counsel from 1974 to 1977, made a thorough study of the legal issues involved. "While the ad hoc committee concerned itself with the 'should-we-or-shouldn't-we' aspect, I was concerned with the legal responsibilities of the Club with respect to anti-discrimination laws. The legal question was thought to be very pressing when the matter first arose, because there was a case before the Attorney General involving the Ingomar Club in Eureka. It was being sued because the Club prohibited women from going there for lunch when it was the only club in the area. There was the possibility of a ruling finding that practice discriminatory. So there was a lot of discussion, a lot of research and position papers were sent out by counsel of the Clubs' Associations. It all led to my opinion that there was no legal requirement; that nobody in California or the United States was going to say to the Concordia Club, 'You have to close up; you can't be treated as a non-profit club.' It was a moot question anyway, because the Club never makes a profit in the first place!"

Neither could the Club lose its liquor license if it restricted its membership to men. At the time there was no law on the books that was being violated. The only penalty to the Club arose ironically, not from any existing law, but from the suggestion of a possible law. "There was a suggestion by the Treasury Department, which supervises the Internal Revenue Service, to deny tax deductions for business luncheons or anything else at a club if the club discriminates under federal law. However, the regulation was never issued and I doubt it ever will be during the Reagan administration.

"However, the result of that suggestion was that large corporations — the Bank of America, Wells Fargo, Standard Oil, and so forth — used this as an excuse to cancel their corporate memberships. The Club has — all clubs have what might be construed as — corporate memberships permitting the corporation to join for its president or another officer. He's the member. but the corporation pays his bill as a business expense. More often, the corporation just reimburses the officer for business lunches and entertainment as a legitimate business expense. But the corporations took advantage of the possible ruling to say, 'We can't do this anymore; we don't want to get involved with the IRS.' We lost quite a few members, which at the time, when we were worried about membership, was more significant than it would be now."

•       •       •

Since Club members feel they were — and are — under no legal obligation to promote women's privileges, and since they nevertheless opened their doors to women during the prime time of the day, most members feel they have gone as far as they can go.

This attitude was prevalent in a poll of the membership taken in the fall of 1979. Adrian Scharlach who, along with Allen Meier, was chairman of the House Rules Committee, reports: "There was quite a bit of feeling that there should be some sort of membership for women, not necessarily wives of members. A number of women judges, attorneys and bankers were coming to the Club as guests of members. They couldn't come by themselves and some members, like Jerry Falk who is an attorney, felt very strongly that we should devise a social membership that would allow the women these privileges. We outlined a proposal for a method by which we'd start with twenty or twenty-four women. But we soon realized the problems: How do you limit it; what about wives of members; and what do you charge? In presenting our proposal, we suggested that the membership be polled. The Board rejected the proposal and told us to formulate suggestions on which to poll the membership.

"We got the plebescite out soon thereafter and the response was about half and half — 50% of our members favored establishing a category of membership for women and 50% didn't. Because there was no clear-cut response and because we were currently at our membership limit, the whole matter was dropped."

Herb Leland voted with the half that felt women should not be offered membership of any kind in the Club "because philosophically, there is every reason to have a men's club, just as there is every reason to have a women's club. Suppose, finally, we reached a decision to let the ladies in. Maybe a law was passed so that we'd lose our liquor license if we didn't. Now, how would you go about doing it? Are you going to charge them the same initiation fees and monthly dues and then say, 'You pay the same amount but you can only swim during such-and-such hours, and you can't come in on Wednesday night because that's the men's club night?' In other words, what kinds of limitations are you going to give them for paying the same dues?

"If you change the dues structure, on what basis do you do it? If you give them a lower rate because they use the Club less, then why shouldn't a member who only uses the Club for lunch pay less? I can name you twenty guys who have never gone downstairs in the Club, who never use the athletic facilities. And conversely, there are those who only use that side of the Club and have never gone upstairs to the dining room. They could say, 'just let me pay for the limited use I make of the Club. I'll take just the dining privileges . . . or I'll take just the athletic privileges.' But once you make a change, the whole financial structure will take a loss.

"Now, there's a certain amount of hypocrisy in the suggestion that we should solve the whole problem by taking women in on an equal basis. Charge them the same rates we are charging the men — $4,000 initiation fees and $120 a month — and tell them realistically we have only limited facilities, but they can come in, so there's no discrimination. How many women are going to join for what they're going to get?"

Certainly not Ellen Newman, director of a top consumer affairs consulting agency and wife of Walter Newman, whose roots go back to the very beginning of the Club.

"I haven't been to the Concordia Club for lunch yet. Why would I want to go there? What does it offer me that a thousand other places don't? Does the fact that it is prohibited to women make it better?"

Ellen doesn't resent the fact that the Club discriminates against membership for women. On the contrary, she fully subscribes to the philosophy of separate clubs for men and women.

"I think today's young people have taught us a whole lot about having space. Everybody needs a little privacy. This may sound sexist, but as a woman, I like a space where there aren't men around, where I can be with my network of women friends. I think men deserve the same thing. Unfortunately, clubs sprung up at a time when women weren't equal, so there aren't as many women's clubs. But I think, given an equal number of men's and women's clubs, women wouldn't feel discriminated against. A hundred years from now, if things continue as they are, none of us will want to go to a men's club. I think women will like their clubs better. Their purposes will be served better."

Mrs. Newman sees Concordia-Argonaut as serving the needs of her husband and her sons very well. "My role in the Club had been to drop the children off on the sidewalk at Van Ness to go to their classes. I love, and respect the wonderful relationship the boys had with their father at the Club. That was their space together. I had a lot of time with the boys when Walter was busy. His time with the boys involved the Club. They are grown now, but to this day they look forward to Thanksgiving Eve and to gambling with their father. They look forward to the domino tournament, where they can play with their father at the Club. Why spoil that? For what? I think father-son relationships are very special and I credit the Club for providing that between Walter and his sons. Oh, Walter had that relationship other places — they were together in Boy Scouts and other things — but one of the things that goes on through life, that matures with them, is the link with the Club, and I have a very high regard for that."

Ellen also has a high regard for the potential development of women's clubs along the same lines. "There are beginning to be women's networks of all kinds. I belong to Women's Forum West, a group of women who 'excel' in their fields. We meet at the Metropolitan Club, which is essentially a women's club. We need our space, too . . . ."

PART FOUR

# THE SUM OF ITS PARTS

## CHAPTER TWENTY

# THE NORTHSIDE JOCKS

 HERE IS A STORY ABOUT a man who interrupted a card game at the Club to announce. "I feel wonderful! I just came from a swim in the pool." And the card players exclaimed "Pool? Where? You mean this Club has a pool?"

There is some truth to the fact that there is more than a geographical division separating the north end of the Club, the location of the Athletic Department, from the south side, the card-playing and eating side. For many years the Athletic Department was ignored because the Board of Directors mainly consisted of men from the Southside. What attention was directed its way centered on juvenile programing. The Athletic Department was an appendage to the Club, but not a very important one for many members. Today, by contrast, the Athletic Department is the tail that wags the dog, and is credited for the long membership waiting list. But that is a very recent development.

"I was so unimpressed with the Club's athletic facilities when I was interviewed for a job that I was about to turn it down," recalls Everett Whitney, who took over as Athletic Director in 1950 and served until 1975. "I made a long list of the things I was concerned about — I went right down the line — and I said I have to have answers to these things. Jack Voorsanger, who interviewed me in Sacramento, where I was working at the YMCA, agreed to make the changes.

"My primary responsibility was to develop a program for the children from eight years of age up — these were all youngsters who grew up during the war. We had a lot of kids here then. About thirty little kids eight years old; about the same number of ten-year-olds and a few of the intermediates, and about twenty-five to thirty of the high school kids — about 100 all together. And it kept increasing. After a few years, we developed a program for women and girls."

"After Hoyt Wood died the Club hired a young fellow, Ray Janassi, and he was here for just a short period. The reason he didn't stay, he told me, was that he hated kids. I guess he let them get out of hand. When I came here, they'd get up on the balcony and dive into the pool. They had a habit of taking balls from the pool tables, throwing them in the water and diving for them. They'd throw nuts and bolts in — the bottom of the pool was pretty well chewed up. First thing I did was make up a list of rules."

Whit, a warm, friendly man, who had over twenty years of experience working with kids at the YMCA, quickly instituted programs that channeled all that young energy into competitive sports. The boys were divided into three groups: cadets, preps and high schoolers. Competing within their own groups in a full range of gymnastics, swimming and basketball, they also competed in the Bay Cities Boys Athletic League, swimming or playing basketball against teams from the Buchanan "Y," The Booker T. Washington Center, Potrero Hill Neighborhood Center and the Oakland "Y." "We had the kids from the Buchanan "Y" here frequently as our guests — all of them black kids.

In 1953 – 56 the Concordia juveniles were the champions of the whole group, and the juniors won the trophy in '54 and '56."

Competition within the Club centered around winning the coveted "Athlete of the Year" award. The kids competed within their own age groups in a range of skills that included broad-jumping, high-jumping, free-throw basketball, rope climbing, plus various events in the swimming pool. The youngster with the most points was named the Athlete of the Year.

"The awards were presented at the Annual Father and Son night. We put on a big exhibition in the gym. Each kid had certain activities. Every boy was in it, and his father was there to watch. Then we came down to the swimming pool for the competition there. At the conclusion we had dinner, and I gave out ribbons for the first, second and third place awards and announced the Athlete of the Year."

Watching the swimming was particularly hard on Maurice Knox one year. His young son, Johnny, collided with another youngster who dove in after him. When Maurice realized what happened, he nearly climbed over the railing, clothes and all, to rescue him. Whit, at poolside, calmly scooped up one kid in each hand making light of the whole thing in order to reassure the boys.

Among those receiving the Athlete of the Year title were Rick Colsky (1957), Rick Meyerhoff (1958), Peter Block (1959), Paul Meyerhoff (1960), Ron Mack (1961), Louis Constine II (1962) and Ken Grabstein (1963).

The goal of the Athletic Committee was not only to develop athletic expertise in the youngsters, but to build character. Whit has some bright memories of how he accomplished that aim.

"Ricky Colsky was a little rascal, always getting into difficulty. I always gave the kids five minutes to get out of the pool and I remember one day they all left except Ricky. He said, 'Whit, what are you going to do if I don't get out?' I said,

'You stay in one minute more and I'll show you what I'll do!' He jumped out. It was a good thing because I never could have caught him — he was an excellent swimmer."

"Then there was Dr. Milton Pearl's son, Louie, snapping towels across other boys' backsides. It pains, and I know it, but I wanted him to know it, so I walked up and, ping — right across his butt. He cried and said, 'I'm gonna tell my father.' 'That's exactly what I want you to do as soon as you get home, and tell your dad to come down and see me, because I wanna talk to him,' I said. He was an angel after that."

Recalling an incident involving Johnny Peiser, Whit said, "It was during a birthday party. Kids would often celebrate their birthdays at the Club. Their mothers loved it because we had a nice program. Took them to the gym first for any kind of games they wanted to play. Then to the pool for a swim and then up to the Dining Room for the party . . . cake, ice cream, drinks and so forth. By the time the kids were ready for refreshments, they were pretty exhuberant. Well, while I was in the kitchen, I heard all this noise in the Dining Room. I discovered Johnny and his friends tossing ice cubes at one another, cake was flying, the room was in one big mess. I really blew the whistle, and they had to stay and clean everything up."

How the athletic program was used to build character is also evident in a letter written to one young member by Robert Zelinsky, chairman of the Athletic Committee at the time:

June 23, 1954

"Dear Keith:

"Your recent action in taking the elevator from the first to the second floor while the operator was not in the cab is grounds for suspension from the Club. However, in taking positive action, it is not the desire of the members to suspend you without taking other means to see if the rules of proper conduct can be properly observed.

"Your Club is composed of men who by proper, honest action in this community have been accepted as members. It is believed that you, as a Junior member, can benefit from association with them. Your recent action, however, does not bear this out and it is the action of this committee that you be removed from a position of responsibility, member of the Junior Athletic Committee, until your action proves that you are in a position to assume leadership of your friends and associates. Your membership in the Club for other purposes is not affected unless, however, your future actions require further discussion by this committee.

"Your parents are being sent a copy of this letter. We sincerely regret this action, but believe it to be in the best interests of all members. It is hoped that no further discussion of the above will be necessary.

"If you have any comments to make to the Committee relative to the above incident, will you make arrangements with the Club Office to be present at the next meeting.

Yours very truly,

Athletic Committee
Robert D. Zelinsky, Chairman

•     •     •

On Saturday mornings, Whit had special classes for non-swimmers. John Rothmann remembers when he attended it. "I was deathly afraid of water, but Whit was very positive in his encouragement. I remember sitting on the edge of the pool and shaking so much I vomited all over him. He just cleaned it up and went in the pool with me."

Vernon Kaufman, who came in with his twin boys one Saturday morning, told Whit his family was leaving for Lake Tahoe the following week and he wanted his boys to learn how to swim. "These two little red-headed rascals, about seven or eight, they just shook all over," Whit recalls. "Scared to death. I told their father I'd do the best I could. I got them in the water, and while I couldn't make swimmers out of them in that short time, I did get them over their fear of the water."

Whit also instituted a class for wives and daughters. "They came in every Monday. About a dozen or more women and a raft of girls. Mrs. Roger Coffee was one that stayed with it, and Eleanor Wollenberg, a nice little swimmer. Mrs. Newman came for a short time. Eventually we had about thirty-five young girls. . . . Carole Shorenstein (I read about her in the papers all the time now — a big show producer now, she was a little rascal then), and her older sister, Joan, were good swimmers. And Barbara Ruth Rogers (her mother, Mrs. Ernest Rogers, used to come regularly), and Linda Pearl, and Jo Constine, are a few who stand out. The girls had competition one time with the Oakland Athens Club.

They stayed with it for four or five years, and then the girls went to high school and began being fussy about hair-dos. . . ."

While the activity in the Athletic Department during these years centered on kids, the men also used the facilities, although to a lesser extent. As Whit explained: "We had volleyball at noontime two days a week, but that broke up because we didn't have enough men to make up two full teams. We had a night group that played on Friday at five o'clock, a very good group, and the Monday and Thursday nights groups that Jim Abrahamson and Larry Nestel played in. We used to play volleyball with the Central "Y," the Jewish Community Center, the Oakland "Y" and occasionally, the Berkeley "Y." We held our own. The players included Mel Marx, Jr., Walter Miller, Jim Lee and Herb Lane.

"They played a lot of basketball on Wednesday nights informally. There was no competitive basketball with other clubs. We had a lot of handball, then gradually racquetball came in. . . . There wasn't much swimming at noontime, but there was in the evenings, so the boys had to be out of the pool by five o'clock. We had instruction for men in swimming on an individual basis as well."

Toward the end of Whit's time at the Club, in the early Seventies, he said "the kids had grown up and there was no feed-in of kids at the bottom."

One who had grown up to become the chairman of the Athletic Department in Whit's last year was the once devilish Rick Colsky. "What happened was that the facilities were no longer used by the younger people of grade school and high school age. The lives of young people today are much more complicated," said Colsky.

At the same time, many young men began joining the Club primarily for its athletic facilities. Fortunately, there was a man around who could supervise the activities. Joe Ferrereo — sometimes affectionately called "Super Joe" — a tall, lanky young man, was the assistant director during the two years before Whit's retirement. Joe, a one-time golf pro and the Athletic Director's son-in-law, stepped into Whit's job on a temporary basis. He proved so popular with the members that Rick Colsky's Athletic Committee, after considering a number of other applicants, voted unanimously to offer Joe a position as a permanent staff member. He accepted.

The new Athletic Director faced many challenges, the most important of which was to acquire more modern sports equipment. The Universal weight machine was the first item purchased. After it was installed, Joe began staying late on Wednesday nights to develop individual programs for members to reduce flabby middles, strengthen biceps and tone calf muscles. Before long, a knee and thigh machine was added to the equipment.

Despite the improvements, substantial remodeling work was needed in both gym and swimming pool areas. As Colsky noted, the condition of the facilities were destined to get worse with increased usage, and the problem of locker space was critical.

By 1980 the facilities had improved considerably. Work was completed in the sauna, steam and cooling off rooms, then in the shower and utility areas. That year efforts to transform the old handball courts into modern, regulation-style racquetball courts also began. Joe instituted a full program of sports for the men in volleyball, basketball and racquetball in the mean time, while a volleyball clinic brought new players into the fold. Volleyball games on Monday and Thursday night had long been a Club tradition. "The Thursday night group has its own tee-shirts," says Nestel, an original member. "At one point we were almost a club within a club. We had the longest, established floating game in history! Now we're not that exclusive. Anyone who shows up on Monday and Thursday nights between 5:15 and 6:15 can get in a game. We play four on a side, and Joe is always there to keep score. We're a mixture of ages and abilities, and we have a lot of fun playing together. Some of the guys, in addition to Jimmy Abrahamson and myself, are Jesse Levy, Carl Pearlstein, Bob Appleton and Bill Green. The players change from time to time, but the game goes on."

In addition to the individual fitness programs and the sports clinics, Ferrereo organized a racquetball tournament, and by the spring of '79, sixty-three members were participating. "The Concordia racquetballers are among the best of any of the organized racquetball clubs in the Bay Area," said Al Rossi, a nationally-ranked player.

Basketball tournaments were also organized. The first year of play ('77), thirty-nine signed up for thirteen teams of three men on three. By 1979, the number of participants increased considerably. Four teams made it to the finals under the team captains Lou Rovens, Marc Spiegelman, Wayne Lesser and Tom Moellerich. Spiegelman's team was the winner.

George Moscone, the handsome young Mayor and a basketball regular, used his honorary membership to work out in the Athletic Department. Assassinated in November 1978, Moscone's loss was felt deeply by members of the Club who had enjoyed a sense of camaraderie with the gregarious politician. Stan Diamond, echoing the sentiments of many members, wrote a memorial poem which appeared later in the *Concordian*:

> *This symbol of his City*
> *Perhaps the symbol was the City*
> *His vibrant heart*
> *Beat in cadence with his City*
> *At Post and Van Ness—even here.*

*Three on three in basketball*
*With all that yelling,*
*George, Lou, Tom, Hal, Mike, Joe*
*Yell, yell, yell*
*A lay-up — a fifteen foot swish*
*And in between*
*The usual bounce offs and the roll outs.*
*In the sauna, shared stories, experiences, gags, laughter*
*And on occasion — George — alone*
*At noon — alone — in the sauna*
*With myriads of faces*
*Jamming the neuron net for attention*
*Singly, in groups and in crowds*
*"We want this," — "you said that," —*
*"I disagree with him," — "with them,"*
*"All of us disagree with each other."*
*Once in a while a face appeared,*
*"I love you, George," it said.*
*The City and George — congruent,*
*A unity, an identity — one*
*Then the muffled drum*
*And the name George*
*Is in the roll call for the dead.*

The only competition Concordia-Argonaut athletes engage in outside of the club circuit is in baseball. For three years, beginning in 1979, the Club has fielded a team in the City Softball League. Slamming the slow pitches into the field for runs in their gray Club shirts with blue lettering, the team, representing the only private club in the league, came in third in its first year and went to the playoffs in its second. Since the fire, the team has been in limbo.

●    ●    ●

As the years progressed, the demand from members to use the athletic facilities intensified. To accommodate Concordians the department took steps they hoped would cut down on the amount of guest use. In 1977, the Club resolved to charge $1 per guest, but when that brought no substantial decline in the number of patrons, the price was raised to $5 two years later. That furnished an additional source of revenue for the department, little else. "Until the fire, we were getting about $500 a month from this source. Actually, we barely came out when you figure the soap, towels and wear and tear on the equipment," said Joe.

In 1977, the year of one of the most severe droughts in California, the department was faced with serious challenges. "Conservation" became the name of the game, and the atheletes were told to maintain their vigilance and go "easy on the towels and the showers. Turn off the faucets when through shaving. Try Navy showers, it's just as easy and cleansing," Joe urged.

Another problem was the whirlpool, which quickly became a Club joke. "We have a waiting list of thirty-five members to get into the Club and a waiting list of 350 to get into the sauna," President Rick Colsky reported to the membership in 1980, five years after construction had begun on the unit. The problem which Harry Hilp, Jr., House Committee chairman, and Renny Colvin, Club Counsel had to deal with was the leak in the whirlpool. Not only had water seeped through the Club's foundation but it threatened to flood the bookstore next door. The manufacturer made a number of attempts to correct it and couldn't.

"Finally," said Colvin, "we made an agreement at the end of '78 to have the thing finished by January 5, 1979. He never could get it straightened out, and we finally took him off the job and gave it to Steve Sankowich of Alta Roofing."

"To tell you how frustrating this whirlpool incident is," Colsky told the membership, "It would be like Renny fighting all the way to the Supreme Court to get Allan Bakke into Medical School and then finding out Bakke couldn't stand the sight of blood!"

By 1980 Club members were finally able to immerse themselves. The bubbling, invigorating, hot water was at last churning in the whirlpool, which had been dedicated to the memory of Roger Coffee, "a man of deep conviction, unswerving loyalty, firm courage and constant strength. . . ."

Joe, who now had two assistants to help him run the increasingly popular department, was pleased by the evolution of the Club's facilities, yet he would have liked other athletic features added to the Club, notably a jogging area and tennis courts. "We thought about putting them on the roof, but we had structural experts come in who told us the roof just wouldn't support it."

As far as Colvin was concerned, that was just as well. "The attractiveness of membership — especially for the young members — has been based upon athletic facilities, but gives the Club what I consider to be a false character. That is to say that the Club was never really intended to be an athletic club. It did not develop facilities in keeping with that and even given the rosiest estimate anyone can make, it really cannot furnish such facilities on a large scale. The athletic facilities were meant as a kind of incidental convenience for members, but they are not the heart of the Club."

"Super Joe" had no quarrel with that. He said, "People are on a health kick. While the facility here is not as elaborate as at the Olympic Club — that place is like a zoo — this one makes people feel 'it's my own private club.' Use it when you want to use it, with no prior reservations. Small enough to be personal but large enough to be efficient is our aim. We want the fellows to feel you can have a good time, a good workout and enjoy your friends here."

## CHAPTER TWENTY-ONE

# THE PALACE OF THREES, FOURS AND FLUSHES

HERE IS A LEGEND, often told in the smoke-filled rooms of the Club's Southside, about a man who slumped over the Pinochle table and expired, whereupon, one of the anxious players asked, "What should we do?" The response was, "Take out the sevens and eights!"

The story — at least part of it — does have a basis in fact. Philip Sichel had made his fortune in Los Angeles, where he had been a City Councilman in the early 1860s, then moved to San Francisco and joined the Concordia Club, where he died in the cardroom one September morning. The following is an account of the man's unfortunate demise, as it appeared in the *San Francisco Alta California* on September 7, 1868:

"A few minutes after ten o'clock yesterday morning Mr. Philip Sichel (of Fleischman & Sichel, hardware dealers, on Front Street) met with his death in a most sudden and melancholy manner. At the time he was playing a social game of cards with several friends at the Concordia Club rooms on Sutter Street. After having played his last card he gasped and fell back in his chair. His friends, thinking he had taken fits, carried him to the windows and sent immediately for medical aid, which, however, arrived too late to render him any assistance, as he had already expired.

"The coroner was notified and the body conveyed to his office, where he held a post-mortem examination, and the cause of death was found to be aneurism of the aorta. The deceased had been up the night before until a very late hour, at a ball given by the Concordia, and seemed to be in perfect spirits, although he had been complaining . . . for some time. He was of a quiet and social disposition, about forty-five years of age, and leaves a wife and four children to mourn their untimely loss . . . ."

With the exception of the unfortunate Mr. Sichel, the second floor parlors have been the scene of good-natured fun and relaxation for most cardplaying men of the Concordia-Argonaut, even during times of stress — like fires. Jack Lipman swears the following story is true: in the early Fifties a fire broke out somewhere in the building. The firemen responded quickly, dragging hoses through the windows of two cardrooms. The card players, only momentarily nonplussed, got up to rearrange their chairs to fit over the hoses, and, as the firemen fought the flames, the intrepid bridge players carried on with their game!

The well-being of the card players was given priority on the agenda of the Board of Directors meeting in June 1948, as evidenced by the following action: "Board o.k.'s telephone jack in poker room, $18 installation fee plus $2 a month on the phone bill. This would be a great convenience to the card players in this room as they complain about the distance to the telephone booth."

The continuous — and rigorous — use made of the second floor facilities prompted a wise decision by Judge Milton Shapiro during his presidency. The Board minutes of January 17, 1951 read: "The Card Room chairs are being re-seated and re-backed with sponge rubber and a hard-wearing fabric at about $18.50 a piece. These will be sent out in small numbers from time to time so that no large expenditure will be noticed." And perhaps more importantly, so that no disruption of the game would ensue.

•          •          •

While journalist Choynski has referred to the Concordia as "the palace of threes, fours and flushes," poker is only one of the games popular with members. Pinochle was the favorite of Carl Plaut, a Club vice president in the Thirties, who played with Dr. Louis Green, Dan Stone and Harry Weiss. Plaut, retired president of the Union Ice Co., was renowned for his flowing mane of thick white hair. In a humorous poem dedicated to his memory, Adrien Falk, after devoting the first two stanzas to his virtues, exposed Plaut's antics at the pinochle table:

> "But this is the epus; cut free from deceit;
> The two-timing bastard's a fraud and a cheat!
> When a blue chip in the card game is lost,
> He recovers a white, worth a tenth of the cost!
> There is peace at the Club since he went home to rest,
> The round-table insults are devoid of zest!
> The suckers depart with their dough — more's the pity!
> There's no need to guard the cigars or the kitty!
> Yet we all miss the tightass and long for the times
> When he'll again purloin our nickles and dimes ..."

Bert Rabinowitz's game was bridge. He tells of a Monday night game shortly after the merger of the Argonauts with the Concordians. "Once in a while I would be asked to join in a game with the former Argonauts. I rarely did it because I couldn't afford to lose. This particular night, Jake Blumlein, Louis Lurie and George Jessel, who was visiting, asked me to make a fourth. I said I'd love to, but I couldn't afford the stakes. They told me it was all right, they'd carry me. "When the evening was over, I wished I *had* played their stakes, because they played bridge like it was poker. If they could bluff someone out it was fun. It didn't make any difference what the final outcome was, because when it was over, they'd just write a check—two, three, four hundred dollars. They'd play five or ten cents a point and they had a lot of fun."

On Wednesday night, the traditional Club night, Rabinowitz played with the same group. "We were all second class players: Irwin Stern, Al Lobree, Frank Goldsmith, and two or three others. There were five or six revolving players, so we always had a quorum. Groups were established either according to friendly affiliations or skill. You would find the same people at this table and that table. If one of them were missing, you'd phone to see if he were ill.

"Harry Hilp played on Wednesday nights in a bridge game with Merv Cowen, Fred Zelinsky, Emil Brisacher, Charles Erhman, Ben Rosenthal, Lawrence Dickson and Dr. Franklin Harris. They accommodated their game to fit the needs of Ben ("Pinky") Rosenthal, who was totally deaf. "The way we bid was that if you bid a club, you would clench your fist; a diamond, you'd point to the third finger of the left hand; a heart, you'd point to your heart; and a spade, you made a motion as if you were digging. To indicate the number you were bidding, you held up the same number of fingers and to double, you took your right hand hand and made thumbs down. We had a lot of fun."

The bridge players in the Ivy League and the Garbage League also had their good times, as Lloyd Liebes, a former Argonaut, can attest: "The Ivy League played in the small room where they played dominoes before the fire. The players included the Ransohoffs, Lloyd Ackerman, Stanley Sinton and Morgan Gunst. I'm the sole survivor of the Ivy League. Now I play with the Garbage League. That's the name Harold Brown gave them because their bridge game smelled," he laughed. "Dave and Lawrence Livingston played in it, too."

The kibitzers would add to the fun. Raymond Anixter remembered Barney, the waiter who was a great kibitzer in the bridge games. "This fellow would waltz around the players, checking out their hands. One night, after sizing up the situation, he studied Lou Brounstein's hand and said, 'You just can't make it, Lou!'"

Sanford Treguboff also enjoyed kibitzing. "I used to do it rather often. I was there every Saturday. Six or seven of us met there for lunch: Walter Haas, Lloyd

167

Ackerman, Sidney Liebes, Adolph Meyer, and a couple of others. I kibitzed a very good bridge game!"

"In those early years — in the Thirties and Forties — we also played on Saturday afternoons and on Sundays," said Rabinowitz. "On Sundays the Club served a wonderful brunch and there would be a dozen or so older men who would play nonstop, while the younger ones would go in and out."

The present Saturday bridge players include Jack Lipman, Dave Falk, Jack Davis, Herb Leland, Stubby Goldsmith and Ernest Benesch.

But Wednesday night, Club night, is the time the loudest card-shuffling is heard. Renny Colvin described the scene: "People enjoy dinner and then the card games begin. It's rather sedate, an atmosphere of informality. People who are members of a group that has a game eat together and then play."

Dick Goldman is a member of such a group, who has been playing together for thirty years. According to Goldman: "We started to play poker together when we were kids: Ernie Rogers, Bill Peiser, Harold Baer, Bill Green, Alvin Hayman, and a few others. We play once a month. It's always the same nucleus. We've never had a serious argument. No one ever stormed out of the room. It's a very friendly game. For example, one night recently we had to make a judgment about a mistake one fellow made, whether to treat it critically or perhaps make some concessions. We worked it out and everybody was happy. It's the camaraderie that's important."

Not everyone plays cards; there are also the devotees of dominoes such as Neville Rich, Jr., Dan Stone, Jr., Edgar Gould, Don Magnin, John Golden, Al Miller, Ben Gollober, Vernon Kaufman and Harold Baer. In addition there is Walter Newman who, with his sons, invariably turns up in the winner's circle, whether inside the Club or out. In 1979 Walter and his son John won the Club's doubles tournament, and they also represented the Club in the finals of the Hunter's Point Boys' Club World Domino Tournament.

Among the Club's past domino greats was Harold Linfield, who would arrive each day to challenge the Club's best players. When he passed away in 1977, Harold's friends paid a fitting tribute to him by establishing a Harold G. Linfield Memorial Trophy in the World Domino Tournament.

Herb Leland is another Wednesday night regular who plays in a bridge group. He dines and then plays a rubber or two with Clubmen Ed Rothschild, Ted Israel, Sid DeGoff, Phil Kirschner, and Irwin Stern. Leland's late partner and brother-in-law, Henry Robinson, has erroneously attained immortality as a card player. A wall of the third floor bar, until the fire, was decorated with an oil painting depicting four men engaged in a game of cards. A gold plaque affixed to the painting indicates that it was donated in memory of Henry Robinson, leading one to suspect that perhaps it was given as a tribute to Robinson's prowess at the gaming tables.

"No, that's not so," laughs Leland. "Henry was a very casual player. Once in a while he would play a game of gin, but he was never a Wednesday night regular. No, the reason for the picture is that Henry had been Club Counsel for many, many years. He was a well-loved man. He could have been president, but he refused the nomination. When he died, the members took up a collection for something in his memory. The committee decided they wanted a memento everyone would see when they congregated in the bar. They went in search of a painting and thought the one depicting the card players was appropriate for the bar. People would look at it and say, 'Henry? I didn't know Henry was a cardplayer . . . .' "

## CHAPTER TWENTY-TWO

# THE FINEST FOOD IN TOWN

HE ONE ACTIVITY most Club members would accord even higher rank than card playing is eating. Food at Concordia-Argonaut has always been considered a fine art, and members take a great deal of pride in the Club's reputation for its excellent cuisine.

A newspaper description of the New Year's Eve dinner which ushered in 1896 is an early example of the kind of dining for which the Club has always been noted. *The Morning Call*, describing the repast as a "dainty supper," printed the following menu:

First there was "California oyster cocktail, consommé, frogs à la Poulette, squab on toast with fresh mushroom sauce." This was followed by "shrimp salad, paté de foie gras with gelée, ham and tongue with gelée, pickles and olives." Then came "roast duck and roast turkey." And last there was dessert: "Plombière ice cream, assorted cakes, candies, salted almonds, pistache cream cake, camelia cream cake, mocha cream cake, fruit and café."

After this "dainty supper," the newspaper account continued, "the ladies took over, the new year being a leap year, and the merry dance was . . . to be kept up until daylight."

Mention of the Concordia-Argonaut dining room in modern times conjures up that feature for which it is most renowned, the buffet table. A beautiful display of more than thirty foods, the buffet, both before the fire and during the interim at Concordia East was and will continue to be meticulously arranged not only to please the palate but the eye, according to Club Manager and former Maitre d', Douwe Drayer. Soft lights and pale shadows, and the blending of fresh flowers arranged by Club Secretary, Carolyn Tokusato, create an intoxicating effect. Beginning at one end of the long, oval table, diners often first choose a bowl of piping hot soup prepared by Chef Niels Ploug, who serves a stunning variety of soups. There is his lobster bisque, or on Friday, Boston or Manhattan clam chowder. During the rest of the week the soup of the day might be cream of mushroom or asparagus or a fragrant French onion. To circle the table is to be dazzled by an array of smoked salmon, several varieties of herring, shrimp, crab and gefilte fish. There are platters of roast turkey, roast beef, ham, tongue and sliced cheeses. Next to a huge bowl of lettuce are all the ingredients to make a tempting salad. Beside a mound of cottage cheese the eye rests on an assortment of fresh and stewed fruits. Then there are molded salads, cold artichokes, and other fresh seasonal vegetables. At the far end of the table from the soup are a selection of cheese and chocolate cakes, mocha tortes and eclairs, Napoleans and fancy fruit tarts. There are puddings, custard and, for those whose will power remains strong, bowls of strawberries, fresh raspberries in season and grapefruit.

In a quiet plea to members in an edition of *The Concordian*, shortly before the fire, Chef Niels Ploug asked their help in maintaining "this warm, appealing scene by: 1) When with your children, either please accompany them to the buffet table or caution them to handle foods carefully so that the food arrangements remain clean and neat. 2) Smokers, please don't smoke while going to the buffet table. The smoke affects the food taste (smoke gets absorbed) and occasionally one may drop ashes in and around the buffet dishes. That is very unappetizing."

"Despite the escalating price of food, the Buffet has remained the same," said Douwe Drayer. "The last time we changed anything was five years ago when we had to cut out prawns. The price was just out of sight. We'd like to cut out smoked salmon for the same reason, but it would create a civil war! We also have lobster tails, but we only put them on the buffet Wednesday nights."

The buffet, with its thirty items and its arrangement of tantalizing desserts, is a constant feature at luncheon and at the dinners served by the Club. During lunch, diners may choose to have the buffet alone, or as a first course before the hot entree. At dinner, it is always the first course.

"We started the Buffet right after World War II to attract members here for lunch. Most of them worked down on Montgomery Street. If they didn't get something different here than down there, it was useless for them to come way up here for lunch," said Steve Blumenthal, creator of the Buffet.

Among those coaxed from downtown by the Buffet were the Liebes brothers, Sydney and Lloyd, and David Livingston. "I remember the first time Mr. Livingston came to lunch," said Steve. "I walked up to him and said, 'It's nice to have you here.' And he said, 'Well, Chef, don't think I came up here for your food. I just came to have a game with the Liebes brothers.' 'I'm surprised at you,' I said. 'Your industry and mine are those that made civilization. Without them we could be like the Eskimos and the Hottentots in Africa. They don't need cuisine and they don't need style either.' 'By golly,' he said, 'I never thought of that!' "

Lloyd has a singular complaint about the Buffet: "If you can read braille, you can read your way around the table. Everything is in the same place all the time!"

"That's because people in this Club are so accustomed to certain things that they don't even like you to move the lox from this side of the table to that," said Frank Passantino, past Vice-Chairman of the Food and Beverage Committee. "When we made changes, they were very subtle changes. We'd add a dish or subtract one and people by and large would go with it."

Other members who frequent the Club's buffet table, especially on the third Thursday of every month are Stanford Class of '24, Concordia-Argonaut branch, who meet regularly, including at their big, round table are Bob Goldman, Richard Gross, Bert Bley, William and Edward Bransten, Walter Levison, Charles Fleischman, Bert Levit, Herb Sommer and Jerry Newbauer. In former years the group also embraced the late Judge Mathew Tobriner, Paul Wolf, Richard Coblentz, Bob Mann, Charles Rosenbaum, Edgar Kahn and Richard Sloss.

•　　•　　•

The Gourmet Dinners, now a Club tradition, have become thoroughly identified with Jack Lipman, who has been responsible for them since 1968. Jack, the Club's resident gourmet food and wine expert, a real estate developer and former Stanford track and field star, travels each summer with his wife Ruth to Europe. There, they make the rounds of all the fine restaurants and vineyards.

"There are twenty-one restaurants in France that have three stars," says Lipman. "When we started, there were only twelve." The walls in the Lipman home leading to Jack's distinguished wine cellar are covered with menus from those restaurants.

"When we travel, we keep Concordia Gourmet Dinners in mind. When we are in a restaurant and see something that's different, we ask to talk to the chef or the owner, such as Claude Tourel, owner of Tours d'Argent, who we originally met through Lloyd Liebes. We've been there twelve times. Ruth and I decided it would be nice for our first Gourmet dinner to have a menu with all his recipes.

"We sat in his kitchen for over an hour going over the details with him. He was great, even on the little things. We had peppered duck, and he sent me to a special place in Paris to get these peppercorns. He wrote a long letter to Tony Pels, who was Club manager at the time, telling him how to do these different dishes. Impulsively, I said, 'Look, it would be wonderful if you could possibly be at the dinner.' He said, 'I would love it, but that is the time of the year I hunt, and

I hope to be hunting then. But if anything happens, I'll come.' When I saw Lloyd I told him we better hope nothing happens, because if he does come he'll expect us to pay his way!"

While Tourel missed the dinner, his dishes, executed by Chef Joseph, Theodore's successor, and beginning with La Terrine de Canard au Porto, ending with L'Orange en Surprise, lost nothing in the translation!

In recent years, it has been the custom to honor past presidents at Gourmet dinners. In 1973 Donald Magnin was the guest of honor one night when the menu began with "Caviar sur Glace," was followed by "Noisette d'Agneau," the entrée, and ended with "Surprise au Chocolat."

The 1975 dinner at which Jack was honored as a past president featured his own favorites: "Saumon fumé du Pacifique," "Fonds d'artichauts Nantua," "Poularde a l'Estragon à la mode de Chez La Mere Charles," and for dessert, "Crêpes Boneur."

The dinner honoring Larry Nestel in 1977 was prepared by Chef Niels. The menu was brilliant: "Crab Bruxelloise, Paté de Canard a l'Orange, Quenelles de Sole, Le Filet de Richelieu, Boeuf à la Wellington, and Les Crêpes au Chocolat." The champagne was a Piper Heidsieck and the wines included a '73 Meursault and three excellent Bordeaux vintages.

French "nouvelle cuisine" has crept into the Club's gourmet menus. "This means new ideas, explained Ruth Lipman, "and the food tends to be less fattening, too, because it is less rich. For instance in cuisine minceur, they've taken cottage cheese and added yogurt to it instead of using rich cream and butter."

"The menu for the 'nouvelle cuisine' dinner was dishes that I have prepared myself . . . dishes that were successful with my friends," said Jack. "I told Chef Niels, 'This is the dinner we are going to do.' I told him exactly how I did it, but I didn't dare say, 'This is how *you* are to do it. So what I got out of it was that he cooked things his way, and believe me, it was fine!"

Many of the recipes Jack and Ruth have brought back for the Gourmet Dinners now are regular features of the Club menu. Like the Crêpes Bonheur (crepes with sugar and honey), and Artichauts Moscovitz, which are hearts of artichokes, with sour cream and caviar.

The Gourmet Dinner is held in the fall. After that long anticipated evening, Jack and Ruth get busy planning the Wine Festival held each spring since 1969, the offspring of the wine appreciation courses offered by the Club.

"What happened was that after four years of wine appreciation courses the Club had become wine-oriented. When I was elected to the Board in '69, and they made me Co-chairman of the Entertainment Committee (along with Norman Grabstein, Neville Rich, Jr. and William Lowenberg) I said, 'We are going to have to have a wine-tasting.' To be very honest, what I did was work out something like Steve Simon did for Simon Brothers at the Fairmont and other places. They would invite their customers to sample their new wines, serve some cheese, some of their famous nuts, and that was about it. I decided to do what they did, but since Club members are going to pay for this, I thought, they will want something special. We'll have a wine-tasting, with gourmet foods. That was the theory of it. It was a wine-tasting, but a real Concordia event — which means a lot of 'fussing.' "

The Concordia event is held annually in the large dining room, which for the evening, is decorated to evoke the feeling of a wine garden. Trellises heavy with grapes, checkered tablecloths and strolling musicians lend authenticity to the scene. There are five tables, each numbered, of fine wine. Opposite them are tables of food which are paired with the wines. "There are reserved tables for everybody, but the food service is all buffet. So you take a little of what you want and come back to your table and sit down. You do a lot of walking around, and you do a lot of drinking — as much wine as you want," said Jack. "The important thing about it is that there is just a mass of food, and the thing that I insist upon is that the waiters never let those trays get depleted."

The predominant wines at first were French, although the selection was augmented by several California vintages. By 1978 Jack completely switched to California wines. "I figured the French ones were just too high," he said. "We chose four varietal grapes which are most popular with local wine experts. All the wines we selected represented those in our Club cellar so that people, once they were familiar with them, could ask for them again when they dined at the Club. We had three tables of white wines and two of reds."

At the 1980 wine-tasting, Jack was back with both California and French wines. Again, they were all selected from the Club cellars. He noted on the menu that "For your very special occasions, the Club cellars maintain a limited amount, but an excellent selection, of most of the great wines of France. These wines are expensive, but more reasonable than current restaurant prices indicate."

"The members felt it just wasn't a real wine-tasting without the French wines. They weren't that concerned about keeping the price of the event down," he said.

Bert Tonkin, who served as entertainment chairman when Jack began his Gourmet Dinners and wine-tastings, said, "It was Jack's great personal interest in these things that has made epicureans out of us." Jack, who is modest about accepting praise, says, "These evenings are a tribute to Chef Niels Ploug, Manager Douwe Drayer and their staffs."

The Chef and the Manager have earned accolades for another food festival that has become an Entertainment Committee favorite in recent years, the International Night Dinners. Again, the initiative for the event came from members who evinced a strong personal desire to turn an idea into a reality. Stanley Diamond is one such Concordian, the man responsible for the Argentine Night held in May 1975. Diamond's wife Maria is a native of Buenos Aires. Her family and Diamond's, distant relatives of one another, own wine vineyards there. Together, the Diamonds planned and carried through one of the most successful International Night affairs the Club has sponsored. Even the ambience seemed South American. The moment a doorman in gaucho uniform ushered the guests into the Club, they were transported south.

During the cocktail hour, strolling troubadors sustained the Latin mood with background music. Guests sampled hors d'oeuvres, drank Argentine liquors, and viewed a display of the country's art and artifacts lining the walls of the lounge. Before long, the guests moved upstairs to the dining room which was set with perfectly matched appointments in blue and white, Argentina's colors. After Maria Diamond welcomed the guests in Spanish, Vernon Kaufman, chairman of the evening, introduced Ricardo Elizondo, Argentine Consul General.

The dinner began. Guests feasted on splendid Argentine dishes adroitly prepared by Chef Niels under the instruction of Maria and Renata Piompi, a well-known Argentine business man and the Diamonds' friend. Dinner included "Carbonada," squash stuffed with lamb, sweet potatoes and other vegetables. There was entertainment provided by a South American Folklorika Group, and then guests performed the tango, rhumba and samba to the beat of an Argentine orchestra. When the night ended, the guests brought away momentos of the delightful evening—albums by the Folklorika Group for the men and Spanish perfume for the women.

Sam Camhi wanted to give Club members a taste of "the elegance of Spain." Being extremely proud of his Sephardic heritage, he arranged a "Sephardic Festival" held November 5, 1977. There were Latino musicians, singers and dancers and the sweet, succulent food traditional of Mediterranean Jews. Sam, whose wife is not Sephardic, searched far and wide to come up with recipes for dishes he remembered fondly from his mother's kitchen. He located them in a cookbook published by the Sisterhood of a Sephardic congregation in Seattle; they were faithfully reproduced by Chef Niels.

Frank Passantino had a less difficult time planning for a "Night in Old Vienna" in May 1978. His Viennese wife arranged the menu, from the 'Liptauer Kase," to the "Huhner Ragout Suppe" and "Grune Bohnen Paprika" to the dessert which consisted of three kinds of tortes plus "Apfel Strudel." The several courses were capped by "Kaffee mit Schlag." Following dinner there was entertainment patterned after the salons of Emperor Franz Joseph. The strings of the violinists filled the air with the music of "Old Vienna" and "The Whisperings of the Vienna Woods." There were sweet-voiced sopranos and throaty tenors to sing the music of Johann Strauss and Franz Lehár with selections from "Die Fledermaus" and "The Merry Widow." And there was slivovice to toast the performers and the guests of honor, Consul General and Mrs. Francis Seidler; the former Consul General Karl Webber; and North American Manager of the Austrian Airlines Hans Schneider.

•       •       •

Gourmet Dinners and theme dinners are not exclusively reserved for Entertainment Committee events. Members may hold private "Silver Plate" dinners, so called because silver plates are used as table liners at these plush affairs, which began after Tony Pels became Club Manager. Before the fire, they were usually held in a private room on Tuesday and Thursday evenings (minimum number of guests is fifteen), or in the dining room on Friday, Saturday or Monday nights when the Club dining room was closed (minimum number of guests is sixty-five). There is a set price for the Gourmet or theme dinners (French, Italian or Latin cuisine). Included in the dinner is one hour of unlimited cocktails, hot and cold hors d'oeuvres, seafood salad, prime rib steak, roast sirloin or filet mignon, with unlimited house wines, plus dessert and coffee. The price of the dinner is not more than the cost of the food alone at a fine restaurant, so it is no wonder that private parties are heavily booked and are considered by the members "the best thing going in town" for entertaining.

How can the Club afford to give one hour of unlimited cocktails and endless wine at dinner? "That is because Jewish men do not drink very much," says Douwe Drayer. "While members at these Silver Plate dinners have outside guests, they are predominantly Jewish, too, and the drinking is not very heavy."

Tony Pels, from his vantage point as Bohemian Club manager, compared the drinking at both clubs this way: "Biggest drinking night of the year at Concordia is Stag Night. The amount of liquor consumed that night is about what we average every Thursday night at the Bohemian Club."

If ethnic conditioning were not enough to moderate Club members' drinking, Chef Niels recently offered this caveat in *The Concordian:*

"Smoking, what it does to the lungs, heart, arteries, is bad enough," he writes. "What it does to your taste buds is a disaster. Smoking dulls the tongue's taste buds. Food flavors are weakened or lost. Sorry too, about you gin, whiskey, vodka and Scotch drinkers. These also numb the taste buds. I recommend light wines or an aperitif before dining. I want you to really know and feel my kitchen art."

In 1965 when Richard Reinhardt wrote an article for *San Francisco Magazine* surveying the City's men's clubs, he said Concordia-Argonaut had "the best smorgasbord and the least patronized bar in the City." It still hold true.

Perhaps the most elaborate of the Club's feasts is the annual Stag Night buffet, held traditionally each year on Thanksgiving Eve. There is no record of when it first began. "Started 'way before my time," the oldest of the old-timers will tell you.

About half the Club's senior membership — about 300 men — can be counted on to attend. Out-of-town members from as far away as New York, Seattle, and Los Angeles fly in especially for the event. It is an annual reunion; an opportunity to catch up on the year's news; and to renew old friendships dating back to grammar school.

It is also a time for non-stop gaming. Through 1981, this was the way it looked: Before the ten o'clock buffet, every available space on the second floor was filled with card tables and chairs. In the lounge, the billiard table was transformed into a crap table where the younger members threw dice until the wee hours of Thanksgiving Day.

But at ten p.m., when the bell rang to signal the opening of the buffet, all the action stopped. While the members were busy playing bridge, poker, pedro, pinochle, dominoes and other games of chance, the kitchen staff, under the guidance of Chef Niels, had been preparing food on huge, silver trays to grace the U-shaped table set up in the Sylvan Room.

They prepared a feast fit for kings: the kings of industry, commerce, finance, medicine and law; men whose families go back to San Francisco's birth. For them, and for the others who have been accepted as members in one of the City's leading social clubs, the kitchen staff yearly unveiled these regal dishes: a large, glazed and beautifully decorated whole turkey, in the center of an enormous tray of sliced breast of turkey; ham, garnished with glazed white flowers of aspic with leek stems, surrounded by thick, pink slices of succulent meat; a beef tongue ornamenting a tray of sliced tongue; two large ice trays of bluepoint oysters and cherrystone clams; attractively garnished platters of fresh cracked crab, lobster, and prawns; patés of duck, ham and veal; stuffed pheasant, and platters of cold duck; beautiful shrimp, fruit and vegetable molds. But there were two hot dishes that also have become a Stag Night tradition because, said Niels, somewhat ruefully, "the boys love them:" enchiladas and hot dogs.

Opposite the clams and oysters, at the other end of the U-shaped table, there was a bucket filled with cold beer and wine. At the round end of the table, an ice sculpture carved by an artist ornamented the setting.

For lack of space the pastry chef set his table of sweets in the main dining room. There were cheese, Chantilly and Black Forest cakes, plus assorted French pastries, fruits and a dozen varieties of imported cheese.

President Marvin Nathan and Manager Douwe Drayer, surveying the scene of Stag Night 1981, were duly proud. The manager was thinking of the words his predecessor, Tony Pels, used to describe the Club. "The Concordia is a little jewel." Tonight, thought Drayer, the little jewel is really sparkling.

What the two men could not know was that Stag Night 1981 was the last Stag Night when the jewel would sparkle in the same setting.

## CHAPTER TWENTY-THREE

# THE GREATEST SHOWS

N MARCH 7, 1947 LOUIS NEWMAN, son of one of the Concordia Club's original founders, wrote a letter to the Board of Directors, congratulating them on "the splendid entertainment the Club gave Thursday night." Newman's letter concluded with the comment, "It proves that a good clean performance is more successful than the smutty ones put on in past years."

When Mr. Newman spoke of "smut," he was probably referring to the shows of the Twenties and Thirties, including such plays as "He Got What He Wanted," written by Adrien Falk and produced by Milton Marks, which was staged on February 25, 1931. A satire of "Outward Bound," the production's program notes that "Big Harry Levy wanted a Club theatrical .... For plagiarism, violation of copyright, indecencies and chutzpah the author and producer offer humble apologies. There is no other redress."

Big Harry Levy and the rest of the audience got more than they bargained for. They roared with glee over Max Fredrick playing a rabbi and Paul Bissinger as a minister. Milton Marks portrayed a writer and Adrien Falk personified "Henry Lehachlis Levy."

Preceding the era of "smutty" plays was a period of pretentious "musical comedies," like "The Royal Bluff" and "A Musical Comedy in Two Acts, Written by Anybody with Music by Everybody." According to the program notes, "The Royal Bluff" was a "Two-Act Musical Nonsensity, written to amuse, not to educate. It will be acted, sung and danced with gusto by all to welcome the year 1899." The show's cast included Sam Jacobi, as King Bluff the XLII; Henry Ahpel as the Major Domo; Leo Davis, as Maximilian, Duke of Thrace; Max Koshland, a shoemaker; Milton Bremer, his son; Hilda Rosener, the Princess; Mollie Simon, her maid; and Florence Levy and Hattie Simon playing Tutti and Frutti, Ladies of the Court.

Despite the success of early shows, the greatest era of theatrical entertainment in the Club's history was that of the Sloss-Glikbarg-Bissinger years, which began in 1941 and continued through 1966. These "good, clean performances" were much more than that. They were hilariously funny without being offensive — original musical comedies without a shred of pretension. While they were certainly written to amuse, their story lines, so cleverly aimed at contemporary issues, also educated.

The shows, which were quite expensive productions, never showed a profit despite sold-out houses each night of their three- or four-night runs. Losses often ran as high as $10,000. But the productions attracted large numbers of participants, which is one of the reasons the Club happily absorbed the losses. "I bet I made one hundred new friends as a result of those shows," said Walter Newman, a veteran of Concordia footlights.

Each production featured lavishly designed stage sets sometimes with special wings built to extend the existing stage on either side and a full orchestra led by Jack Seltenrich. A professional make-up artist, sound man and lighting technician were hired, and costumes were rented from Goldstein & Company.

"It was great fun to be in those shows," recalls Arthur Simon, whose specialty dance numbers were show-stoppers in four of the productions. "The spirit of the cast was wonderful. It was an exercise in tolerance. Even now when I see people that I've been in plays with, there is a special feeling of camaraderie, like being part of a football team."

"Rehearsals were hard work, but there was also a lot of horseplay," recalls Walter Miller, who appeared in many of the plays. "We rehearsed many, many weeks before the show. After each rehearsal the Club would provide a good buffet with lots of cold cuts and beer."

● ● ●

Like Manny Brandenstein, of an earlier period, all three impresarios would have much preferred to devote their full-time energies to theatrical careers. Sam Glikbarg, educated in law, was president of Pacific Intermountain Express, a large trucking corporation. He wrote the scripts for all nine productions, which spanned two decades.

"One thing about Sam," recalls Miller, "was that he hated to see any of the lines he wrote for a show changed. When one of the players had a suggestion for a change, he would really die hard before he would agree to it. He was also his own best audience. He'd go into hysterics when he heard the players deliver the dialogue he wrote."

Paul Bissinger, whose father had a successful business in meat packing and tanning, headed for Broadway as soon as he graduated from Stanford, after promising his father he would join the family firm if his first theatrical venture was less than a complete success. It was, and the young man — with great reluctance — kept his part of the bargain. But his heart would always remain in the theater. Bissinger was a member of the Special Events Committee which booked the entertainment for the 1939 Exposition on Treasure Island.

"Paul, who directed the shows, was a very patient man, with a nice smile and a terrific knack for getting people to work together," Miller said. "When he pleaded, 'Come on fellas, just one more time,' it always was said gently!"

"Bissinger was a perfectionist," adds Joel Horowitz, also a show veteran. "He spent $6,000 on one play just for props."

Lyricist Richard Sloss was a member of one of the City's most prestigious law firms, the firm once headed by his father, Judge M.C. Sloss. "It was from his mother, Hattie Hecht Sloss, who had her own radio shows — one on the symphony and one on poetry — that Dick inherited his creativity," said Horowitz. "He was a Gilbert & Sullivan buff, and many of his lyrics were written to music from those operettas. Dick could make anything rhyme. At rehearsals, he would play the piano, sing the lyrics and practice with us until we learned them perfectly. But he never performed himself in the shows."

Following "The Little Foxes" (1941), and "Dream Boy" (1947), the trio presented "Mid-Winter Madness," a spoof of psychiatry, in 1948. Several of the Club's medical members, including Drs. Harold Rosenblum, Franklin Harris, William Auslen and Al Cohn ("who pulls teeth") played themselves. The plot which treated the difficulty of distinguishing the crazy from the sane, concludes with these lyrics, sung to the tune of "Inside U.S.A.":

> *Do you ever raise and later draw four cards?*
> *Bid at bridge without a look at the score cards?*
> *Throw away the stuff you needed in gin games?*
> *Let opponents meld four aces and win games?*
> *Do the kibitzers ever say what's wrong with your play?*
> *Does it rattle you when they talk about your poor play?*
> *("Look, here's the sure play!")*
> *Do you teach the game when coming out winner?*
> *Do you, when you lose, act like a beginner?*
> *These, and lots of traits I'm able to mention,*
> *Do not call for psychiatric attention.*
> *Are you proud whenever you cop a point,*

> *Cowed whenever you drop a point?*
> *You're not the pest of the club,*
> *Jest of the club;*
> *You're like the rest of the club.*
> *In every way,*
> > *Since first Concordians*
> > *Met in audience*
> *Gay,*
> > *Most of us have rated*
> > *Rather pixilated —*
> *How far it's gone it's risky to say.*
> *And though it may*
> > *Seem inconvenient,*
> > *Let's be lenient,*
> *Pray;*
> > *For if we started out to cure nuts,*
> > *It could be that I'm nuts and you're nuts,*
> *And so let's call it O.K.,*
> *And stay*
> *This way*
> *Until the judgment day.*

"Getting Nowhere" was staged in 1950. Glikbarg's script was a burlesque of the origins of the Club, replete with inside jokes about the Reckendorfers and the Ichenhauseners and their determination, after leaving Bavaria and arriving in New York, to settle in California. One group went by land (the Argonauts, in a "canasta" wagon); the other, by sea (in a boat named "Concordia"). When the Concordia group is marooned on a South Seas island, Richard Sloss's lyrics, adapted to the music of hit songs from "South Pacific," poke fun at their gambling proclivities in a song called, "There Is Nothing Like A Game." Jovial, rotund Louis Freehof (later director of Sinai Memorial Chapel) was cast as Bloody Mary, cavorting in a muumuu and singing "Me Go Too" to the tune of "Dites-Moi."

When the Argonauts, traveling overland, are stranded at Donner Pass, Glik-barg's dialogue is spiced with good-natured banter about the grammatical errors made by the descendents of the Reckendorfers ("unto the fifth generation"). When the actors bemoan the fact they have nothing to eat but an old bear bone, the retort is, "It was either he or we." That became the introduction to the "Pronoun Song," sung to the music of "Always True to You Darling In My Fashion." Sloss's inspired lyrics began:

*I was made to learn by rule*
*In an unprogressive school*
*They would lick me when my grammar got too free.*
*So I trained my tongue to talk as the teacher taught me*
*And I've never had a teacher tough as her.*

The song ended:

*Now I'm off to lands of gold*
*Where the people, I've been told,*
*Need a man of style to guide their motley crew.*
*Well, I've trained my tongue to talk as the teacher taught me*
*And I know I'll get my name in the next "Whom's Whom."*

In the finale to the show, set at the 1915 dedication of Concordia-Argonaut, Glikbarg wrote this prediction for toastmaster Jack Davis to deliver:

"Well, we finally arrived in San Francisco. By land and by sea we came — but we made it. . . . Our children and grandchildren will thank us for creating this Club on this spot. . . . In the vista of the future I see it: always immaculate, neat and clean, serving small portions of delicate food to gourmets with fastidious appetites — quiet men of culture and distinction sipping apéritifs while calmly engaged in intellectual conversation. Well-groomed, peaceful men sitting in beautifully lighted rooms listening to the strains of fine music, the walls adorned with the finest productions of the old masters. That is our vision of Concordia-Argonaut. I predict it will come to pass."

The dialogue sent not only author Glikbarg into hysterics, but the entire audience as well!

"Valley Forgery," staged in 1951, was a minstrel show that made learning world history a delight. Freehof, dressed as a revolutionary maiden, was cast as Betsy Ross; Albert Cohn played Mr. Interlocutor; and Harold Kroloff was Mr. Bones. Others in the cast included Jack Davis, Julius Irving and Milton Lees, Jr., plus "The Gamest Troupers in the World, the Concordia Choristers." One of the numbers adapted to "Hostess With the Mostess on the Ball," from "Call Me Madam," took the "Mystery Out of History." It went, in part:

*Do you think that hist'ry's highbrow?*
    *Do you dread that kind of book?*
*Pause before you raise that eyebrow —*
    *Better take another look;*
*You've been frightened by some academic snob*
*Making myst'ry out of hist'ry for the mob.*

*Every victim who has shunned it*
  *Has derived his deep disgust*
*From a dreary classroom pundit*
*Of the sort that's dry as dust;*
*It's a shame to see an uninspiring slob*
*Making myst'ry out of hist'ry for the mob.*

"Me and Trygve," performed in 1953, was a farce about public relations and advertising. By that time, the show's producers had a steadfast group of Concordia players who turned out for each casting call. Jack Davis returned to the stage as Mr. Bunker, of the P.R. firm of Bunker, Bunker and Bull; Harold Kroloff played Trygve, his assistant. Other repeat performers included Albert Cohn, Julius Irving (playing himself), Milton Lees, Jr., Louis Freehof (as Congo) and Allen Meier, Jr., previously a Concordia Chorister, who moved up to a speaking role as La Zongo. The most memorable song from "Me and Tryve" was "Trio for Committeemen," which Sloss wrote to the music of "I Got Da Horse Right Here" from "Guys and Dolls." The number included lyrics like the following:

*The bunch of members there*
*Keep getting in our hair,*
*The way they quarterback from their easy chair:*
*They kick — they kick —*
*They say that we make 'em sick —*
*They say that we make 'em sick —*
*They kick — they kick.*
*Now take the dining room —*
*It fills 'em full of gloom,*
*But you should see the portions that they consume.*
*They kick, etc.*
*We can't arrange a thing*
*Without their arguing;*
*In fact, there's just one song they know how to sing.*
*They gripe — they gripe —*
*They think that our job's a pipe —*
*They think that our job's a pipe —*
*They gripe — they gripe.*
*There's not a thing we touch*
*That doesn't cost too much,*
*But if we cut the service, we're still in Dutch.*
*They gripe, etc.*

"Three To Get Ready" was staged in 1957. Each participant had his favorite show; Joel Horowitz thought the '57 production was the most outstanding.

"It had everything: a great script based on the Pygmalian legend — three shoe-shine boys (I played one of them) who were groomed to pass as Concordia members; fantastic lyrics from the music of "My Fair Lady;" terrific stage sets representing familiar San Francisco locales; and great costuming — everything from gym suits to white tie and tails. The best of everything was in that show."

The cast included Dan Stone, playing Abe Shragge; Dan Stone, Jr. playing his father; Meyer Heller (then assistant rabbi at Temple Emanu-El) portraying John Blumlein; Bert Green as Fred Zelinsky; Jack Voorsanger as Julius Irving; and Walter Miller as B. Charles Choy. "They thought a six-foot-four Chinese fellow named B. Charles, for B. Charles Ehrman, was pretty funny," said Miller. Other players included Herbert Ross, Richard Dinner, Don Auslen, Robert Heller, Joe Leon, John Meyer, Larry Sanford, Allen Meier, Stuart Erlanger, Dick Alberton, Herbert Jackson, Neville Rich, Jr., Howie Miller, Arthur Simon and Charles Weinshank, III.

"After the last performance," reminisced Joel, "we all went back to Jack Voorsanger's house and we sang the songs from that show into the wee hours of the morning. We hated to see it end. As a matter of fact, there was some talk about Louis Lurie booking us for a run at the Curran. But it fell through. None of us had that kind of time. We had to get back to making a living."

"The Four Founding Fathers" was produced as an early celebration of the Club's centenary. The "Four," dressed in flowing white togas, were played by Dan Stone, Jr., Jack Voorsanger, Bradford Liebman and Joel Horowitz. The opening number, adapted to the music of "You Can't Get a Man With a Gun," from "Annie Get Your Gun," extolled the Club's founders with these lyrics:

> *The Four Founding Fathers are legendary figures*
> *Who Belong in the Hall of Fame;*
> *We never can forget them*
> *Because we never met them*
> *They're unknown by face and name . . .*
> *The Four Founding Fathers — the Club that they established*
> *Was a man's world without a dame;*
> *Can we match, as descendants*
> *Their rugged independence?*
> *They're unknown by face and name . . . ."*

The play, a fantasy about establishing a second Concordia-Argonaut Club on the Moon (it was the year of the first Moon landing), featured Moonmen in phosphorescent costumes singing "Leave the Moon Alone, Folks" to the tune of "Pistol Packin' Mama." The script was replete with inside jokes and humorous references to Clubmembers.

When insurance broker Paul Newman sought to insure the new club, the "Mooncordia," the chorus gave a lively rendition of the "Insurance Number" to the music of "I Whistle a Happy Tune" from "The King and I." The song managed to incorporate the names of every one of the Club's insurance brokers. When Louis Freehof, flying to the Moon with trappings for the new club, was halted at the ticket counter for being overweight, he sang a number to the tune of "My Favorite Things" from the "Sound of Music," decrying the temptations on the Club's menu:

> *Filets of sandab and salmon and sturgeon*
> *Crab from Alaska and lobster that's virgin*
> *These are left out of my authorized list*
> *Still, I succumb when I ought to resist ...*
> *Brother, when you*
> *Read that menu*
> *Can you turn from sin?*
> *Concordia's the spot*
> *Where control I ain't got*
> *And that's why I'm not*
> *Too thin ....*

Another highlight of the show, which followed the "Moonstruck" number, was Arthur Simon's specialty dance. Simon, who was born deaf, was endowed with extraordinary grace. His friend Jeanndre Taylor Herst, who has a ballet school in Berkeley, helped him prepare a "moondance."

"Arthur brought me a tape of the show's music and we worked on some movements. He has the kind of grace one is born with, like Fred Astaire. He was also very selective about my ideas and suggestions. Once we settled on a pattern, he just zapped along with it. He loves the theater, loves to perform and he communicates that joyfulness to the audience. He is able to 'feel' the music from the vibrations under his feet and it flows right through his body.

"When Arthur came to me with the idea of dancing in the first show in 1951, 'Valley Forgery,' I knew it could be done. I remembered when I was a child, I knew another deaf man who had the same gift as Arthur. He was the costumer with the San Francisco Opera Ballet and I saw him dance along to the music. So I was delighted to help Arthur. We worked out specialty numbers to tie in with four of the shows and he was a sensation in every one."

Dan Stone, Jr. kept a detailed scrapbook on "The Four Founding Fathers." From the memos he preserved, he recalls that rehearsals for the show, which was performed March 16 – 19, 1963, began in late November. On January 7, the fitter arrived at the Club to take measurements for costumes. After the first of the year, rehearsals were rescheduled from 7:30 to 7 p.m. "sharp." In addition to the Monday night rehearsals, there were also daytime "spot" rehearsals during the lunch hour.

A memo from Paul Bissinger, dated January 30, stated: "We have exactly six rehearsals left before dress rehearsal. I am sure you all realize the amount of work to be done to have a smooth show. Please learn all the songs and business and those with speaking parts learn their lines by February 4."

Dress Rehearsal night finally arrived, and the cast got these instructions: "Start promptly at 8 p.m. Be ready in costumes as we do not want to run into overtime for musicians, electricians and sound men. Performance Nights: Dinner for cast at 6 p.m. promptly. Report for makeup backstage by 7 p.m. Please be prompt as there are thirty-one to be made up.

"We have a serious problem backstage. Immediately after your numbers, please get off stage as fast as possible . . . stage hands have a real problem . . . I feel confident you will have a great show. *Wait* for your *laughs . . . hold* it for the *applause*. Thanks again from Sam, Dick and myself. Paul."

Stone's scrapbook reveals a tradition faithfully observed at the conclusion of each show. The "Big Three" would give their thanks to the cast in song — usually a reprise of the last number of the show — and the cast, in turn, secretly would have prepared their own lyrics to thank Bissinger, Sloss and Glikbarg. There was an extra stanza by the cast that year, honoring Neville Rich, Jr., whose thirty-fifth birthday coincided with one of the performances.

•     •     •

Three years later, in 1966, the Club mounted another production, called "A Real Good Scout." The plot involved a baseball scout (the Giants — and Willie Mays — were still new in town), the FBI and intrigue and tomfoolery set in exotic locations.

Two features distinguished the production. First, the cast included a professional soloist Tommy Harris. A Club member, Harris had once been an NBC radio singer and one of the City's top performers before illness forced him to retire from the stage to become a restauranteur. Second, a new name was added to the production staff: that of Theodore Seton, a stockbroker and relatively new member of the Club who had joined after moving from New England three years earlier. Seton was credited with "a major assist" to Richard Sloss in the writing of the show's lyrics.

"My first meeting with the triumvirate was like having an audience with the Pope," recalled Ted. "Afterwards I remember Dick Sloss telling me that, as a result of my participation in the show, 'You will be accepted among Concordia members in a way you could never have hoped to be.' And you know, he was right!"

The cast, who were costumed variously as blue-suited G-Men, the Giants baseball team, Hawaiian maidens in muumuus and straw hats, included Jerrold Ladar as the Scout; Tommy Harris as Golden Voice; Joel Horowitz, John Leipsic, Edwin Berkowitz and Kenneth Birnbaum as Mexicans; Walter Newman, Bradford Liebman and Dan Stone, Jr. as G-Men; and Lou Freehof as "the man on the mountain." Others in the cast were Jack Feder, Jr., Robert Bransten, Dr. Alan Abrams, Paul Bissinger, Jr., David Bloch, Dr. Les Fink, Jacques Adler, Leon Blum, Stanley Diamond, N.J. Friedman, Pierre Gamburg, Morris Green, Robert Heller, Donald Kahn, Dr. Joseph Kushner, Melvin Lichtman, Dr. Stanley Reich, Claude Rosenberg, Jr., Herbert Ross, Laurence Sanford, Lloyd Sankowich, Ted Seton, Dr. Albert Steiner, and J.H. Voorsanger.

Two years later, in 1968, when the Haight-Ashbury hippie movement was in full flower, that phenomenon became the subject of "How to Succeed at Concordia Without Really Trying." The script, based on a hippie's successful bid to gain membership in Concordia-Argonaut, was written by Claude Rosenberg, Jr., directed by Theodore Seton, with lyrics by Richard Sloss, Claude Rosenberg, Jr. and Theodore Seton, and produced by Lew Tilin. For the most part the lyrics were set to Beatles' music.

Due to Paul Bissinger's illness, the era of the "Big Three" was over, but because of the legacy they left behind, their students were able to carry on.

"Actually," said Seton, "I thought I was just going to *help* Paul direct, but when he became ill, I had the whole thing to do myself. First thing I did was to go to the Mechanics' Library and check out six books on play directing for the theater." Seton's dedication led him to utilize the cardboard inserts from his laundered shirts to block out stage directions.

In a real about-face, Walter Newman was cast as a hippie, along with other Haight-Ashbury "residents" Morris Green, Arthur Simon, Jacques Adler, Martin Aufhauser, John Leipsic and Arthur Schwartz. Bradford Liebman portrayed the hippie who succeeded in making it into the Concordia, courtesy of his uncle, Harry Hasgelt, played by Matthew Weinberg. Others in the cast were Dave

Sachs, who played himself, John Ritchie, Tommy Harris, Claude Rosenberg, Jr., Louis Freehof, Joel Horowitz, Stanley Diamond, Kenneth Birnbaum, Allan Sommer, Maurice Knox, Jr., Donald Kahn, Robert Heller, Lee Blum, Stan Lipschultz and Charles Breyer.

Rosenberg's book had the usual inside jokes, the lyrics were bright and catchy, and the new Club manager, Tony Pels, was most cooperative. However, the music was a problem for the director. "Jack Seltenrich was not with it," said Seton. "He just couldn't get the hang of the Beatles' music. But we had to have him because it was a Club tradition."

"How To Succeed" was the last show to be produced by Concordia-Argonaut.

"We didn't mean it to be that way. Five years later, in 1973, we decided to have another show," said Seton. "The Club members loved the idea. It was a great arena for participation, for displaying talent and for having fun.

"Because I didn't have the time to direct — nobody had the kind of time the 'Big Three' could devote to it — we brought in an outside director, Paul Blake, an assistant director for A.C.T. He put a script together — not a great one, but one we could work with — and we put out a casting call. We even invited the wives and daughters of members to participate. It was the first time that was done.

"The first evening we got two dozen people — out of our entire membership. The second time, only twenty-two people showed up, and the third time, we had fifteen. Well, it just wasn't the Concordia approach. The shows should generate a lot of Club participation. We decided we couldn't do it, and the idea fizzled out like a very soggy firecracker . . . ."

Seton doesn't think the poor response necessarily means "it's curtains" for Club theatricals. "The shows were immense fun," he said. "A team effort. It's an exciting moment when the horseplay subsides and you realize you have a responsibility to the ticket-holders to provide a polished performance . . . The moment when you go from a group of well-intentioned people, having fun, into a cast who can produce . . . ."

The "Big Three" have all departed, but from the legion of troupers they left behind, surely there will be those in the future who will be willing to heed Bissinger's call for "just one more time."

## CHAPTER TWENTY-FOUR

# THE FINEST PROFESSIONAL STAFF

E ARE "BLESSED with the finest professional staff that can be found anywhere," declare Concordia Club presidents in their Annual Reports year after year. That the Club not only has attracted top-notch professionals but has been able to keep them over remarkably long periods of time is a great source of pride among members.

Steve Blumenthal, a Gentile despite his Jewish-sounding name, cooked for Concordians for thirty-eight years. Born in Switzerland, where he trained as an apprentice cook, Steve's first job was at the Palace Hotel in St. Moritz, Europe's finest hotel. After coming to the U.S. as a young man, he worked at the Plaza Hotel in New York, the Brown Palace in Denver and the St. Francis Hotel in San Francisco before accepting the job as sous-chef at the Concordia. He was promoted to chef before long.

"I could have had quite a few jobs at much more money, especially during the war," he admitted, "But I had no desire to quit. It was like cooking for a family. While we had to watch our costs, costs were not number one. For instance, when Mr. Shragge was president he said to me one day, 'Steve, why don't you make a bouillabaisse again one of these days? I have a friend who thinks you make the best bouillabaisse.' I told Mr. Shragge, 'I'd gladly make it, but we don't sell more than three or four.' And he said, 'Steve, if you can make three or four people happy here that's all we want.' So you see, I never would have fit in at one of the hotels with all their efficiency.

"When my little boy was stricken with polio, the Club members insisted I bring him in on a regular basis to exercise in the pool. He had to undergo seven operations. For me it was a big expense. Through Judge Wollenberg, we got the boy into Shriners Hospital for one of the operations at no cost."

Steve loved the personal contacts with the members, another reason he never left the Club. "I knew them all so well. Like Mr. Kauffman from the H. S. Crocker Paper Company. He would always come in, saying hello to no one, not even to the men at the table where he sat down. Then he went away for a couple of weeks and when he returned, I said, 'Welcome home, Mr. Kauffman.' 'How in hell did you know I was away?' he grumbled. 'Because, Mr. Kauffman, without you it was like a morgue here,' I told him. He broke into a big grin and we became good friends."

Steve loved walking around the tables at lunch time taking the members' good-natured jibes about his "rotten" dishes. At the annual Stag Nights he fixed his "boys" take-home packages of turkey. "Everyone would say, 'Steve, don't forget me tonight!'

"I could never work at a big hotel where you are only a machine. I have a friend who was a chef at the St. Francis for twenty-five years and he never saw a soul. Who could work like that?"

Among Steve's souvenirs are letters and a clipping he received in 1954 on this thirtieth anniversary with the Club.

One, signed by Marcel Hirsch, read:

> You and I started going after each other thirty years ago.
>
> We both must be pretty strong, because we are both on our feet and we are still going after each other.
>
> I should therefore like to observe your thirtieth Anniversary on the basis of one buck per year, because it has been worth at least that to have the privilege of fighting a champion.
>
> Seriously, Mrs. Hirsch and I send our congratulations and our affection.

Dan Stone commemorated the occasion by writing:

> "You lousy drunken bum, you have been annoying me and all other good members of Concordia for thirty years trying to poison us with your rotten cooking. So congratulations, you old s.o.b., and may we have to put up with you and your awful disposition another thirty years!"

Ben Baum, with whom Steve and his family still maintain a close friendship, expressed his sentiments as follows:

> "An uncle of my third cousin on my wife's side was at the Club about three weeks ago and claims that while at lunch, he was served something that was fit only for pigs to eat. Being an intimate friend of yours, I thought it only wise on my part to advise you of the many complaints that I have been hearing about the vile food you have been serving to the many good members of our Club. I likewise wish to advise that after having had to put up with you for thirty years, that your miserable disposition, if anything, is becoming more so, and that unless

this notice will straighten you out, I doubt that either Mrs. Baum or myself will permit you the privilege of working and cooking our next buffet. I hope that you will be around thirty years from now, and that your disposition is no worse than it is today.

With best regards on your thirtieth anniversary at the Club.

And, as local celebrity of note, Steve provoked a few lines in Herb Caen's column, to wit:

"ASK A SILLY QUESTION DEPT.: Speaking of anniversaries, Steve Blumenthal this week celebrates his thirtieth year as chef at the Concordia-Argonaut Club on Van Ness — so the other night, member Louis Lurie asked him how he felt about his long service. 'Well,' said Steve, running a finger thoughtfully over the edge of his cleaver, 'thirty years on one job isn't so much if you're working for the City Hall or Uncle Sam — but cooking thirty years for the same old crabs is different!' Mr. Lurie mumbled congratulations and left hurriedly."

When Steve retired eight years later, he was given a solid gold watch, a pension and a check from the Club members for $6,000. Ben Baum, who felt Steve's pension was inadequate, largely because the pension plan had been in effect only a few years, led a successful move to increase it.

Two other long-time staffers served concurrently with Steve. One was Norman Kelk, the Club Manager from 1924 until he died suddenly in 1944. Kelk was meek, mild-mannered and kind, but ran the Club with an iron fist. Dan Stone, Jr. remembering two incidents from his childhood about Kelk recalled, "My father would take me to the Club on Saturdays after I spent the morning polishing desks at Stone & Youngberg to earn a little allowance. I must have been about ten or twelve. It was in the days before they cut up the dining room, when the portable bar that we now use in the main lounge for parties used to sit in the corner of the Club overlooking Cedar Street and Van Ness. I'd sit at a big round table up front with my father and Marcel Hirsch and Max Frederick and some others. This one day, a gentleman came in — I've forgotten who it was — and sat next to me, looking at the menu. Mr. Kelk came over and said, 'The lamb chops are very good today.'

'Thank you for telling me, Mr. Kelk,' the man said, 'but I really don't want to eat lamb chops today.' He returned to the menu and Kelk kept saying, 'The lamb chops are very good today.' Then the waiter came up, the man gave him his order, and Mr. Kelk said, 'No, Mr. So-and-So is going to have the lamb chops.' By God, the man got the lamb chops, and by God he ate them and signed his check!"

Shortly after that, when Dan was in Mt. Zion hospital with appendicitis, Mr. Kelk paid him a visit. "It was Thanksgiving Day, and Mr. Kelk brought me what was my first wild duck, complete with wild rice and other wonderful things. My father, seeing the dish, said, "Mr. Kelk, I didn't have any wild duck stored in the refrigerator at the Club.' 'I know,' Kelk said. 'Where did you get the wild duck?' my father asked, to which Kelk replied, 'What you don't ask you don't have to get answers to.' I never have found out whose duck it was. I'll never forget his thoughtfulness either."

The other man serving with Steve, Arnold the Bartender, who retired in February 1981 after fifty years, still holds the record for the longest continuous service.

Arnold Robleto's career at the Club illustrates how capable staffers could move through the ranks. Coming to this country as a young man from Nicaragua with his wife and baby, he started at the Club moonlighting as a dishwasher. "I was working daytime for a Jewish firm at that time. My nephew worked at the Club as a storekeeper. I needed to earn extra money for the family, so my nephew got me the job here washing dishes. Next I worked in the pantry. Then I was moved to the kitchen where I helped the cook for seven years. Just before Norman Kelk passed away, he asked me to try being a waiter in the dining room. From there, I was moved up to head waiter during the war. Then I watched the bartender. When he needed help, I filled in. Some time later, I was made head bartender."

During the half-century Arnold has been at the Club he has seen at least two generations of membership grow to manhood. "I know most of the present members from the time they were kids and I waited on their fathers. Ricky Colsky, Ricky Friedman . . . ."

As for the modest drinking habits at the Concordia he said, "The bar never loses money — the dining room never made a nickel. Wednesday night is a big drinking night. The members drink a lot of wine. The favorite is Christian Brothers Chablis."

Arnold also tended bar at the private parties held at the Club. "Almost every week there are two or three of them — weddings, bar mitzvahs, anniversaries. There is now a waiting list for dates. We have the best here that can serve you. We do everything to please." The most impressive private affairs to Arnold are the seders held at the Club each Passover by Temple Emanu-El. "They are the most memorable."

Looking back on his years at the Club, Arnold commented "If I were to have another fifty years of life I would be glad to work here. Jews are the most beautiful people in the world. The Club is just like one family."

Eugene Buenzly was the Maitre d' who retired because of failing health in 1968 after serving for thirty-five years. "That was also the year that our manager, James Carey, a most capable man, left," recalls Dr. Stanley Reich, president at the time. "Then Chef Theodore had a heart attack and he was forced to retire."

Replacing a manager, a chef and a maitre d' in the same year would have left most clubs in total disarray. But the transition at the Concordia worked smoothly. When Chef Theodore left, the second cook was promoted. Joseph, previously a pastry chef at the St. Francis Hotel, had been trained by Steve Blumenthal, becoming thoroughly acquainted with the operation of the kitchen and the tastes of the members. Joseph stepped in, but after two years was forced to retire due to ill health. But here again the transition went smoothly: Niels Ploug, who had come to the Club as Chef Theodore's assistant, was elevated to chef, a position he has filled with distinction ever since.

Ploug, a Dane, has been at the Club since 1964. He arrived the same year as Chef Theodore, whose assistant he was at El Prado in the Plaza Hotel. His longest and most strenuous working day at the Club is Thanksgiving. The eve before the holiday is the annual Stag Night, when he and his staff of seven, prepare the Roman feast.

"I work Wednesday from eight a.m. until one a.m. the following day. Then I must come back a few hours later to get Thanksgiving dinner. The turkeys must be ready by 4:30. We serve dinner in two shifts on both the third floor and the second floor. Thanksgiving, along with Easter and Mother's Day, are the biggest days in our dining room."

●     ●     ●

The search for a Club manager and maitre d' was more difficult. Walter Newman, Chairman of the Search Committee, said, "We decided we had to get ourselves a top manager. I did a national search. We went out to the 'head hunters' and talked to people all over the Bay Area. Somebody told me about a very capable man who was the Wine and Beverage man at the Mark Hopkins. His name was Anthony Pels. I interviewed him and he was just great. We made him an offer and told him all the pitfalls of a Jewish Club and he didn't care. He came on, and he was able to bring a maitre d' with him. He had wonderful connections all over the hotel and club field. Through Pels, we were able to hire Hans Fallant. Hans has since gone on to become the manager of the Metropolitan Club and, later, the head of the St. Francis Yacht Club. When Hans left, Pels got us Douwe

Drayer as maitre d'. And Douwe, of course, moved up into Pels' place when he left to manage the Bohemian Club."

On the wall in Tony Pels' office at the Bohemian Club is a brass plaque presented to him by members of Concordia-Argonaut "in grateful appreciation for your dedicated services" during the twelve years he managed the Club.

"There is a fine atmosphere at Concordia-Argonaut between employees and the membership," said Pels. "The employees respect all that's going on, respect all the traditions and are certainly impressed by the generous gifts they get from time to time — Christmas, for example. And every time there are special functions at the Club they get a little extra.

"It's like a little jewel, that Club. Like anywhere else, the employees have to go along with the management, but it was always in the spirit of, 'Let's do these things together. You know, that is not in line with what we used to do.' And they would understand. They'd accept that."

Pels, who went on to manage a club three times the size of "the little jewel" cherishes the training he received at the Club. "I learned a lot about financial management from men like Norman Grabstein and Ben Baum. The Club also sent me to seminars for additional training." That training further sharpened his own outstanding managerial capabilities, which were recognized in 1975 when Pels was named president of a state-wide organization of club managers.

Douwe Drayer, an ideal choice to manage the Club with its new, youthful image, stepped up to the position of Club manager. Clearly he was young enough to identify with the needs of young members and seasoned enough to serve the older ones.

A handsome, urbane, yet understated man, Drayer, had all the excellent credentials of the classic European maitre d's. Born in Holland, he studied at the Hotel and Restaurant School in Amsterdam, and from the age of twenty to twenty-five worked on Holland-American ocean liners as a dining room and bar steward. "I wanted to get out of those wet socks," Drayer said, so he came ashore and spent the next few years at the Amsterdam Carlton Hotel and the Haarlem Brinkman restaurant as a waiter and assistant maitre d'. He left Holland for the United States in 1965.

"My choice was San Francisco, because I had heard and read so much about the City, its beauty, charm, population mix and its restaurant and dining sophistication."

The young man worked the night shift at the Sheraton Palace at the front desk. During the day he attended San Francisco State University, majoring in psychology. At night, as new opportunities arose, he drew from his reservoir of psychological insight in his job at the Fairmont. Later he was named maitre d' at the Blue Fox, which, after six years, he left when Pels persuaded him to come to the Concordia-Argonaut.

An opera buff and a student of classical music, the Club manager, who is fluent in many languages, often discusses opera with the older members. By contrast, the younger members are intrigued by the fact that, until recently, their manager biked to work on his motorcycle from his home in Orinda. "I stopped after I had an accident. I hit a dog and fell off. I had my arm and my leg in a cast. It caused too much embarrassment," said Drayer sheepishly. Now he commutes in a more conventional way.

Drayer supervised a staff of thirty-seven employees at the Club. Among them is a husband and wife team, Paul and Carolyn Tokusato. Paul Tokusato, a native of Hilo, Hawaii, came to work at the Club in 1959 as an assistant to Everett Whitney in the Athletic Department. Initially, his duties were to keep the pool and the Athletic Department clean. Paul, who had once been a first rate boxer, and, during World War II, a member of the 442nd "Go For Broke" U.S. Infantry division, rose through Club ranks to the position of Head Houseman. Today he and his staff of three are responsible for the state of the Club's social wings. From his office on the second floor, he also supervised many banquet room setups.

Carolyn, who also comes from Hilo, joined the Club staff following the death of long-time Club Secretary Peggy Court. "They had a few other secretaries in between Peggy and me, but they didn't last long," said Carolyn, who soon became an indispensable part of the Club. Carolyn, previously a secretary with an agent for the Matson Navigation Company in Hilo, Hawaii, had been hired by the company in San Francisco upon arriving in the City. Through Paul, her fiance at the time, she learned of the job at the Club.

Carolyn, known for her pleasant personality and cheerful willingness to perform various "girl friday" tasks, is an expert flower arranger. Every Monday morning she would cover the billiard table with plastic, cut open the bunches of fresh flowers ordered by the Club manager and, in a brief while transform them into graceful displays to adorn the Club. "I do the flower arrangements. Paul takes care of the plants," smiles Carolyn. The two are parents of a son, who shares his father's enthusiasm for sports.

Clifford Nott became the Club's chief bartender after Arnold Robleto's retirement. He is another staffer who gained advancement because of the opportunities the Club offers capable employees. Like Paul, Cliff, in 1950 also started as a swimming pool attendant. Two years later, he was promoted to second floor cardroom waiter; then was elevated to second floor bartender. Cliff is an easygoing, friendly man whose youthful appearance belies the fact that he is a grandfather of twins.

Ellys W. (Bill) Layton, who had been tending the Club's books since 1958, is also a native of Hawaii, although he moved to the mainland as a youngster and was graduated from Galileo High School. An army master sergeant with the 1st Cavalry Division in Korea, Bill used his G.I. benefits to attend Golden Gate College where he majored in accounting. He came to Concordia-Argonaut after six years at the San Francisco Commercial Club, and over time has consolidated and streamlined the tasks within the financial office. While members rarely question the statements Bill mailed each month, many would pay him a social call to view the display of calendar art on the walls. Bill's retirement went into effect January 29, 1981, two days before the fire.

Layton's retirement enabled Tito Villamarin to step up and fill the vacated position. Tito, a native of Manila, has been a Club employee for twelve years, starting as a part-time switchboard operator on weekends. Later, he worked as a houseman and one of his duties was to help Layton in the accounting office. Now he is working on Club financial records full time.

Two other long-time staff members are housemen Rodolfo (Rudy) Selva and Saturnino (Nino) Gamez, who have been at their posts thirty-two and twelve years respectively. Both men are natives of Nicaragua. Rudy learned of the Club from a fellow Nicaraguan, Cortez, houseman at the Club in 1947. "He told me it was a nice place to work and they had an opening. So I applied and got the job," says Rudy. Nino, who got his position through the Hotel and Restaurant Workers Union, was delighted to find another Nicaraguan as a co-worker.

• • •

A contented staff is vital for a smoothly run club and a satisfied membership. Only once during the more than 100 years of the Club's existence has the balance been upset. The scales were tipped in 1946 at a time when a new policy regarding gratuities was to go into affect. Lawrence Livingston, in a furious letter to Maitre d' Gene Buenzly December 7, stormed about the waiters "so surly and so insulting to the members present that I was ashamed of my Club. I have been in the dining rooms of practically every club in San Francisco. I have been properly and respectfully served. I have never seen anything remotely resembling the attitude of our waiters. I should like information as to whether the Board of Directors intends to take any steps with reference to this complaint. . . ."

On December 9 Werner Hartman, Club Manager, forwarded Livingston's letter to Gene with this comment:

"To say that I was surprised and disappointed is to put it mildly. The waiters, no doubt, know by now that I am putting a considerable raise in wages in effect as of December 1. I have also suggested to the House Committee that we will give all the employees a very worthwhile Christmas present. You and I know that the boys have a very good job here and to have a thing like the above happen only reflects on you and myself.

"The membership has recently been notified that tipping in the Club is to be discontinued. However, I expect you to see to it that *all* members will receive courteous and prompt service. In other words, there will be no more discrimination between members who tip and those who do not tip. Please see to it that all of your boys read this letter and advise them, that if I receive any further complaints like the above, the waiter in question will be immediately discharged, regardless how many years he has been at the Club.

"I look forward to the time when our new dining room will be open to the members, and it will be your job and mine to see to it that the service rendered by the waiters will be as near perfect as we can make it.

"I know that you will cooperate with me, and hope the boys will all fall in line."

Fall into line they did. The only complaint with regard to the new policy was voiced by Steve the Chef.

"That policy works against the Club on the special days when we need outside help, like Thanksgiving, Mother's Day and Easter. Every waiter who is worth something has a job at the Fairmont or the Mark Hopkins, so we would get what was left in the barrel. But I don't know if it is that way still. I noticed when Mr. Baum's son got married not long ago and my wife and I were invited here, they had very good waiters that night. Very efficient. I don't know if it's always that way or not."

But the Christmas bonus policy has continued to be a "very worth while present." Said Larry Nestel, "Lots of people would ask (when I was president), 'What should I give?' We did a survey. We found that the average contribution was 'x' percent of the member's total bill for the year. So we said that, for your information, the average contribution was 'x' percent. Immediately, everybody raised their contribution up twenty to twenty-five percent. The Club has a very gentlemanly, respectful attitude towards its employees."

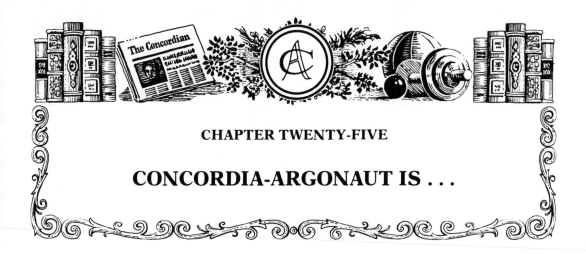

## CHAPTER TWENTY-FIVE

# CONCORDIA-ARGONAUT IS . . .

E ARE WHAT WE ourselves choose to be," Ted Euphrat told the membership in his annual report of April 1966, following a tumultuous year in the Club's history. And Concordia-Argonaut chooses to be "a luxury club formed decades ago for the sole purpose of social intercourse," he said.

Members, however, describe the Club in more simple terms. "Concordia is my other home," they explain.

For bachelor Dan Stone, Jr. the Club serves much the same purpose it did so long ago for another bachelor, founding member Levi Strauss. "To me the Club is essentially a place where I meet a lot of friends and where I like to go to entertain people," he says.

On occasion he likes to entertain members of the Stanford football team at his Club. "I have a great interest in the team, and after the season is over, I invite three or four of the boys up at a time and let them loose at the buffet table. They wreak havoc with the Club's budget for that week! I'm very jealous of the Club's reputation as a nice place to be invited, an enjoyable place to go. Perhaps because I use it as much as I do—albeit in streaks—I am much more conscious of what goes on or the way it looks in certain areas than a lot of people who use it very casually."

To Stone, "one of the little signs of class is to have genuine things," which is why he championed the cause of quill toothpicks.

"A few years back, when Tony Pels was manager, we ran out of quill toothpicks. At the time the only other place that still had such toothpicks (made from duck quills) was the Stock Exchange. All the other places—the Bohemian Club, the University Club, Trader Vic's—had already converted to plastic toothpicks. Tony and I had a long session over whether we should stick to quill. The only place to get the toothpicks is from France. Should they be domestic plastic or French quill? I held out for the real thing."

According to Stone—and the Club members concur—other important touches of class include "hand towels that are laundered rather than disposable paper; tablecloths made of linen; napkins that are pressed; silver plated, rather than plastic, eating utensils and serving pieces; fresh flowers on the dining tables, and when you have candles on the table, they are lit."

The management also keeps smoked salmon on the table, despite the price, because the members demand it, and features bouillabaisse on the menu to please the three or four members who like it. The Club fills the pool with salt water (until the suppliers go out of business) because the swimmers insist, no matter how the plumbing suffers.

Concordia-Argonaut is a luxury club and members are willing to pay for its expense.

"The stance that I have taken — and it is a proper one — is that we should not accept anybody into the Club who can't afford to belong," says Ben Baum. "Nobody has a gun to anyone's back saying you have to belong. If you can't afford it, don't join it. You cannot run a business based on the man least able to produce; you cannot run a charity drive on the basis of the man least able to give, and you cannot run a private club on the man least able to pay.

"If bonds are needed for refurbishing, if the costs of maintaining the Club increase because of inflation, higher food costs, labor costs or whatever, those costs should be absorbed by the members. We shouldn't have to apologize to anybody because we are raising dues to meet them."

Concordia-Argonaut exists for rest and relaxation.

"We maintain a tradition of 'no business' — not in the saunas, the gym, the lounge, or anywhere else in the Club," says Larry Nestel. "We do not allow any solicitation of our membership list, nor does the roster specify members' occupations."

Until very recently the policy not to disclose such information was perhaps moot, since the members were acquainted with each other since grammar school, knew the maiden names of each other's grandmothers and were probably related to one of them.

However, the Club does provide a change of pace for the ninety-one attorneys, five judges, thirty-four doctors, twelve dentists, and scores of stock brokers, insurance agents, accountants, business executives and other top professionals who comprise its membership. It is a second home, where they find a masseur to relax their tense muscles, a barber to tend to their tonsorial needs and a manicurist to care for their hands.

●　　　●　　　●

"Don't make the mistake of attributing greatness to the Club because of the accomplishments of some of the names on the membership rolls," warned Renny

Colvin. But there is no gainsaying the importance the Club's role has been — and continues to be — in the sustenance and revitalization of those great men.

Daniel Koshland, in his younger days, a vigorous, athletic man, regularly used the Club's pool and gym to maintain his high energy level; energy that in 1977 earned him the University of California's "Alumnus of the Year" award from among the thousands of distinguished University alumni throughout the world. He received the award for "guiding Levi Strauss to a world-rank manufacturer, pioneering in training and hiring minority workers, the creation of a blueprint for the education of San Francisco's handicapped, a founder of the San Francisco Foundation and the Council for Civic Unity, serving three governors as a member of the California Industrial Commission, evolving a humane approach to the treatment of alcholism and mental retardation. . . ." These accomplishments were in addition to his work in the Jewish community.

Equally illustrious is his brother, Robert Koshland, who explains modestly, "We are only carrying out Mother's example." The younger Koshland, who was a partner in the family's wool business in Boston until the business was liquidated, moved back to San Francisco in 1930. Here he has devoted most of his time to civic affairs and philanthropic interests, including the California Conference of Social Welfare, the Jewish Home for the Aged, the Peninsula Hospital and Medical Center, the Bay Area Social Planning Council, Services for Seniors, the Advisory Council to the State Commission on Aging, and the University of California Alumni Council.

Another distinguished family member was the Koshlands' cousin, Walter Haas, who often relaxed at the Club over a game of bridge. Haas, who had been president of Levi Strauss from 1928 to 1955, the years of its expansion from a regional business to the world's largest manufacturer of men's clothing, had a record of service to his City equal to his business accomplishments. Haas had been president of the San Francisco Chamber of Commerce, the San Francisco War Chest (now, United Crusade), the Jewish National Welfare Fund, the Manufac- turers' Association of San Francisco, he Jewish Welfare Federation and the San Francisco Parks and Recreation Commission. Among his many honors and awards have been those from the University of California, the Boy Scouts of America, the City and County of San Francisco, the National Conference of Christians and Jews, Hebrew University of Jerusalem, the Board of Supervisors of San Francisco, the United Bay Area Crusade, and the (Israeli) Prime Minister's Medal.

Harold Zellerbach, who contributed so richly to San Francisco's cultural, artistic and religious life was another distinguished Concordian. Zellerbach be- came president of Zellerbach Paper Company in 1929 and later, executive vice president of the parent Crown Zellerbach Corporation. Paralleling his active business career, Harold Zellerbach was president of the San Francisco Art Commission for twenty-eight years. He was vice president and a member of the Board of Governors of the San Francisco Symphony Association, a director of the San Francisco Performing Arts Center, President of the Newhouse Foundation, and a trustee of the San Francisco Ballet Association.

In the religious life of the community, Zellerbach was president of Temple Emanu-El from 1948 to 1953, and a president of the Jewish Community Center. Also active in Democratic politics, Harold accepted appointments to national commissions and special projects from Presidents Roosevelt, Truman and Johnson. Two such appointments were to the Zellerbach Commission, which studied European refugee problems, and as a delegate to the Atlantic Congress. (Referring to his Republican brother, James Zellerbach, appointed by President Eisenhower as Ambassador to Italy, Harold commented, "My brother and I sometimes took different political positions. That happens in all families.")

The Club's pool was often filled with three generations of Zellerbachs, when Harold, who had been a member of the University of California's track and swim teams, and his sons Bill and Stephen, and his grandsons would swim laps together. On those occasions when his friend, Senator Jacob Javits, was in the City, Zellerbach would work out with him.

Concordia has been a respite for a benchful of distinguished judges, including Max C. Sloss, Albert C. Wollenberg Sr., Milton Shapiro, Mathew Tobriner, Donald Constine, Jr., and John Molinari.

The Club has been a place of leisure for the area's leading rabbis, who are accorded clergy membership. The Club's files contain a thank-you letter from Rabbi Alvin Fine, dated shortly after he assumed the pulpit of Temple Emanu-El in 1948. It reads: "I would appreciate it greatly if you would inform me of any formalities or obligations that I must fulfill in connection with my membership in Concordia-Argonaut." Rabbi Fine's letter brought this response from Richard Sloss, then Club secretary: "There is only one formality with which you have to comply as a member of the Club — to have a good time here as often as it is possible for you to come in."

Concordia-Argonaut represents a legacy handed down from father to son throughout generations in a number of illustrious families: the Newmans, the Zellerbachs, the Branstens, the Steinharts, and the Haas's. It is also a legacy in the Ladar family.

Sam Ladar, a distinguished San Francisco attorney, was raised in the Pacific Hebrew Orphan Asylum, a favorite charity of the "First Families." How proud they would be of Sam's accomplishments! In 1980 he was honored with the American Jewish Congress' Community Services Award in recognition of his years of service to the City and the Jewish Community as President of the San Francisco Board of Education, the San Francisco Police Commission, the Jewish Welfare Federation, and the Jewish Community Relations Council as well as his activity as a director of the American Jewish Committee. Currently three generations of Ladars are active in the Club: Sam; his son Jerrold, also an attorney; and his two grandsons, Jonathan and Jeffrey.

Concordia-Argonaut has evolved with the passage of 130 years of history, and yet its essential character has withstood the test of time.

"People tend to conform to the spirit of the club they join," Larry Nestel points out. "They join because they are attracted to it, not to change it. This is still a club in which the membership takes great pride. They respect it and tend to conduct themselves in that way. Concordia-Argonaut was run by a smaller, closer group in the past. It is still very conservative . . . very gentlemanly. The new people are blending in very well with the old-timers."

Such new people include members like Carl Pearlstein, a quiet, well-loved man who heads one of the largest horticultural companies in the country, Nurseryman's Exchange. His is a modern Horatio Alger story. Born on the Lower East Side of New York, Pearlstein first learned about horticulture from his father, who, during his vacations, worked on a farm in the Catskills in order to become a farmer in Palestine. Carl's stamina and inspiration derived from his mother, who at an early age taught the boy to be self-sufficient. After working his way through the University of California, Pearlstein got a job as an accountant with a seed company. When he informed his boss he wanted to quit his job to go into business for himself, Pearlstein's boss reminded him he had no financing. So he remained, sold seeds and at the same time built up a business by buying bulbs on credit from local farmers.

"I sold the bulbs for cash and paid back the farmers. At the Home of Peace Cemetery, they let me have the lily bulbs for nothing if I dug them up and cleaned them out. My wife and I — by this time I was married to Virginia Simon — went to the cemetery, and we dug for weeks. We had no place to store all those bulbs. It was late in the '40s and we were living in a small apartment. We put them under the bed, in the living room, anyplace we could find space. My mother-in-law was aghast. 'For this I had to send my daughter to Stanford,' she moaned."

From this humble beginning, Pearlstein's nursery business began to flourish. Today he delights in inviting Club members and their families to visit his hothouses at Half Moon Bay. One memorable November day, ninety-three members and their guests left the Club in two buses for the jaunt. At the nurseries they walked through a fragrant, colorful wonderland of poinsettias, chrysanthemums, house plants, ferns, and exotic plants. When the visitors left, each departed with Carl's gift of a poinsettia for his home — with plenty left over for the Club's holiday decor.

Carl, who is president of the San Francisco chapter of the Anti-Defamation League and a director of the San Francisco chapter of the American Jewish Committee, is committed to share the inspiration his mother gave to him. "I feel an obligation to pay back my good fortune. I believe showing people how to help themselves — giving them the tools — is the best thing you can do for them."

Recently, Carl joined with Glide Memorial Church to launch a job-training program for indigents, teaching them to garden and landscape, and then finding the trainees jobs after completion of the six-week course. The first graduates landscaped "Wino Park" on Sixth and Harrison Streets. Pearlstein is presently offering training to Vietnamese refugees.

Other "new" people who have been well-integrated in the Club include the German-American refugees from Hitler's Europe, such as real estate broker, philanthropist and Jewish community leader William Lowenberg, attorney Norman Weil, ladies' dress manufacturer Ernest Benesch, and architect Max Garcia. Garcia, along with Jay Darwin's wife Lonnie, founded a Holocaust Library and Research Center in San Francisco so the atrocities committed in their former homelands will never be forgotten.

•        •        •

Concordia-Argonaut is a club devoted to pleasure — even concerning the selection of its reading material. Arthur Simon, who has been Club librarian for the past fifteen years, recalls, "When I took over from Dan Stone, Jr., he told me never to buy non-fiction, that reading in the Club library should be purely for pleasure. Members enjoy books like *Sophie's Choice*, by William Styron; *Covenant*, by James Michener, and the three Howard Fast books about a San Francisco family." Simon issues library bulletins from time to time, categorizing his new selections as "Mystery Check List," "Books People Have Been Screaming For," and "Good Reading for the Women — and Their Husbands."

Back in 1948, at the height of the Great Books Discussion movement that swept the country, a member proposed a book club be started in the Concordia. Notices advertising a reading group were sent out to members. "Great," responded attorney Lawrence Livingston. "I think it would be very nice for some of our members to find out what is inside a book!" But his was one of a total of four responses received. The proposal was dropped.

The following year, Nat Schmulowitz, another well-known attorney and longtime active Club member who was Club librarian at the time, hired Frances

Lang Paap, head librarian for the City, to "discriminate, discard and rearrange the library." She did this on week-ends, spending ten working days to make her evaluations. She found that: "One-third of the collection should be disposed of because they are in bad shape, unusable and have not left the room in three or four years . . . . The classics: no one reads these leather-bound sets, but they make for a comfortable and pleasant atmosphere . . . the *Who's Who* is of dubious use, as is a telephone book more than fifteen years old . . ."

Concordia-Argonaut is a Club where the emphasis at lunchtime is still on camaraderie. Although many of the members — particularly the younger members — use the noon hour for a "business lunch," entertaining clients or associates, there are still groups like the Wednesday Group, who have met to-gether for lunch at the Club for more than thirty years. They include Bill Green, Allen Meier, Alvin Hayman, Jr., John Greenberg, Jay Hamerslag, Stuart Erlanger and Bob Bloch. (Until his recent death Harold Getz was the informal leader of the Wednesday lunch group.) The group, who became acquainted through boyhood memberships in the Club, first formalized their Wednesday lunch ritual after World War II. Occasionally a member of the group will propose to change the day or place of their luncheon. Someone will second the motion and call for a vote. The motion is promptly and inevitably voted down.

The "Cabinet Table," is a second group of men who have lunched together for decades. Not as closed a circle as is the "Getz" group, the "Cabinet Table" is comprised of "wise gentlemen with sensitive palates." Those who predictably have "Cabinet" posts include Jack Lipman, Maurice Oppenheimer, Ed Bransten, Willie Bransten, Edgar Sinton, Fred Zelinsky, Jack Davis, Al Grossman and Ernie Lilienthal. (Until their deaths Marcel Hirsch, Mel Spiegl, Joe Mittel, Irving Breyer, Lloyd Hanford and Joe Bransten were also "Cabinet" men.) A special table seven feet in diameter with a lazy susan in the middle was constructed for them so the "Cabinet" men need not struggle to reach seasonings or appetizers. The table is open to any member who wishes to join the privileged circle. So many do that the "Cabinet" frequently expands to two or more tables.

Concordia-Argonaut continues to satisfy evident needs. Says Walter New-man, "As the only Jewish club in the City, this in its own way gives us an equal opportunity to enjoy the good things that a private club can give you. There are only a handful of Jews in the Bohemian Club and a couple or three in the Pacific Union, but that's it. All the rest of us would be out looking for a place . . . ."

Concordia-Argonaut is a Club that has taken on "a much more youthful approach," says Newman, who doesn't necessarily favor the change. "It's much more relaxed. I find it much less formal . . . much less proper."

Some of those contributing to the "youthful approach" — men in their early thirties who could comprise the Club's future leadership — include Brian Getz, son of Harold Getz; Andrew Colvin, son of Renny Colvin; and John Rothmann, son of Dr. Hans Rothmann, and Mike Mendelson, a newcomer to this area, who says, "The Club was a good introduction to San Francisco for me. It has opened doors to friendships that I could not have made otherwise."

Concordia is a club with a sense of permanence. Rick Colsky recalls the plaque hanging in his office which states his son Jason will be given "honorary membership" as soon as he is old enough to become a juvenile member. The plaque was presented to Colsky by Vice President Adrian Scharlach on behalf of the Board in recognition of the fact that Colsky was the first president in the Club's history to become a father while in office. "I'm glad the Club was here for my father," he told the Board that night. "I'm happy to be part of it now. It's nice to know it will be here for my son and his son."

●　　　●　　　●

Concordia is a club susceptible to internal divisions. When Marvin Nathan succeeded Rick Colsky as president in 1981, his election came as a surprise — even to Nathan. He received the news while at a meeting in Oregon.

The surprise move occurred during the course of the Annual Meeting that year. For the first time in the Club's history, there was a contested election of Club directors. Adrian Scharlach, who had served as Vice President for three years, seemed the likely choice of the presidency of the new directors. When he wasn't renominated to the board, a petition was circulated to place his name in nomination to the board. If he were re-elected, it would then have been possible for him to become the president. The movement failed, and, as a result, Marvin Nathan became the president.

The new president was born and educated in Virginia. His army service brought him to California in 1952, when he was stationed with the Army Audit Agency in Berkeley. He later enrolled at the University of California, where he received his MBA at the same time he earned his CPA credential.

Nathan met a San Francisco girl and was first introduced to the Club through his future father-in-law. He has been a member since 1966. Nathan's activities in the Athletic Department led to a request that he serve on the Athletic Committee a short time later. In the mid-Seventies he served on the Finance Committee for five years, was nominated to the Board in 1978, and became assistant treasurer, a post he held for two years. Re-elected to the Board, he served a year as treasurer before being elected to the presidency. Nathan's leadership would soon undergo a baptism of fire.

May our eyes, well pleased, behold
A work to prove us not unskilled
Wield the hammer, wield,
Till the frame shall yield!
That the bell to light may rise,
The form in thousand fragments flies.

# A NEW BEGINNING

T WOULD BE NEARLY TWO YEARS before the members, "eyes well pleased," would behold their restored Club. Twenty months filled with frustrations, complications and hard decision-making. There was never any question, as the members watched in anguish as the flames devoured their Club, that it would be rebuilt. The only questions were how long it would take and how much it would cost. The answers to both, when they were finally known, were far, far in excess of what members had anticipated.

The morning following the fire, when President Marvin Nathan strode into the Metropolitan Club for the emergency Board meeting, he came equipped with a plan of action.

"We have three immediate objectives," he told the assembled members: "one, to find temporary facilities for our members; two, to retain and accommodate our loyal employees; and, three, to restore the building."

"We sat there still in a state of shock, perplexed and distressed by the enormity of the disaster," said Rick Colsky. "Then Marv, displaying great leaderhip, spelled out what we had to do, assigned us roles and we fell into line."

Nathan organized a Task Force of eight committees, with a Steering Committee comprised of himself, Vice President Ted Euphrat and Secretary Allen Meier. In order to expedite decisions, he told the men, the Steering Committee would approve the work of each committee unless substantial sums of money were involved, in which case the approval of the full Board would be required.

Nathan selected the best that the Club had to offer by way of expertise to serve on the eight committees. Leading insurance experts, lawyers and CPAs were asked to sit on the Insurance Recovery Committee; men knowledgeable about the hotel and restaurant facilities in the City were appointed to a Temporary Site Location Committee; architects and engineers were selected for the Structural Integrity Study. Other committees, each comprised of members carefully chosen for their experience in the respective matters, included the Office

Location and Finances Committee; Dues Structure Committee; a committee to select a contractor to clean up what remained of the building as well as to select an architect for the rebuilding; an Employees Retention Committee; and finally, a Site Use Committee to decide on the best possible plan for rebuilding the Club.

The latter committee, chaired by Walter Newman, currently a member of the City's Urban Renewal Board, was immediately showered with a variety of suggestions. One idea was to raze what remained of the Club building, using the site for a highrise in which the club would retain several floors for its own use. (The City had just granted permission for two highrises to be built across Van Ness, on the next block from the Club, thereby increasing the value of the adjacent land.) Others wanted to keep the existing structure intact, but add one or more stories to it. A group of younger men wanted to see more athletic facilities built.

"The fire made the membership conscious of the fact that this is an historical building," Colsky said. "Most of us wanted to retain its old world charm."

By Tuesday, the second day following the disaster, President Nathan sent a letter to the entire membership enclosed with the monthly bills.

"The Club anticipates continued services for you within the next few weeks," he wrote. He listed the clubs who had invited members to use their facilities in the interim. He promised that "Club bulletins will be sent to you regularly reporting our progress." He informed the members of the Board's actions in establishing the Task Force, and of the letter sent to the Fire Department's Chief Andrew Casper "expressing our deepest appreciation for their heroic and diligent efforts demonstrated in controlling the fire," together with a check in the amount of $500 "in the name of your Club to the 'Fire Fighters for Youth Program,' a juvenile program sponsored by the Fire Department to educate young people in the danger of fire hazards." He reported that perishable foods and other foodstuffs which were qualified as edible by the San Francisco Health Department were contributed to St. Anthony's Dining Room and the Salvation Army.

"We, at Concordia-Argonaut, have entered into a new era," the letter concluded. "During these first few days of the crisis, many members of the Club have contacted the Board to share their expertise, offer assistance in solving the problems caused by the fire and to express their feelings about the unfortunate loss we have realized.

"The warmth and depth of concern expressed by so many of you in this crisis shows all of us that our spirit and mutual brotherhood at Concordia-Argonaut guarantees we have the synergism amongst us to achieve a beautiful and successful restoration of the Club. . . ."

Bulletin No. 2, which was mailed the following month urged members "not to pay too much attention to rumors, heresay and speculation floating around the

City. Watch for these bulletins. They will be timely and accurate."

The progress report then went on to state—accurately—that "President Marvin Nathan, the Board of Directors and a host of Ad Hoc Task Force subcommittees are working days, nights and weekends putting together scores of parts of a reconstruction program. And the parts are falling into place."

One part that had fallen into place was that the Club would remain at the Van Ness-Post location and that "facilities would be similar to those we now have i.e. style, tone, ambience. Changes will be in modernization with advanced technology."

By that time the architectural selection committee, chaired by Jack Lipman, had chosen the firm of Hertzka & Knowles, one of the finest architectural firms in the City, to provide the designs for the rehabilitation of the Club.

Structural engineers had ascertained that the Club's Athletic Department, having sustained the least damage in the building, could be readied for use within a few months. Although the bulletin did not state a firm reopening date, President Nathan advised, "Jocks, don't throw your sweat glands away. You'll be using them again soon."

The Bulletin listed a long list of clubs offering Concordia members their athletic facilities for the time being. But most of the younger men took advantage of a deal Rick Colsky had arranged between two new athletic clubs with superb modern equipment, the San Francisco Bay Club and the Telegraph Hill Club, where the men were given a greatly reduced initiation fee based on the temporary nature of the arrangement.

"Even though these clubs had the finest facilities—the Bay Club even had tennis courts—far better than our Athletic Department, there was not the slightest fear that any of our men would defect. Not a chance. You don't make you 'second home' in a gymnasium!" said Colsky.

All dues were suspended as of February 1, 1982, and a Building Reserve Fund set up under which seniors and limited-privilege members were to be billed in the amount of $50 a month, and the other categories of membership would be billed for lesser amounts.

• • •

Club business carried on. The Board announced the names of members chosen for the 1982–83 Nominating Committee, and the Bulletin mentioned with sadness "the passing of the following members: Raymond T. Anixter, William Blackfield, Marcus Glaser and Harry Hilp, Jr."

By April 1 cleanup work at the Club had been completed. Bulletin No. 3 noted that "the damaged portion of the building had been removed and salvage-able contents have been stored away from the Club site."

Discussion about alternate methods for restoration of the facility continued unabated. Proponents of the highrise solution and the fourth-floor-addition advocates continued to press their cases. The Board carefully evaluated all proposals. Bulletin No. 3 explained the process whereby the Board arrived at its decision.

"The Board of Directors has carefully considered all these alternative proposals and has determined that for reasons entirely too numerous to relate in this bulletin, our proper course of action is to proceed with the rapid rebuilding of our Club to establish it in essentially the same form as it was prior to the fire. The membership should be aware that the Board of Directors is extremely sensitive to the needs and desires of our entire membership and is making this decision to reflect those requirements."

A decision was made to have "an entire new third floor with the second and first floors structurally remaining essentially as they were prior to the fire. The building will have sprinklers throughout, and a new second stairway will be constructed to separate exits to facilitate departure from the building in case of emergency."

To expedite the job, the Board was willing to bypass the most cost effective means in favor of a process known as "fast tracking."

"The Board of Directors is aware that the most cost efficient means of construction is to direct the architects to prepare complete plans and specifications of the work and then put them out to bid. We have been advised, however, that this would take a number of months and would significantly delay the rapid restoration of our facility."

Instead, as architects Hertzka & Knowles completed sections of their work and it was accepted by the Club, the contractor (Herrero Brothers was the firm chosen) would instantly execute the plans as they were approved by the City.

"Our initial stage of construction," the bulletin continued, "provides for a new roof on the building. Expected time of completion for this project is approximately three to four months. Concurrent with this effort, work will begin on the Athletic Department to expedite our return to use of this area of the Club."

Meanwhile, the Temporary Site Location Committee, under the chairmanship of Rick Colsky, had found what seemed to be an ideal place for Chef Niels to establish interim operations. The dining room of the Hotel David, located on Geary Street across from the Curran Theater, had formerly been used for private parties and political banquets. It offered a fully equipped kitchen and accommodations for approximately seventy-five diners.

"It is our intention to serve lunch with our familiar buffet table and other hot dishes available on a daily basis Monday through Friday with the possibility of also adding certain nights for dinner later," Bulletin No. 3 announced. It continued with the all-important news that, "The facilities will also provide for daily card-playing and will give us the flexibility to schedule committee meetings and other functions that may be appropriate. We will also try to have these facilities open on Saturday for lunch and card playing."

Club business proceeded as usual. The Annual Meeting, scheduled for May 19, was convened in the auditorium of Temple Emanu-El. Plans were finalized for a winery tour and bridge tournament. "We are also looking for a location for a Game Night, and are exploring the possibility of resurrecting an old Concordia-Argonaut favorite — a Club musical show. . . . ."

Bulletin No. 4, issued within a week of the prior one, was brimming with good news. First, the "fast track" approach had been given verbal approval by the City. "Reconstruction of the roof will commence on May 3."

Second, operations at Hotel David would begin on Monday, April 12, and the Club's liquor license, being transferred to the temporary facility, would be available in May.

Members had little difficulty locating the new facility. From the first day, security guard Ted Loeffler, dressed in his usual navy blue blazer with its white "C-A" emblem, stood outside the building on Geary to welcome Club members back to a clubhouse of their own. Upstairs, in the pleasant, airy facility, they were greeted by a sign reading, "Welcome Concordians to Concordia East." In the center of the room, which was divided into three sections, Clifford the Bartender, presiding in a gazebo, was ready to prepare their favorite drinks. At one end of the room stood the buffet. All the familiar delicacies were back — the lox in its usual place. Only one thing was missing from the selection: the gelatin molds. Although the men surely noticed its absence, they were too polite to mention it. "We have a quarter of the refrigerator space I had before," apologized Niels.

"I have to buy my fruits and vegetables every morning," he continued. "It is a challenge to buy just the right amount — too little and we are embarrassed if we run out, too much and I have to throw it out. It is the same with the hot entrees. We limit them to steaks, chops, hamburger, fish and omeletes. In my old kitchen we had five refrigerators and three freezers. Here we had room for two refrigerators which we bought, in addition to the built-in chest already here."

Niels, who in the interim between the fire and the opening of David's, confined his duties to a weekly shift of guard duty outside the ravaged Club, found confinement to a tiny kitchen fifteen feet long by three feet wide gave him claustrophobia. "I have no place to walk around," he said. But he happily antici-pated his new domain. By the mid-April he had had three meetings with the architects and talked excitedly about the new changes planned for the kitchen.

"We will have a special corridor from the kitchen to the dining room for the delivery of food — something sorely lacking before. I will have my own office — a glassed-in area — tiny, but where I can leave my papers on the desk, shut the door and know where they will be when I return the next morning. The cooking area will have a self-cleaning exhaust system which will automatically shut down in case of fire. The kitchen will have a new type of fire extinguisher system. It is different from the kind now used in most restaurants which, when the tempera-ture reaches 250 degrees an alarm goes off and sprays powder all over the kitchen. This new system will emit fog — a very high pressured fog. In case of fire there would be no messy dust to clean up."

●     ●     ●

Beneath the white dining cloths which covered the tables set with the silver bearing the familiar "C-A" initials (the flatwear and some of the serving silver pieces were salvaged from the fire unharmed) each table had a green felt cloth. As soon as lunch was over, Paul, the Houseman doubling as a waiter, would whisk away the linens and the room would be transformed into a card room. The dominoes and the cards would come out and the games would begin.

More or less happily ensconced in their temporary location, it appeared the membership would wait patiently for the fast-tracking to begin. But the news in the next communication, that of April 29 — a thick information packet pursuant to the Annual Membership Meeting of May 19, brought the fast-tracking to an abrupt halt. Construction on the roof and all that was to follow would not begin as scheduled on May 3. An enclosed petition, signed by thirty-five of the younger men, urged that all building stop until the membership could vote on two important changes. One called for the earthquake proofing of the building. The other called for the addition of a fourth floor.

The petitioners were headed by two insurance men, Jerold Rosenberg and Donald Williams. After dismissing the idea of "the total replacing of the Club with a new structure," as not being feasible, they emphasized the age of the original building and declared that "potential loss of life poses a serious problem for the Club which could be substantially mitigated by seismic reinforcement to the building."

The reasoning behind the addition of an extra floor was to allow for expanded athletic facilities on the second floor, the removal of the card rooms to the third floor and for enlarged dining facilities on the new fourth floor.

The Board, after studying the proposal thoroughly and rebutting it point by point, asked the membership for a vote reaffirming its original plans.

With regard to the seismic proposal, the Board's letter said, "Reduction of fire hazard was our first priority . . . . We carefully considered the possibility of seismic retrofitting . . . . The work involved many structural changes to the interior of the Club, estimated to cost between $650,000 and $1 million . . . . and would delay construction three to six months . . . . But most importantly, the seismic work is no guarantee of a 'safe structure.' Depending on the size of the quake, there are no totally safe structures of the age of our building. The roof we are installing will act as a diaphragm and will serve to stabilize the building considerably."

The major objection to a new fourth floor with its enlarged dining room was the result of parking requirements. "City Codes require a minimum of one parking space for every 200 square feet of new dining area. We could find no way to incorporate this requirement into our structure without going into a basement configuration which would have to disrupt the pool area, if not destroy it. Costs could easily exceed $2 million and we could lose the use of our facilities for more than two years."

The Annual Meeting, held at Temple Emanu-el, was well attended. Feelings were running high on both sides, but President Nathan saved the discussion about the new building for the Special Meeting he would convene immediately following his President's Report.

"Tradition has it," he told members, "that the President reports to members once a year following the April 30 fiscal year closing. Tonight we are not only following tradition, but we are also repeating history. Again members of Concordia-Argonaut are meeting away from their home at 1142 Van Ness. The last time the Club met outside of its premises was after the April, 1906, earthquake and fire."

Declaring that as a result of the January 31 fire, "the Club has experienced a truly bifurcated year," he gave his report in two parts. During the eight months prior to the fire, members used the Club for 72 private room luncheons, 119 dinner gatherings, 12 dinner dances, 11 cocktail parties and two teenage dances. Entertainment Committee chairman Mel Lichtman and his committee sponsored 11 functions, including an Income Tax Forum in December, chaired by Past-President Larry Nestel who brought together a group of tax experts all of whom were Club members. The last Gourmet Dinner in the old building was held on

October 15, planned by Jack Lipman and executed by Chef Niels. They held two separate test dinners before arriving at the final menu. Hailed as the finest one yet, the dinner was given in honor of Past-President Richard Colsky.

The untimely death of Reynold Colvin precipitated two board changes. Clifford Barbanell was appointed a director and assumed Colvin's duties as House Committee chairman. And since Colvin had also been serving as Vice President, the Board elected Ted Euphrat to serve out Colvin's second term.

Describing the Club as it began 1982, Nathan said, "The real spirit of Concordia-Argonaut was expressed in the 150 members serving on 19 committees and subcommittees." It was also expressed in the number of potential members waiting "as much as three to five years before becoming full members." In order to facilitate the process, the Board established a "Limited Privilege Membership" in September, under the leadership of the co-chairmen of the Food and Beverage Committee, Dr. Frank Passantino and Sidney Konigsberg.

During the year, eight members resigned (all prior to the fire) and not a single member had resigned since, Nathan reported. Sixteen new applicants were accepted to the waiting list, bringing the total to 71 who had been approved and were waiting for membership openings.

Before moving to the post-fire part of his report, Nathan reflected that "the fire may have been a blessing in disguise, notwithstanding the enormous inconvenience to all. We had overwhelming problems that needed to be resolved."

Uppermost among them was fire safety in the building.

He reminded members that when the Board met on January 27, 1982, just four days before the conflagration, it was well aware that the Club was unprepared for a fire crisis. Board members were considering that night a proposal from Hertzka & Knowles, architects, for a study of building integrity. The study was to include the exterior and interior of the structure, code compliance, mechanical and electrical systems and the matter of installing an automatic sprinkler system.

"We were deeply concerned over the safety of members and guests in the fire emergencies. We long recognized that one staircase could become a flue for a fire should such an event occur. Inasmuch as the elevator would not operate in a fire, we could only assume that we would be operating in a fire trap. Thank God that what occurred on January 31st did not occur during a full house. . .Thank God that no one was killed or seriously injured."

At the same time the Board was considering the Hertzka & Knowles proposal with its costs that could not be predetermined (probably around $1 million), it was also trying to make decisions on the five-year deliberations regarding the redecorating of the Club and the selection of an interior decorator at a cost of another $1 million.

While the events of Sunday morning, January 31, brought a painful resolution to those problems, Nathan stressed this point: members knew that even if the fire had not occurred, they would still have been faced with a substantial building assessment as well as much inconvenience while major repairs were being made to the building.

But once the fire had occurred, the idea of an assessment engendered resentment among many of the members who felt that the money recovered from the Club's insurance should pay for all the necessary work. When it was becoming increasingly clear that it would not, rumors began circulating that the Club had been underinsured. Nathan sought to dispell those rumors by explaining that the Club had building, personal property and contents as well as business interruption coverage, which each year was increased to offset inflation. The three policies had an aggregate value of $2,204,971. "We expect to collect the entire amount, although we recognize that there will be a battle. We believe the insurance carried will cover all the fire damage sustained."

He was right. The insurance companies did come through for the full amount. But while that amount covered the fire damage sustained, it was far from enough to put a 1909 building back together with 1983 state-of-the-arts technological improvements.

Turning his attention to the hectic months following the fire, Nathan asked members to give a standing ovation to Club Manager Douwe Drayer for his dedication to the Club under the most trying circumstances. He termed the unflappable manager "our Rock of Gibraltar" who had worked under "more pressure than most of us will ever realize in a lifetime." Also singled out for praise were the 15 members comprising the staff's core group: Carolyn Tokusato, her husband Paul Tokusato, Rudy Selva, Nino Gamez, Eddie Salguero, Cliff Nott, Tito Vallamarin, Douglas Carvell, Joe Ferrero, Niels Ploug, Romeo Rodriguez, Earnest Bettencourt, Drayer, Ysmael Jarquin, Chiu Au — an average of 17 years of employment per staff member. An employee retention program, developed by Clifford Barbanell, Donald Magnin and Jay Darwin (since deceased) kept the core group intact until the reopening of the building.

Moving on to the Special Election, Nathan said, "Reasonable men may reasonably disagree, and this is the case with those who favor a fourth floor and or doing extensive seismic work. If the Board's position prevails, installation of the roof trusses will begin tomorrow. Whatever the outcome, let us resolve to come together and complete the rebuilding harmoniously and in accordance with the wishes of the majority."

The Board's position did prevail. After all the arguments were heard, and the vote taken, the petition was turned down. Installation of the roof trusses began the next day.

Once the construction resumed, the attention of the membership centered on how much it was going to cost and how they were going to pay for it. The July, 1982 bulletin announced that an Assessment Committee was being formed under the co-chairmanship of Larry Nestel, and Sidney Konigsberg. By August, with two thirds of the architectural drawings completed, the newly-formed group met to discuss the "not to exceed" price prepared by the general contractor.

The membership received the bad news in the September bulletin. The price, including the redecoration, was a whopping $6,948,000. "But we are confident that this outside maximum will be substantially reduced to $6,000,000." To aid in this, Club member Paul Epp, a general contractor, was named Construction Manager for the project.

The Bulletin reminded members that "the new Club will have air conditioning, and it will be fully sprinkled. All the plumbing and electrical wiring will be replaced and we will be virtually occupying a new building — except that we do not have to provide off-street parking. Admittedly the cost of reconstruction is high. . . . .but to replace a facility with such ambience today would cost at least two and a half times the amount being spent."

To cover the shortfall of $4 million (the amount between the funds from insurance and the total construction costs) the Board planned to apply for a bank loan.

Some quick arithmetic indicated that each senior member's share of that loan would be approximately $8,000.

The Bulletin assured members the Assessment Committee would be studying several alternative methods of financing that bank loan. One alternative it had already discussed was to fund the payment with a "modest assessment" accompanied by a substantial increase in dues. Another was "a package involving some type of Proprietary Membership, where under some circumstances members could receive repayment of a portion of the funds paid by them."

Early in October, Jack Herrero, the general contractor, escorted members through the Club pointing out the scope of the reconstruction and how the numerous problems discovered following the fire have been resolved. The tour evidently accomplished its purpose because it was proposed that additional tours be scheduled so more members could have the opportunity to see at first hand the magnitude of the reconstruction.

Meanwhile the Assessment Committee, in an effort to get as much input from the membership as possible, mailed out a questionnaire in October to help them determine how the assessment might best be handled. The returns indicated that the majority of members preferred the entire assessment be financed by adjusting the dues structure. In answer to a question relating to increasing the number of senior members, 75% voted they were in favor of it.

In regard to the idea of proprietary memberships, 61% were attracted to such a program — even with the condition that the Assessment Committee could only consider such a program if the entire assessment were paid up front.

Along with the results of the poll, President Nathan promised the member-ship that the Assessment Committee would study the results and formulate a plan to be presented at a Special Meeting a few weeks hence. And, for the first time since the 1970's, there was a discreet pitch in the bulletin for people interested in being listed "for a future membership."

While the Assessment Committee was formulating its plan, and the social activities at the Club continued (the annual pre-Thanksgiving Party was planned for November 24, at the San Francisco Commercial Club and a Club dinner dance was scheduled for early spring at the Fairmont Hotel, among numerous other events), Howard Fine and his Decorating Committee were holding frequent meetings with Interior Designer Robert Hering, the decorator chosen for the enormous task.

Hering was no stranger to the Club. He had been called for his opinions long before the fire when the Club was deliberating on redecoration "So I knew what had been there before and what they wanted to preserve," he said. His work had been entirely confined to private residences before. He stressed this fact with the Decorating Committee when he was first contacted.

"I've never done club work before, I told them. I've never done a commercial job. They said they didn't want a commercial look. They wanted a residential look. So that's why I was selected — to create a residential look that reflects the needs of a club."

The residential look for which Hering was noted was one of traditional, low-keyed elegance, achieved largely by the use of English antiques.

"I like to use antiques in my interiors because they give a feeling of stability. I think that was particularly appropriate here because we were not just building a new building. We were reconstructing a building which had a great deal of the sense of the past."

The choice of Hering, the "residential" interior designer, was an appropriate choice for another reason. He fully understood what Club members meant when they called the Club their second home.

"I felt that it was important that the Club be masculine but not so masculine that women do not feel comfortable there. Concordia-Argonaut differs from other men's clubs in town which only appeal to men — which *want* to appeal only to men. This club certainly wants to reflect that masculine image, but, because it is also a family club, women must also feel comfortable in it. I accepted that as an additional challenge."

Explaining that interior decorating is not simply a matter of "putting in furniture", he saw his task as including the creation of "tremendous amounts of interior architecture to the building which didn't exist or was ruined by the fire."

The third floor, which was totally destroyed by the fire, was one of the places that afforded him such an opportunity. His sketches for the dining room (which were eagerly adopted by the Committee) called for replacing the former stage with a curved wall behind which would be a service area for the dining room. In his sketch, he detailed raised panelling on the wall. "I envision it as a wonderful background for a speaker or whatever." In addition, it added length to the room as well as supplying them much-needed service area.

Another architectural detail was the frieze he proposed to run around the top of the dining room walls. Decoration on the frieze, painted in the blues, golds, yellows, whites and grays of the specially woven floor covering in that room, repeated the medallion design in the rug. Adding sliding panels in the wall separating the dining room from the Sylvan room, he made it possible to use the Sylvan room as an extension of the main dining room for banquets or other large affairs.

While Hering went off to England on an antique shopping expedition, the Board of Directors and the Assessment Committee convened a Special Membership meeting to present the Assessment Committee's plan.

At that Special Meeting, held on January 12, 1983, the membership approved a recommendation that Senior members be assessed $2500 each, payable March 15, with a 10% discount if paid all at once. Lower assessments were provided for other categories. Widows, Clergy and Junior Members were exempt from any assessments.

For the balance of the reconstruction costs, members had the option of paying the entire amount at once, including the assessment ($7250 with the discount for early payment) or paying the $2500 assessment and the remaining $5500 in monthly payments added to their dues over the length of the bank loan ($250 per month for 26 months.)

Nothing had yet been formally proposed for proprietary memberships. There was great concern among the membership that there be some method of acknowledging those who had been members prior to the reopening of the building and their desire to be eligible for some sort of a refund of part of the payment on that building on termination of their membership. In the interest of harmony, an amendment to the assessment resolution was proposed and approved. The amendment provided for the formation of a committee of twenty members to formulate such a plan and to report back to the Board by March 1.

The Committee of Twenty grew to be a Committee of 31. Richard Maltzman headed one group exploring alternative financing, while Alan Axelrod and his committee concentrated on the proprietary membership concept. And the Special Membership meeting was delayed until April 27, while the Board's deliberations with both groups extended through "four lengthy meetings and included among the attendees guests, past presidents and spokesmen for the committees." The board also deferred the initial payment of the $2500 assessment from March 15 to April 15.

The Proprietary Investment Capital (PIC) program, endorsed with Board approval, was presented to the membership at a packed meeting on April 27 at Temple Emanu-El. Essentially, it provided for setting up a PIC account for each member who had joined prior to May, 1983. The PIC account consisted of half of the amount paid for the assessment, plus half of the amount paid toward the reconstruction loan. It provided that, upon termination of membership after May 15, 1985, unless the termination occurred earlier because of death, the money in the PIC account would be returned to the member or to his estate. The refund paid to him would be paid only out of funds received from new members. Two other provisions were typical of Concordia-Argonaut tradition. One was a provision for the waiver of a PIC refund simply by written communication declaring such a waiver, reminiscent of the spirit behind the turning in of Abe Shragge's debentures. The other provision was for the transferring of all or part of the PIC account's value to "a direct lineal descendent who subsequently becomes a member."

The PIC program passed overwhelmingly by 90% of the membership in attendance and by those who sent in their proxy votes.

Despite the fact that a "Phoenix Fund" was being set up under the co-chairmanship of Harold Dobbs and Claude Rosenberg, Jr. to solicit contributions from the more affluent members so that no member would resign for financial reasons, there were, of course, many resignations. On the other hand, there were members like Edgar Sinton. The ninety-four year old member, stating that, "I may only have twenty more minutes to live, but I want to pay my share." handed over his full assessment and Reconstruction Fund payment. About 100 others did the same thing.

Things were looking up all around. There was great jubilation in the Athletic Department. Forty new lockers graced the mezzanine above the pool. The pool area, with its soft grey tiled walls (to tie in with the total color scheme of the Club as designed by Robert Hering), was once more filled with the splashes of happy swimmers. The Monday night volleyball team was back working out in the gym on a floor so highly polished they could see their own reflections on it, and the weight lifters were muscle building in a newly expanded, all-mirrored surrounding.

There was elation too, at the Annual Meeting that May, 1983 when members were reminded that it was the last time they would be meeting outside their home.

"In the achievement of our goal to reach home," said President Nathan that night, "I dedicate this meeting to your Board of Directors. The Board's excellent judgment, reflecting a sense of harmony and cooperation and sensitivity to the needs of the membership, respect for each other and respect for the ideals of Concordia-Argonaut. . .assures that the Club will flourish in the years ahead." Nathan reported that the Board had convened at "twelve regular meetings, four special Board meetings, two Special Membership meetings and participated in seventy various Committee meetings — a record which, hopefully, will never need to be broken."

In addition, Nathan singled out for special thanks these members: Ted Euphrat, Ben Blum, Larry Nestel, Herb Leland, Jack Lipman, Harold Dobbs, Jack Scott, Judd Weil, Paul Epp, Alan Minkin, Eddie Goodman, Don Werby, Dick Maltzman, Justice John B. Molinari, Claude Rosenberg, Jr. and Richard Goldman.

In June, members were taken on another tour of the building. They saw the changes made on the main floor. . .the alcove to the right of the entry hall staircase where a communications center would replace the old switchboard room. . .the Club's office area closed off from public view. . .the double doors from the Main Lounge into what was formerly the Billiard Room. They saw samples of the oak paneling to be used for the wainscotting in these rooms, as well as in the Lobby and Library.

On the second floor, they saw the bar room which had been enlarged by four feet. . .a walk-in stainless steel refrigerator and freezer for extra storage space for banquets. . .the former lightwell that had now been turned into a pantry and storage area. . .they saw their cardrooms unchanged except for better lighting, wood molding and aluminum sash windows duplicating exactly the old wooden ones.

In the Main Card Room, they heard Gene O'Sullivan, the building superintendent for Herrero Brothers explain how they had been able to preserve the Roman columns and how O'Sullivan was able to recreate those too badly burned.

But it was on the third floor that they saw the most changes. To make room for the new corridor from the kitchen into the dining room, the original floor plan had been altered. Getting off the elevator, guests would still enter the dining room from the right, as before. But in the corridor to the left, there was a jog. In the foreshortened area (which allowed more space in the kitchen) was a bank of telephones. Across from that, an enlarged and fully tiled men's room. The third floor bar was back in its original place, but made somewhat smaller because of the double doors required by the fire code. Walking through the Sylvan Room into the enlarged dining room, the visitors could see how the elimination of the stage had added to the length of the room.

The kitchen was worthy of a tour all by itself. Club Manager Douwe Drayer, who had formerly worked in some of the finest dining rooms both here and in

Europe, proclaimed it the "best kitchen anywhere." The walls the members saw were all tiled in the same soft greys as the swimming pool area, forming a harmonious background for the stainless steel equipment. Everything Chef Neils had envisioned was here. From his raised, glassed-in office, he could orchestrate lyrical gastronomic symphonies, drawing on such instruments as two convection ovens, a micro-oven, plus a section of broilers, grills, deep fat fryers, warming ovens, an enormous walk-in freezer and a walk-in refrigerator. The refrigerator also had a side window into which huge trays of salads and deserts, made up ahead of time, could be kept cold and ready for serving. There were separate areas for pot cleaning, for dishwashing and for a storage pantry.

Already, in anticipation of the opening of the dining room, Earnest, the maitre d', revealed that he had been beseiged with letters and phone calls (one all the way from London) from former Club waiters wanting to have their old jobs back.

Behind the new, curved wall, past what had once been the Club's stage, members walked into the small space which was formerly a balcony overlooking the gym. It was the place where performers in the Club's shows had waited for their entrance cues; it was also a storage area for all sorts of used decorations, menus, and other relics of past affairs. This area, which had long been a fire trap was now a fire escape. It formed a solid passageway (the side exposed to the gym was now a solid wall) to the new staircase that extended from the roof to the basement.

O'Sullivan explained that the new staircase, all solid concrete and steel, was made from space occupied by the old spiral staircase that went from the gym to the roof, plus some space "borrowed" from behind the handball court and some of the locker space in the basement.

Walking up the wide staircase, members got a good look at the new roof. Behind the new redwood fenced-off sun-deck, they could see the steel braces that reinforce the entire perimeter of the roof forming part of the earthquake-proofing of the building. They could see the air conditioning equipment (now five times as large as the former air conditioning unit) which had taken a helicopter eight trips to put in place.

They left satisfied with the knowledge of where their money had been spent.

As Fall began and the shipments of furniture started to arrive, there was great excitement among the members. The building at 1142, the wooden sidewalk blockades now removed, suddenly sprang to life again. The historic edifice, which for three quarters of a century since the earthquake, sat so regally on the south-west corner of Post Street, emerged from its nearly two-year confinement looking like an elder statesman who had just returned from a magical Fountain of Youth.

When members finally entered the premises, they were transported into a tranquil world of paneled woods and light colors — oyster whites and beiges and blues and antique vases and parquet floor forming borders around rich, specially woven rugs. A familiar uniformed staff member sat before an unfamiliar com-munications console set in an alcove.

In the Library, the same pictures of past presidents smiled down at them, but from elegant new surroundings. The Library seemed to flow into the Main Lounge, with its sofas and chairs arranged in inviting conversational groupings, which in turn, blended harmoniously with the Billiard Room. Billiard Room? Only the name remained the same. Instead of the old table which dominated the room before, there now stood a glorious Georgian English mahogany bookcase cabinet against the main wall. In the base of the cabinet was a television set suitable for those times when children were in the Club or when the doors to the Main Lounge were shut.

More pleasant surprises awaited members on the second floor. The Main Card Room, its familiar columns back in place, looked twice its former size now that pale linen-colored walls replaced the old dark-green ones. The tweedy sofas, the rust mohair card chairs insured that kibbitzers as well as card players would be comfortable here.

The smaller card rooms were restored to look the same, only better. All unified in design, the rooms had vinyl covered walls that could be wiped clean, brighter overhead lighting and wood-slat Venitian blinds to adjust for daytime sunlight.

But it was the Second Floor Bar that caused the most comment, one of the two rooms in the Club Designer Hering deviated purposely from the harmonious over-all color scheme he had created. Here members were engulfed in a totally masculine atmosphere with paneled wood ceiling and wainscotting of dark wood going half way up the wall. The rest of the walls Hering papered in dark green with a small repeat pattern with bits of rust. On the floor he used a plaid rug, woven in the dark greens and rusts, and overhead he hung an antique English chandelier in polished brass. The bar was moved to the back wall and lined with a row of bar stools with side arms upholstered in rust. Behind the bar were three specially-designed glass-etched panels, sitting in polished brass boxes. The etch-ings depict building elevations — front, north and south — taken from Gus Lansburgh's architectural drawings of the 1915 building. They show all of the exterior embellishments as they existed until 1949, when a City earthquake ordinance called for the removal of all parapets and ornament that could fall off a building in the event of a strong tremor.

The unusual back-bar treatment was used, said Hering, because it reinforced the feeling that the Club had been there a long time.

The other room in which the decorator departed from his overall theme was the Ladies Lounge on the first floor. This room was as strongly feminine as the Second Floor was masculine. Widow members and wives of members were delighted. Highlight of the room was a beautiful antique pine fireplace from England. Painted in pale rust, it supplied the dominant color theme of the room. The walls, painted by a muralist, were done in "faux marble" in parchment color. The drapes, made of silk tafetta, were the same parchment color with rust and blue designs in them. The standing card table of pine matched the fireplace. Wood-framed chairs with seats upholstered in blue completed the card table corner. The rest of the furnishings inclued a velour sofa in pale rust, a glass topped coffee table with a gold metal frame and two round tables skirted in printed silk.

But the room which caused the most delight was the elegant new dining room, now capable of seating up to 280 guests . . . the beautiful oyster-white room with its coved ceilings, its brilliant chandeliers and its inviting high-backed Queen Anne chairs.

Members viewing their newly-opened Club left with the same feeling a *Chronicle* reporter must have had when he described the original Concordia Club that opened in 1891. He wrote: "The Club has now if not the absolutely ideal clubhouse, certainly something as nearly approaching it as can very well be. . .the appointments are peculiar to a place of rendezvous and entertainment used by men, but in innumerable other features, the beautiful interior nearly resembles the private interiors of the wealthy and cultivated. . ."

We began this story at the end — the end of Concordia-Argonaut's first 130 years. We end now at the beginning — the beginning of a new era in a beautifully rebuilt historic landmark. After all the months of discussions, debates, disagreements, harmony once more prevails. Concordia-Argonaut again stands ready to offer its members a "second home," one completely modernized, yet with the same aura of genteel living from a cherished past.

It is a Club which has remained faithful to its original purpose of "promoting social intercourse" and "healthful pursuits."

During the period of their "homelessness", Concordia-Argonaut members had a chance to appreciate their Club for what it is: a place where camaraderie, warmth and tradition abound. . .a place where he is proud to bring his friends because it reflects his own good taste and gracious way of life. A Club, which, if it lacks certain of the accoutrements of some of the "athletics only" clubs he joined in the interim, nevertheless provides him with something the others could never offer: a sense of belonging — a feeling of acceptance into one of the leading social clubs of San Francisco; an experience of kinship with members who in the past made their Club and their City great.

And Concordia-Argonaut members enjoy the satisfaction of knowing they've kept faith with their predecessors. They met the challenge of rebuilding, despite all its inherent problems, with the same dignity, courage and faith in the future of their Club and their City that Concordians during the 130 years before them had so nobly demonstrated.

# ABBREVIATIONS

| | |
|---|---|
| AI | American Israelite (Cincinnati) |
| BD | Board of Directors Minutes (Concordia-Argonaut) |
| C-A | Concordia-Argonaut files |
| CHSQ | California Historical Society Quarterly (San Francisco) |
| EE | Emanu-El (San Francisco) |
| PR | Presidents' Reports (Concordia-Argonaut) |
| SCP | Society of California Pioneers (San Francisco) |
| SFJCB | San Francisco Jewish Community Bulletin |
| UCB-ROHO | University of California Berkeley, Regional Oral History Office, Bancroft Library |
| WJHC | Western Jewish History Center of the Judah L. Magnes Memorial Museum, Berkeley |
| WSJHQ | Western States Jewish Historical Quarterly (Santa Monica) |

# NOTES

and the others of German birth seem to have gotten along very well together. Jewish periodicals were printed in German as well as English. 'The Hebrew (published by Philo Jacoby) even had a column called, Rifle Notes, to chronicle sharpshooting events, in German." p.42.

12  "There is one branch . . ." Daniel Levy, "Letters About the Jews of California, 1855 – 1858," WSJHQ, Jan., 1971, p.99.

12  The Frenchman's was a minority opinion. Julius Wangenheim, in *An Autobiography*, CHSQ, June, 1956, p.129, wrote, "In fact, those (Jews) of non-German background were considered rather beyond the pale. The prejudice shown by the German-Jewish group against those from Poland, called Polacks, was as marked as any I have seen on the part of Gentiles towards Jews." Wangenheim was the son of Sol Wangenheim, one of the founders of the Concordia Club.

13  August Helbing: Martin Meyer, *Western Jewry: An Account of the Jews and Judaism in California*, San Francisco, 1916 p.108.

13  Other charter members of the Verein who were Jewish were: Jacob Landsberger, Louis Jacobi, Glanz, p.43.

13  How the Jews were viewed . . . Earl Raab, "There's No City Like San Francisco," *Commentary* Magazine, Oct. 1950, p.371.

13  "Polack" ranked . . ." AI, Vol. 28, 1881, p.229: "One lady wrote that she would as soon marry a Chinaman as a Polack."

13  Jews . . . numbered about 3,000 . . . Daniel Levy, p.93.

14  The "Prentenders . . ." Norton B. Stern and William K. Kramer, *Major Role of Polish Jews in the Pioneer West*, WSJHQ, July, 1976, p.332.

14  "My younger brother . . ." Helen Newmark, "A Nineteenth Century Memoir," WSJHQ, April, 1974, p.209.

14  430 Pine Street — Langley's *San Francisco Directory*, 1870, p.660.

15  Louis Sloss was a member of Concordia: Alice Gerstle Levison, *Friendly Reminiscences*, conducted by Ruth Teiser, 1967, UCB, ROHO, p.54, courtesy JMMM.

15  at a cost of $65,000 . . . *San Francisco Blue Book, 1888 – 1889* p.175.

15  Rabbi Max Lilienthal: *AI* Cincinatti, June 23, 1876, p.6.

## CHAPTER TWO

17  Letter to the editor: *The Hebrew*, Jan. 22, 1864, p.4.

18  The society's objectives . . . *The Hebrew*, Jan. 13, 1865, p.4.

18  A member of that fourth generation, Robert Newman, died in 1981, of a brain tumor at the age of 27. A bright, talented young man who was also a fine athlete, the Club honored his memory by naming its lower volley ball court the "Robert Newman Court."

18  Henry Sinsheimer: Like the Brandensteins, the Sinsheimers also changed their name. In 1917, they became the Sintons. Henry's son, Edgar Sinton, is one of Concordia-Argonaut's "elder statesmen", and had been a member of both organizations before the merger. His late brother, Stanley Sinton, was president of the Argonaut at the time the two clubs merged. Stanley's two sons, Stanley, Jr., and Robert Sinton, are also members of Concordia-Argonaut.

19  "The Club is now . . ." *The Hebrew*, March 10, 1865, p.4.

19    "A subscription ball . . ." *The Hebrew*, Sept. 8, 1865, p.4

19    the "22-piece band . . ." *The Hebrew*, Oct. 5, 1866, p.8.

19    in Dashaway Hall . . . *Streets of S.F.*, Ed. A. Morphy, Vol.IV, page 54, Dec. 15, 1918, SCP.

20    Nearly everyone who bought a cigar . . . *ibid*, p.54.

20    they decorated two floors . . . *The Social Manual of S.F.*, 1884. p.202. Listed as Club officers in 1884 were H. Wangenheim, President; J. M. Rothschild, Vice President; J. Thalheimer, Recording Secretary: A. W. Scholle, Financial Secretary, and J. Sherman, Treasurer.

20    ". . . a social Philistine." Glanz, p.233.

20    "a distinctly German-American atmosphere," Edward Morphy, Feb. 2, 1919

21    "temples of luxury . . ." *Lights and Shades in San Francisco*, B. E. Lloyd, San Francisco, 1876, p.483.

21    The Union Club . . . *San Francisco Morning Call*, Jan. 16, 1887, p.1

22    A livelier club . . . *Olympic Club of S.F., 1860 – 1960 Centennial Yearbook*, S.F., 1960, pp.18 – 19.

22    Their social life was remarkably insulated: Glanz, p.135, talks about "the almost complete exclusion of the Jews from social intercourse with the Gentiles." Choyinski feels it was their own fault. He writes: "Our people as a class have not yet learned to assimilate, to visit the houses of our Christian neighbors and feel at home . . . There are magnates — e.g. monied moguls — among Jews but they rarely invite Christians to their parties, unless wedding parties, and only when they are customers. The consequence is that the Christians ignore our wealthy Jews." *AI*, Vol. 28, 1881, p.282.

23    "An assembly . . ." *The Hebrew*, June 9, 1864, p.4.

23    There were some Jews . . . Frederick Castle: "Our Pioneer Heritage." Norton B. Stern, SFJCB, Jan. 30, 1981, p.7.
Signmund Steinhart: Martin Meyer, p.152.
Philip Lilienthal: *ibid*, p.125.

23    The Standard Club: *AI*, Cincinnati, March 5, 1875, p.6.

23    "I seldom went to Concordia . . ." Alice Gerstle Levison, p.54.

23    "They succeeded." *S.F. Examiner*, Oct. 2, 1881, p.2.

## CHAPTER THREE

25    "leased from Mrs. Mann . . ." *The Jewish Progress*, S.F. April 29, 1887, p.4.

25    "Sixteen members signed the papers . . ." *C-A*

25    "$300,000 to erect the building . . ." *AI* Dec. 14, 1888, p.9.

26    "gambling and banquet hall . . ." *ibid*.

27    "personally directing the erection . . ." *S.F. Chron.*, Oct. 2, 1891, p.12.

28    "On every hand . . . " *S.F. Exam.*, Oct. 2, 1891, p.10.

## CHAPTER FOUR

32    "corner of Post and Franklin . . . " The location of the S.F. Ladies' Protection and Relief Society. The Society, empowered by a legislative act in 1858, apprenticed orphan

children to work in local businesses or in family homes as domestic servants. *California Historical Courier*, published by the CHS, S.F., Vol. 33, No. 1, Feb. 1891, p.2.

32     . . . "was awarded for second place!" The medal was donated to the Club on Feb. 19, 1981, by Mr. and Mrs. Manny Sidorsky, owners of a Pleasant Hill, Ca. pawn shop, after the medal turned up there.

32     "Under the softened glow . . ." EE, Dec. 2, 1896, p.10.

33     on the Club's dance floor. Interview with Edgar Sinton.

33     "California Midwinter International Exposition . . ." *Official History of the Midwinter International Exposition, Jan. to July, 1894*, S.F., Crocker, 1894; also, Millie Robbins, "The City's Midwinter Jewel," *S.F. Chron.*, Nov. 15, 1972, p.20.

34     "Inaugural Ball . . ." EE, S.F., Nov. 18, 1898, p.6.

34     "duplicate gowns . . ." interviews with Edwin Newman and Mrs. S. Walter Newman.

34     "Franklin and Post . . ." interview with Edwin Newman.

34     "The New Year's Eve Ball . . ." *The Wave*, S.F., Jan. 9, 1897, p.1.

35     "thirty-five of the club members . . ." EE, Dec. 3, 1897, p.16.

35     "a popular composer of the day . . ." *Morning Call*, S.F., Feb. 24, 1897, p.50.

35     "a charming young woman . . ." *The Wave*, S.F., Jan. 9, 1897, p.1.

## CHAPTER FIVE

37     "The dance was preceeded . . ." *The Wave*, Jan. 9, 1897, p.1.

38     "little" parties . . . Alice Gerstle Levison, p.53.

38     intermarriages: "If you don't commit incest you've made a bad marriage." *Fortunes and Failures*, Peter Decker, Cambridge, 1978, p.252.

38     "theatrical things . . ." Alice G. Levison, p.15.

38     Libretto by Hugo Waldeck . . . program from CHS, Concordia File.

38     "management of the entertainment . . ." EE, March 6, 1896, p.6.

39     "or fraction thereof . . ." *S.F. Verein By-Laws*, 1902, C-A.

39     "at the S.F. Verein . . ." EE, May 1, 1896, p.14.

39     "prettiest of spring blossoms . . ." *ibid*, March 11, 1898, p.17.

39     "silk-shaded candelabra . . ." *ibid*.

39     . . . "interfere with home life?" *Morning Call*, S.F., Dec. 25, 1892, p.8.

40     "papers of re-incorporation . . ." *S.F. Verein By-Laws*, 1902, C-A.

40     "The Argonaut Club celebrated . . ." *S.F. Chron.*, Oct. 30, 1904.

41     Pres. McKinley's visit: *S.F. Chron.*, May 11 to May 17, 1901, p.1 each day.

41     Newman's 25th anniversary: S.F. news clip in possession of Walter Newman, undated.

42     "magnificent Bal Masque . . ." *S.F. Chron.*, Nov. 23, 1902, p.3.

## CHAPTER SIX

43     "From the Ferry to Van Ness . . ." EE, May 4, 1906, p.1.

44     . . . was strained to its limits. *S.F. Municipal Reports for the Fiscal Year 1905 – 06, Ending June 30, 1907*, published by the S.F. Board of Supervisors, 1908, p.703.

44  "By Thursday afternoon . . ." *The S.F. Disaster and the Mt. Vesuvius Horror,* Charles Banks and Oppie Read, Philadelphia, 1906, p.46.

44  . . . both awesome and appalling. *ibid,* p.47.

45  "to utter strangers . . ." Paul Sinsheimer, "The S.F. Catastrophe of 1906," WSJHQ, April, 1975, p.236.

46  "we had here . . ." Edgar Kiefer, from a letter in the collection of Dan E. Stone.

46  "resumption of their work . . ." EE, May 4, 1906, p.1.

46  J. B. Levison . . . J. B. Levison, *Memories of My Family,* S.F., 1933, p.122.

46  "Totally destroyed . . ." Edward Livingston, Sr., *A Personal History of the S.F. Earthquake and Fire in 1906,* S.F., 1941, p.23, Dan Stone Collection.

46  McIntosh letter: Livingston, p.43.

47  Jacob Stern letter: May 1, 1906, from the correspondence with Toby Rosenthal, collected by Rosenthal's grandson, John Rodes.

48  "Committee of Fifty . . ." *S.F. Muni Reports,* p.756.

48  "Committee on Feeding the Hungry . . ." *ibid,* p.760.

48  "Committee of Forty . . ." *ibid,* p.768.

49  "make the future thine . . ." *ibid,* p.798.

49  Within a month of the catastrophe . . . EE, May 18, 1906, p.3.

49  Members of both clubs . . . *Architects of Reform,* Fred Rosenbaum, Berkeley, 1980, p.57.

49  Concordians promptly rented . . . address listed in *SF-Oakland Directory,* 1907, p.107. Property at that address belonged to Mary L. Treanor, according to *SF Block Book,* Vol. I, Western Edition, 1909, p.604.

49  The Argonauts' used . . . *SF-Oakland Directory,* 1907, p.22. Same address as the residence of Max Brandenstein, *SF Directory* 1905, p.330.


## CHAPTER SEVEN

53  stores demolished in the catastrophe. A notable exception was Livingston Bros. That firm chose, instead, a site on the southwest corner of Fillmore and Geary because, according to Edward Livingston, "from Franklin to the Western Addition, all the homes were intact, and Fillmore Street was in the center of the remaining population."

54  "will not be determined . . ." *SF Morning Call,* Dec. 7, 1908., p.3.

55  of the Orpheum circuit. "G. Albert Lansburgh, S.F.'s Jewish Architect from Panama." Norton B. Stern and William M. Kramer, WSJHQ, April, 1981, pp.210–216.

54  "A very brilliant spectacle . . ." EE, Dec. 17, 1909, p.6.

54  "informal dinners . . ." *ibid,* Oct. 21, 1910, p.7.

54  "that I would be missing . . ." interview with Mrs. Justin Hofman.

55  Julius Kahn of San Francisco . . . EE, March 17, 1911, p.8.

55  Julius Kahn: He became a member in 1916. Bio information *Kahn,* Alan Boxerman, CHSQ, Winter, 1976–77, pp.340–351.

56  "before the House of Representatives." *SF Morning Call,* Feb 2, 1911.

56    "here in S.F.?" *The Story of the Exposition*, Frank Morton Todd, Putnam, New York, 1921, Vol. I, p.35.

56    "alarming national weakness." *ibid*, p.13.

56    "demand that the Canal be dug." *ibid*, p.14.

57    "in perpetuity to another," *ibid*, p. 30.

57    Ways and Means Committee, *ibid*, p.57.

57    individuals and firms . . . *ibid*, p.67.

57    PPIE officers and members . . . *ibid*, p.63.

57    Concordian M. Gunst . . . picture, *SF Chron.* May 2, 1910, p.1

57    totaled $1900! Todd, p.93.

58    "then to the finishers." *ibid*, Vol. IV, p.138.

58    the San Francisco furrier. *ibid*, p.152.

## CHAPTER EIGHT

62    "the facilities were adequate . . ." Harry Hilp, *Reminisces of a Past President* (speech) Nov. 5, 1973, C-A

63    "revival of the old regime." *SF Examiner*, April 9, 1916, p.60.

64    "The House of Concord." Martin Meyer, p.56.

## CHAPTER NINE

65    "accomodate its members." EE, Jan. 15, 1909, p.7.

65    "a very brilliant spectacle." *ibid*, Dec. 17, 1909, p.7.

65    "on Nob Hill." *Coffee, Martinis & San Francisco*, Ruth Bransten McDougall, Presidio PRESS, San Rafael, 1978, pp.103–4.

66    both written by Manny. *SF Examiner*, Feb. 21, 1916, p.5.

66    "explained in Police court," *ibid*, Feb. 24, 1916, p.10.

67    "for a single fellow . . ." McKinley Bissinger interview.

67    "with their father . . ." Roy Van Vliet interview.

67    "Beresford Country Club . . ." Edgar Gould interview.

68    range of international cuisine. From menu in collection of Ruth Bransten McDougall.

68    "about the 'Big Game.' " Robert Goldman interview.

68    "nobody in that room . . ." Robert Levison interview.

69    "bottle in his room . . ." Lloyd Liebes interview.

## CHAPTER TEN

71    Bio material on Mr. Falk: *SF Chron-Examiner*, April 15, 1971, p.55.

71    "Uncle Fred Patek . . ." *Responsibilities & Rewards of Involvement*, conducted by Eleanor Glaser and Louis Weintraub, ROHO, the Bancroft Library, UCB, courtesy JMMM, p.24.

72    the Board approved . . . BD minutes, May 3, 1926.

72    A year later . . . PR, May 3, 1927

73    Harry Hilp bio: *Concordian*, May, 1977.

74    The dining room had troubled . . . Harry Hilp Reminisces.

74    The time was ripe . . . PR, May 9, 1930.

74    By Jan. of 1931 . . . from letter to "All Members", Jan. 14, 1931.

79    In the spring . . . *Mission to Metropolis*, Oscar Lewis, Howell-North, San Diego, p.225.

80    In a humorous speech . . . from the Adrien Falk file, SF Room, SF Public Library.

80    A report prepared by Sylvan Lisberger . . . BD June 17, 1935.

81    A saving from $85 to $100 . . . BD July 17, 1935.

81    "I took it up with . . ." Harry Hilp Reminisces.

81    The financial picture . . . Bert Rabinowitz interview.

83    For four days . . . *Official Program, SF-Oakland Bay Bridge Celebration* Nov. 11 – 15, author's collection.

84    Olympic Salt Water Co: *SF Chron*, This World Section, Jan. 30, 1955.

84    "Synthetic Salt System" . . . BD, July 29, 1936.

84    Three months later . . . BD Oct. 23, 1936.

86    'The year 1939 . . ." *Treasure Island, The Magic City*, S.F. 1941, Jack James and Earl Weller, p.56.


## CHAPTER ELEVEN

87    Marcel joined the Club . . . Glaser & Weintraub, p.33.

87    "Mervin Cowen was captain . . ." *ibid*, p.30.

88    Bert Rabinowitz on Marcel Hirsch: Rabinowitz interview.

88    Dan E. Stone on Marcel Hirsch: Stone interview.

89    Letter to Election Board: Dec. 10, 1948, C-A.

90    "Marcel was very conservative . . ." Jack Lipman interview.

90    The rules were not always convenient . . . Glaser, Weintraub, pp.13 – 14.

91    his leadership in the Jewish community . . . SFJB, March 9, 1980, p.1.


## CHAPTER TWELVE

93    "I merged the Concordia . . ." Glaser, Weintraub, pp.68 – 69.

93    "The reason . . ." Lucille Bush (Mrs. Philip) interview.

93    "The members considered themselves . . ." McDougall, p.103.

93    "The depression helped . . ." Robert Goldman interview.

94    "We kids coming out of college . . ." Edward Bransten interview.

94    "I voted against it . . ." Lloyd Liebes interview.

95    "They brought with them . . ." Steve Blumenthal interview.

96    "When I was discharged . . ." Sam Camhi interview.

## CHAPTER THIRTEEN

## CHAPTER FOURTEEN

130    In his annual report . . . PR, April 30, 1974, CA.

131    "I was concerned with . . ." Nestel interview.

132    Co-Chairman of the new Food and Beverage Committee . . . Adrian Scharlach interview.

133    "Wednesday night is Club night . . ." Nestel interview.

134    "Things began to change . . ." Colsky interview.

135    By 1979 . . . PR, April, 1979, C-A.

135    When Nestel left office . . . PR, April 1977, C-A.

135    In 1977 . . . PR, April, 1978, C-A.

135    "Not only was there . . ." Herbert Leland interview.

136    "Since I was going to the Club . . ." Stanley Diamond interview.

137    At the same time . . . Adrian Scharlach interview.

138    Pres. Leland appointed . . . Herbert Leland interview.

139    "The thing that made . . ." Richard Colsky interview.

139    "Where formerly . . ." ibid.

139    "The proposition that . . ." Reynold Colvin interview.

## CHAPTER EIGHTEEN

141    "We wanted to provoke . . ." John Rothmann interview.

141    "If the attitude changed . . ." Sanford Treguboff interview.

142    "Hiss spoke mostly about . . ." Rothmann interview.

143    "We intended . . ." ibid.

## CHAPTER NINETEEN

145    "By official action . . ." SF Chron, Oct. 1, 1920, p.7.

145    "It seems that . . ." BD Oct. 23, 1936, C-A.

145    The plight of widows: The first group of widows to enjoy dining room privileges were Dora (Mrs. Leon) Judah; Hazel (Mrs. William) Gump, and Hazel (Mrs. Samuel) Gordon. BD. Dec. 27, 1952.

146    "one small step for personkind . . ." Letter from Diane (Mrs. Bertram) Feinstein to Pres. Jack Lipman and Board, May 13, 1974, C-A.

146    "an ideal location . . ." ibid.

146    On the day in question . . . Judge Dorothy von Beroldingen interview.

146    "My offices at the time . . ." Alexander Anolik interview.

147    Two weeks prior . . . LeRoy Hersh interview.

147    "If women are to be allowed . . ." Dan E. Stone interview.

148    Guests in the Sylvan Room: When the room was first opened to female guests of members, the first guest was Judge Isabella Grant, the guest of Lawrence Livingston, whose law partner she once had been. "Lawrence was in a wheel chair by then, but he insisted on coming to the Club and bringing me to lunch so the distinction of being the first woman guest would be mine. It was a lovely gesture and I was deeply touched."

## CHAPTER TWENTY-TWO

## CHAPTER TWENTY-THREE

## CHAPTER TWENTY-FOUR

196    "I was working daytime . . ." Arnold Robleto interview.

197    "That was also the year . . ." Dr. Stanley Reich interview.

197    "I work Wednesday . . ." Chef Ploug interview.

197    "We decided we had . . ." W. Newman interview.

198    "There is a fine atmosphere . . ." Tony Pels interview.

198    Douwe Drayer bio: *Concordian*, and Drayer interview.

199    Paul Tokusato . . . *Concordian*, Dec. 1974.

199    "They had a few other . . ." Carolyn Tokusato interview.

199    Clifford Nott . . . *Concordian*, April, 1975.

200    Ellys (Bill) Layton . . . *ibid.*.

200    Nino Gamez and Rudy Selva . . . *Concordian*, Dec. 1974.

200    L. Livingston letter: BD, Dec. 7, 1946.

200    Werner Hartman letter: BD, Dec. 9, 1946.

201    "That policy . . ." Steve Blumental interview.

201    "very worthwhile present . . ." Larry Nestel interview.

## CHAPTER TWENTY-FIVE

203    "to me the Club . . ." Dan E. Stone interview.

204    "The stance I have taken . . ." Baum interview.

204    "We maintain a tradition . . ." Nestel interview.

204    91 attorneys . . . Tony Pels in the *Concordian*, Feb., 1978.

204    "Don't make the mistake . . ." Colvin interview.

205    Koshland bio: the *Concordian*, Dec. 1977.

205    Robert Koshland bio: the *Concordian*, Dec. 1977.

205    Walter Haas bio: the *Concordian*, Sept. 1977.

205    Harold Zellerbach bio: the *Concordian*, May 1978.

206    Sam Ladar bio: Ladar interview.

206    Rabbi Fine letter: BD, Sept. 7, 1948.

207    "People tend to conform . . ." Nestel interview.

207    Pearlstein bio: Carl Pearlstein interview.

208    "When I took over . . ." A. Simon interview.

208    "I think it would . . ." BD, Dec. 1, 1948.

209    ". . . rearrange the library." BD letter, Frances Paap, May 24, '49.

209    Wednesday Group: *Concordian*, April, '78.

209    Cabinet Table: *Concordian*, Sept. '76.

209    "As the only Jewish Club . . ." W. Newman interview.

210    "The Club was a good introduction . . ." M. Mendelson interview.

210    "The surprise . . ." R. Colsky interview.

210    The new president . . . M. Nathan interview.

## EPILOGUE

213    "We have three main objectives . . ." Bulletin #1, Feb. 9, 1982.

213    "We sat there . . ." Colsky interview.

214    This latter committee . . . Newman interview.

214    "The fire made the membership . . ." Colsky interview.

214    He listed the Clubs . . . On the day of the fire, Lake Merced immediately offered their facilities, one of the first calls Pres. Nathan received. The Press Club's invitation came the next Monday morning, and the Metropolitan Club agreed to let the Board hold its first emergency meeting there. Its facilities were later not available. The full list was given in Bulletin #2 in early March. The clubs included: the Olympic Club, Press Club, The Family, Lake Merced Golf & Country Club, San Francisco Commercial Club, Athenian-Nile (Oakland), Jewish Community Center, Central YMCA, San Francisco Bay Club and the Telegraph Hill Club.

215    "Even though these clubs . . ." Colsky interview.

216    By the first of April, the clean-up work . . . That it took two full months to remove the damaged portions of the building and debris is an indication of just how great the damage was. The rebuilding literally had to begin from the studs.

216    Meanwhile, the Temporary Site Location . . . had found what seemed to be an ideal place: In their search for a site, Colsky and Victor Marcus had several other offers, as reported by Pres. Nathan in his 1982 Annual Report: "a place for $30,000 per month, with a one-year minimum; a $15,000 per month with a one-year minimum and $500 a night with a one-year minimum and a tie-in whereby we would be obligated to use their Chef, waiters and help."

David Apfelbaum, owner of David's, unlike the others, did not take advantage of the Club. Reported Nathan: "The Club has been treated royally by David Apfelbaum, who is not a member of Concordia-Argonaut, but an individual who cares and loves to help others within his power. He was a victim of the Holocaust and survived a three-day hanging by his arms tied behind his back. He is a person who really recognizes emergencies. David indicated to me privately that he would have given us the premises rent free if he could have afforded to do so."

There were other members and non-members who came through in the emergency, and Nathan singled them out: "Eddie Goodman has provided us with over 4,000 square feet to store our salvaged property at no cost; the space where we had previously stored it (immediately after the fire) quoted us a rate of $4,000 a month. Tom Lembo of Adeleine's Bakery, our neighbor and member, provided us with offices immediately after the fire, and Don Werby, an individual on the waiting list, has allowed us to occupy two offices rent free."

217    "We have one-fourth the refrigerator space . . ." Chef Ploug interview.

220    "Limited Privilege Memberships . . ." Because a full membership entitled a member the use of all facilities of the Club, and since the shortage of lockers prevented the full use of the Athletic Department, it was agreed that those on the waiting list who wanted to be able to use the dining facilities should be able to enjoy an interim membership at a reduced price. Later, in the debate over assessment fees, the question came up regarding those long time members whose use of the Club facilities is limited only to the social aspects. Could they be eligible to become limited members at lesser assessments and dues? The answer was no, that the Club does not have social memberships per se. "It is

recognized that the Club must be supported in its entirety and members may avail themselves of all facilities at their own election," was the response.

221     He was right . . . The insurance companies at first refused to pay the "business interruption" damages on the basis that the Club would not suffer an operating loss. The Club refuted that by explaining that dues had been suspended and that the monthly charges of $50 were contributions toward a Building Reserve Fund. Accordingly, the Club argued, it had no operating income from dues as of Feb. 1, 1982. The insurance company reluctantly agreed that the Club had a right to suspend dues, make charges for a Building Fund, pay its employees and continue to operate as it had chosen to do.

223     Hering was no stranger to the job . . . Interview with Robert Hering. Working closely with the interior designer were two Club members, Howard Fine and Robert Appleton, both architects.

# CONCORDIA PRESIDENTS

| | | | |
|---|---|---|---|
| M. Esberg | 1864 – 1865 | H. L. Mayer | 1918 – 1920 |
| I. Steinhart | 1865 – 1868 | Jesse Newbauer | 1920 – 1921 |
| Morris Walder | 1868 – 1869 | Fred Patek | 1921 – 1924 |
| Joseph Naphtaly | 1869 – 1871 | Herman Waldek | 1924 – 1925 |
| Isadore Wormser | 1871 – 1873 | Adrien J. Falk | 1925 – 1928 |
| Henry Goodkind | 1873 – 1874 | Harry Hilp | 1928 – 1931 |
| Abraham Bloch | 1874 – 1877 | Newton W. Stern | 1931 – 1933 |
| C. L. Ackerman (Charles) | 1877 – 1879 | Sylvan Wurkein | 1933 – 1934 |
| Martin Heller | 1879 – 1882 | John J. Goldberg | 1934 – 1935 |
| E. Emanuel | 1882 – 1883 | Dr. Franklin I. Harris | 1935 – 1938 |
| P. Hagan | 1883 – 1884 | Marcel Hirsch | 1938 – 1948 |
| Henry Wangenheim | 1884 – 1889 | Milton D. Sapiro | 1948 – 1951 |
| J. M. Rothchild | 1889 – 1892 | Sylvan J. Lisberger | 1951 – 1953 |
| C. L. Ackerman (Charles) | 1892 – 1894 | Daniel Stone | 1953 |
| Judah Newman | 1894 – 1896 | Sylvan J. Lisberger | 1953 – 1954 |
| Leon Guggenheim | 1896 – 1897 | A. J. Shragge | 1954 – 1960 |
| Sam Sachs | 1897 – 1898 | Roger H. Coffee | 1960 – 1963 |
| Charles Hirsch | 1898 – 1899 | Walter S. Newman | 1963 – 1965 |
| Leopold Michaels | 1899 – 1900 | Harold S. Dobbs | 1965 – 1966 |
| Charles Hirsch | 1900 – 1901 | Edward F. Euphrat | 1966 |
| Simon Newman | 1901 – 1904 | Stanley B. Reich M. D. | 1966 – 1968 |
| Fred Patek | 1904 – 1905 | Benjamin J. Baum | 1968 – 1971 |
| Simon Newman | 1905 – 1907 | Donald Magnin | 1971 – 1973 |
| M. Nickelsburg | 1907 – 1908 | Jack M. Lipman | 1973 – 1975 |
| Herbert Rothchild | 1908 – 1912 | Lawrence A. Nestel | 1975 – 1977 |
| Louis A. Schwabacher | 1912 – 1917 | Richard Colsky | 1977 – 1981 |
| Charles Hirsch | 1917 – 1918 | Marvin Nathan | 1981 – |

# VEREIN–ARGONAUT PRESIDENTS

| | | | | |
|---|---|---|---|---|
| T. U. Basse | 1861* | | Simon Scheeline | 1897 – 1898 |
| A. Walper | 1861 – 1862 | | I. Strassburger | 1898 – 1900 |
| Edward Kruse | 1862 – 1863 | | Gustav Wormser | 1900 – 1901 |
| Dr. J. Regensburger | 1865 – 1868 | | L. W. Saalsburg | 1901 – 1902 |
| Dr. J. N. Eckel | 1868 – 1869 | | J. Regensburger | 1902 – 1906 |
| L. Dormitzer | 1869 – 1872 | | S. C. Scheeline | 1906 – 1907 |
| August Helbing | 1872 – 1876 | | E. Pollitz | 1907 – 1908 |
| G. Muecke | 1876 – 1877 | | Alfred Esberg | 1908 – 1910 |
| Dr. D. Cohen | 1877 – 1878 | | Ben Hecht | 1910 – 1911 |
| H. Bakzar | 1878 – 1879 | | Louis Greenebaum | 1911 – 1914 |
| Dr. J. M. Eckel | 1879 – 1881 | | Maurice Liebman | 1914 – 1917 |
| F. Cramer | 1881 – 1882 | | Dr. Charles G. Levison | 1917 – 1918 |
| Otto Mueser | 1883 – 1884 | | Irwin J. Wiel | 1918 – 1919 |
| I. Gutte | 1884 – 1885 | | B. E. Alanson | 1919 – 1921 |
| John Eckel | 1885 – 1886 | | Albert L. Ehrman | 1921 – 1922 |
| John Altschul | 1886 – 1887 | | Manfred Bransten | 1922 – 1924 |
| I. Gutte | 1887 – 1890 | | Dr. Charles G. Levison | 1924 – 1927 |
| Louis Hirsch | 1890 – 1892 | | Sylvan J. Lisberger | 1927 – 1928 |
| Hugo Rothschild | 1892 – 1894 | | Philip L. Bush | 1928 – 1930 |
| M. H. Hecht | 1894 – 1895 | | Edward H. Heller | 1930 – 1934 |
| M. Ehrman | 1895 – 1896 | | Philip L. Bush | 1934 – 1936 |
| Max Ordenstein | 1896 – 1897 | | William Bransten | 1936 – 1937 |
| | | | Stanley Sinton | 1937 – 1939 |

*No listings were available before that time.

# WORLD WAR I

## CONCORDIANS IN SERVICE

Abrahm, Dr. Henry
Apfel, Herman
Bauer, A. E.
Bauer, Herb
Beermann, W. J.
Bissinger, Fred
Bloch, H. W.
Blum, Chas.
Blumenthal, A. J.
Cowen, M. S.
Dinkelspiel, M. L.
Edlin, Max H.
Epstein, Arthur P.
Fabian, Lawrence
Fisher, Dr. Al
Fox, Harry
Fuld, Edwin B.

Goldberg, Czerny
Goldberg, Walter
Haas, Walter A.
Heller, Walter S.
Hilp, W. J.
Hirschman, Sid J.
Jellineck, Dr. Edward
Juda, Herbert
Katten, Simon, Jr.
Levison, Dr. C. G.
Liebes, Arnold
Loeb, Sidney S.
Lowenberg, Charles
Manheim, Henry J.
May, Louis F.
Metzger, Sam S.
Meyer, Joseph

Meyers, Lloyd
Newman, Lester D.
Rosenshine, Monroe
Ross, H. S.
Rothmann, Dr. Hans
Silverman, Harold
Simon, Gerald
Steinberger, Robert
Stern, Alvin J.
Stone, Daniel
Stone, Richard I.
Sultan, Walter D.
Unna, Walter J.
Weissbein, Julian H.
Wertheimer, Lloyd G.
Wolf, Lester F.
Wolfsohn, Dr. J. M.

## ARGONAUTS IN SERVICE

Ackerman, Robert
Beerman, Dr. Wilfred
Brandenstein, Fred
Epstein, Arthur
Frankenheimer, Dr. J. B.
Gerstle, Mark
Haas, Walter A.
Heller, Walter

Heyneman, Walter
Hirschman, Sidney
Jacobi, A. L.
Kaufman, Joel
Koshland, Robert J.*
Levison, Dr. Charles
Lilienthal, John L.
Mack, Harold L.

Roos, Robert A.
Sinton, Edgar*
Steinburger, Arthur
Wolfsohn, Dr. J. M.

*Currently members of
Concordia-Argonaut

# WORLD WAR II

## CONCORDIA-ARGONAUTS IN SERVICE

Barbanell, Clifford
Berger, Stanley L.
Bibbero, Donald
Bier, John A., D.D.S.
Bransten, Edward Jr.
Brown, A. Lincoln, M. D.
Camhi, Sam
Corvin, William
Diamond, Stanley
Dinkelspiel, John W.
Dugoni, Arthur A.
Ehrlich, Philip, Jr.
Erlanger, Stuart
Ettelson, George W.
Euphrat, Edward F.
Feder, Jack M., Jr.
Fleishman, Ernest†
Foorman, Carl, Jr.
Friedman, Rudolph E.
Geller, Daniel M.
Gold, Rubin L., M. D.
Golden, Jack†
Golden, John R.
Goldman, Richard
Goldman, Robert L.
Green, William
Guggenhime, Richard

Halbert, Randolph W.
Hamerslag, Jay P., Jr.
Harband, Myron J.
Hayman, Alvin, Jr.
Heller, Robert D.
Jacobs, Robert
Kaufman, Oscar D.
Kerson, Mayo
Knox, Maurice, Jr.
Knox, Robert L.
Koshland, Robert J.**
Lipman, Jack M.
Mack, Edward S., D.D.S.
Magnin, Donald
Marks, Alan
Meier, Allen E., Jr.
Meier, John†
Meyerhoff, Richard
Miller, Stephen
Newman, Walter S.
Obermeyer, Walter
Oser, Richard L.
Pearl, Milton, M. D.
Peiser, William S.
Polse, Max L., M. D.
Raffin, Bennett L.
Reiner, Bernard

Ritchie, John
Rosenbloom, Harold, M. D.
Rothmann, Dr. Hans **
Rude, Morton
Scharlach, Adrian E.
Scheeline, Edwin S. Jor
Seton, Theodore R.
Shragge, Harmon
Sinton, Edgar**
Steiner, Philip
Stone, Edgar N.
Sussman, Richard
Tonkin, Bertram M.
Weingarten, Max
Zelinsky, Edward
Zellerbach, William
Zeigler, Sam, Jr.
Zimmerman, Arthur B.

† Killed in action
**Served in World War I
and II

We apologize for any others
whose names were inadver-
tently left out.

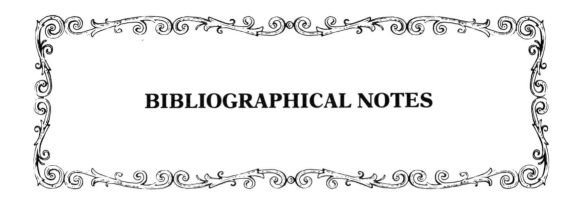

# BIBLIOGRAPHICAL NOTES

AS STATED PREVIOUSLY, Club records were tantilizingly incomplete before 1948. A one-page summary for the year 1911 was compiled by Charles Hirsh; there were Board Minute records from 1930 to 1936 in the Club's storage closets. Nothing at all except the papers of incorporation remain from the merger of the two clubs in 1939. Presidents' Reports on file exist for the years 1925, 1928, 1948, 1954 and 1955. Starting with the year 1959, there is a complete list until the present. These, and assorted memorabilia such as programs, menus and an occasional copy of Concordia or Argonaut by-laws and rosters are all the sources of Club history available. No one thought to preserve any Argonaut records — or if they did, I was unable to unearth them.

Because the two clubs and their prominent members were always good material for newspaper stories, especially in the Anglo-Jewish press, these newspapers served as a prime source of information. Especially helpful were: *The Emanu-El* (San Francisco) 1895 to 1930, which can be found at the WJHC; the *American Israelite* (Cincinnati); *The Hebrew* (San Francisco); *The Progress* (San Francisco); *The Observer* (San Francisco). While some editions of the *American Israelite* can be found at U.C. Berkeley, the most complete collection is available at Hebrew Union College — Jewish Institute of Religion, Los Angeles.

The general community newspapers on which I relied for the early years of the two Clubs and their activities were: *The San Francisco Chronicle, The San Francisco Examiner,* the *San Francisco Morning Call* and *The Evening Bulletin.* These papers can be found at the main branch of the San Francisco Public Library. The California State Library in Sacramento maintains a subject catalogue on the information in all those papers.

References to the two Clubs, their addresses and their members appear in *Langley's City Directories* from 1858 to 1896, and in *Crocker-Langley City Directories* from 1896 to 1916, which can be found at the California Historical Society's library. Two additional periodicals that were useful were *The San Francisco Blue Book,* 1888–1922, and early copies of *The Social Register,* which began publication in 1886. They can be found in the San Francisco Room of the San Francisco Main Public Library.

Another very useful source of Club information was the newsy, entertaining Club Bulletins, *The Concordian*, published in the mid-seventies under the editorship first of Richard Colsky and later, Stanley Diamond.

Much valuable background information about Club members and the role the Club played in family lives was also available in the many oral histories co-published by the Regional and Oral History Office of the Bancroft Library and the Judah L. Magnes Memorial Museum (and available at both these Berkeley institutions). Among them are the oral histories of: Alice Gerstle Levison, *Family Reminiscences* (Berkeley, 1967); Edgar Sinton, *Jewish and Community Service in San Francisco: A Family Tradition* (Berkeley, 1978); Marcel Hirsch, *Responsibilities & Rewards of Involvement* (Berkeley, 1980); Walter Haas, Sr., *Civic, Philanthropic and Business Leadership* (Berkeley, 1975); Elise Stern Haas, *The Appreciation of Quality* (Berkeley, 1972); Mortimer and Janet Choynski Fleishhacker, *Family, Business and the San Francisco Community* (Berkeley, 1975); Marshall H. Kuhn, *Catalyst and Teacher; San Francisco Jewish and Communal Leader* (San Francisco, 1934–1978), and Daniel E. Koshland, Sr., *The Principal of Sharing* (Berkeley, 1971).

Several warm personal memoirs must be given special mention: two books by Frances Bransten Rothmann, *The Haas Sisters of Franklin Street: A Look Back with Love* (Berkeley, 1979), and *My Father, Edward Bransten, His Life and Letters* (Berkeley, 1982); Ruth McDougall, *Coffee, Martinis and San Francisco* (San Rafael, 1978); J. B. Levison, *Memories for my Family* (San Francisco, 1933); and Edward Livingston Sr.'s *A Personal History of the San Francisco Earthquake and Fire in 1906* (San Francisco, 1941).

Finally, I made much use of the countless articles in the Western States Jewish Historical Quarterly which have documented in precise detail the many historical figures in San Francisco who were members of both the Concordia Club and the S.F. Verein. (A subject index for the WSJHQ from its first issue in October, 1968 until 1982 is available.)

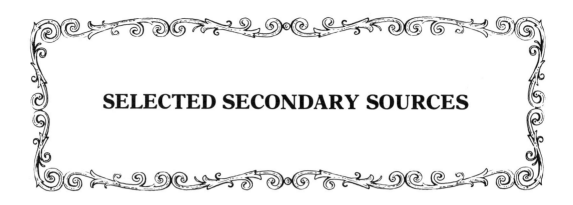

# SELECTED SECONDARY SOURCES

Banks, Charles & Read, Oppie, *The San Francisco Disaster and the Mt. Vesuvius Horror* (Philadelphia, 1906)

Decker, Peter, *Fortunes and Failures* (Cambridge, 1978): "White-Collar Mobility in 19th Century San Francisco"

Glanz, Rudolph, *The Jews of California: From the Discovery of Gold Until 1880* (New York, 1960)

Harris, Leon, *Merchant Princes: An Intimate History of Jewish Families Who Built Department Stores* (New York, 1977)

Holiday, J.S., *The World Rushed In: The California Gold Rush Experience* (New York, 1981)

James, Jack, and Weller, Earl, *Treasure Island, the Magic City* (San Francisco, 1941)

Kahn, Judd, *Imperial San Francisco: Politics and Planning in an American City, 1897–1906* (Lincoln, Nebraska, 1979)

Kramer, William M., ed., *The Western Journal of Isaac Mayer Wise, 1877* (Berkeley, 1974)

Levinson, Robert E., *The Jews in the California Gold Rush* (New York and Berkeley, 1978)

Lotchin, Roger, *San Francisco 1846–1956 From Hamlet to City* (New York, 1974)

Meyer, Martin, *Western Jewry: An Account of the Jews and Judaism in California* (San Francisco, 1916)

Narell, Irena, *Our City, The Jews of San Francisco* (San Diego, 1981)

Raab, Earl, "There's No City Like San Francisco," *Commentary*, (Oct. 1950)

Rischin, Moses, ed., *The Jews of the West: The Metropolitan Years* (Waltham, Mass, and Berkeley, 1979)

Rosenbaum, Fred, *Architects of Reform: Congregational and Community Leadership, Emanu-El of San Francisco, 1849–1980* (Western Jewish History Center, Judah L. Magnes Memorial Museum, Berkeley, 1980)

Starr, Kevin, *Americans and the California Dream 1850–1915* (New York, 1973)

Todd, Frank Morton, *The Story of the Exposition* (New York, 1921)

# THOSE INTERVIEWED

## Members

Anixter, Raymond T.
Anolik, Alexander
Baum, Benjamin J.
Bransten, Edward Jr.
Bransten, William H.
Camhi, Sam
Colsky, Richard A.
Colsky, William A.
Colvin, Reynold H.
Diamond, Stanley
Diller, Philip
Dinkelspiel, John W.
Dobbs, Harold S.
Euphrat, Edward F.
Getz, Brian H.
Goldman, Richard N.
Goldman, Robert L.

Goldsmith, Frank T.
Gould, Edgar L.
Grabstein, Norman E.
Griffin, Noah, Jr.
Hersh, LeRoy
Hilp, Harry, Jr.
Ladar, Samuel A.
Leland, Herbert A.
Levison, Robert M.
Liebes, Lloyd
Lipman, Jack M.
Magnin, Donald
Mendelson, Michael A.
Miller, Walter
Nathan, Marvin N.
Nestel, Lawrence A.
Newman, Edwin S.

Newman, Walter S.
Oser, Richard L.
Passantino, Frank R. D.D.S.
Pearlstein, Carl
Rabinowitz, Bert F.
Reich, Stanley B., M.D.
Rothmann, John F.
Scharlach, Adrian E.
Seton, Theodore R.
Shragge, Harmon M.
Simon, Arthur B.
Sinton, Edgar
Stone, Daniel E.
Treguboff, Sanford M.
Van Vliet, Roy

## Staff

Blumenthal, Steve
Drayer, Douwe
Ferrero, Joseph

Nott, Clifford R.
Pels, Anthony
Ploug, Niels
Robleto, Arnold

Tokusato, Carolyn
Tokusato, Paul
Whitney, Everett

## Others

Bush, Mrs. Philip
Grant, Judge Isabella
Green, Mrs. William
Hoffmann, Mrs. Justin

Lipman, Mrs. Jack
Lisberger, Mrs. Sylvan
McDougall, Ruth
Miller, Elise Shragge

Newman, Ellen Magnin
Newman, Mrs. S. Walter
Russell, Madeleine Haas
Von Beroldingen, Judge Dorthy

# INDEX

# SONG OF THE BELL

by Fredrick Schiller

(English Translation by Henry Wadsworth Longfellow)

Around, around
Companions all, take your ground,
And name the bell with joy profound!
CONCORDIA IS THE WORD WE'VE FOUND
Most meet to express the harmonious sound,
That calls to those in friendship bound.

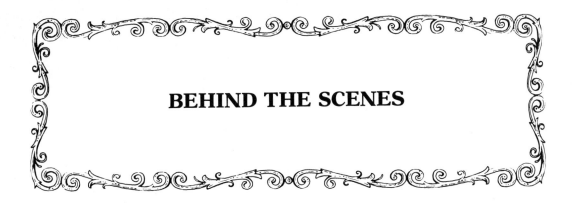

# BEHIND THE SCENES

Every theatrical producer knows the value of the unsung heroes who seldom get the credit for a hit show. The History Committee wants to express its appreciation to some of the many craftsmen who have helped make this book a winner.

Don Lehmann, Marti Lehmann, and Betty Wimmer of Lehmann Graphics for their excellent work in typesetting.

George Caughman, President of Cardoza-James Binding Company cooperated in a wonderful way in doing such a fine binding job.

And to Henry Bettman, sales representative with The James H. Barry Company, our printer, we offer our appreciation for the way in which he shared his knowledge and expertise with us to see that this volume will become a collector's item in the publishing of San Francisco memorabilia.